Lecture Notes in Artificial Intelligence 13408

Subseries of Lecture Notes in Computer Science

Series Editors

Randy Goebel
University of Alberta, Edmonton, Canada

Wolfgang Wahlster
DFKI, Berlin, Germany

Zhi-Hua Zhou
Nanjing University, Nanjing, China

Founding Editor

Jörg Siekmann
DFKI and Saarland University, Saarbrücken, Germany

More information about this subseries at https://link.springer.com/bookseries/1244

Vicenç Torra · Yasuo Narukawa (Eds.)

Modeling Decisions
for Artificial Intelligence

19th International Conference, MDAI 2022
Sant Cugat, Spain, August 30 – September 2, 2022
Proceedings

 Springer

Editors
Vicenç Torra 🆔
Umeå University
Umeå, Sweden

Yasuo Narukawa 🆔
Tamagawa University
Tokyo, Japan

ISSN 0302-9743　　　　　　ISSN 1611-3349 (electronic)
Lecture Notes in Artificial Intelligence
ISBN 978-3-031-13447-0　　　ISBN 978-3-031-13448-7 (eBook)
https://doi.org/10.1007/978-3-031-13448-7

LNCS Sublibrary: SL7 – Artificial Intelligence

This Springer imprint is published by the registered company Springer Nature Switzerland AG
The registered company address is: Gewerbestrasse 11, 6330 Cham, Switzerland

Preface

This volume contains papers presented at the 19th International Conference on Modeling Decisions for Artificial Intelligence (MDAI 2022), celebrated during Sant Cugat, Catalonia, Spain, August 30 – September 2, 2022.

This conference followed MDAI 2004 (Barcelona), MDAI 2005 (Tsukuba), MDAI 2006 (Tarragona), MDAI 2007 (Kitakyushu), MDAI 2008 (Sabadell), MDAI 2009 (Awaji Island), MDAI 2010 (Perpinyà), MDAI 2011 (Changsha), MDAI 2012 (Girona), MDAI 2013 (Barcelona), MDAI 2014 (Tokyo), MDAI 2015 (Skövde), MDAI 2016 (Sant Julià de Lòria), MDAI 2017 (Kitakyushu), MDAI 2018 (Mallorca), MDAI 2019 (Milano), MDAI 2020 (proceedings only), and MDAI 2021 (Umeå).

The aim of MDAI is to provide a forum for researchers to discuss different facets of decision processes in a broad sense. This includes model building and all kinds of mathematical tools for data aggregation, information fusion, and decision-making; tools to help make decisions related to data science problems (including, e.g., statistical and machine learning algorithms as well as data visualization tools); and algorithms for data privacy and transparency-aware methods so that data processing procedures and the decisions made from them are fair, transparent, and avoid unnecessary disclosure of sensitive information.

The MDAI 2022 conference included tracks on the topics of (a) data science, (b) machine learning, (c) data privacy, (d) aggregation functions, (e) human decision-making, (f) graphs and (social) networks, and (g) recommendation and search.

The organizers received 41 papers, 16 of which are published in this volume. Each submission received at least three reviews from the Program Committee and a few external reviewers. We would like to express our gratitude to them for their work.

The conference was supported by the ESADE Institute for Data-Driven Decisions (esadeD3), the European Society for Fuzzy Logic and Technology (EUSFLAT), the Catalan Association for Artificial Intelligence (ACIA), the Japan Society for Fuzzy Theory and Intelligent Informatics (SOFT), and the UNESCO Chair in Data Privacy.

June 2022

Vicenç Torra
Yasuo Narukawa

Organization

General Chair

Jordi Nin   ESADE, Universitat Ramon Llull, Catalonia, Spain

Program Chairs

Vicenç Torra   Umeå University, Sweden
Yasuo Narukawa   Tamagawa University, Japan

Advisory Board

Didier Dubois   Institut de Recherche en Informatique de Toulouse, CNRS, France
Jozo Dujmović   San Francisco State University, USA
Lluis Godo   IIIA-CSIC, Spain
Janusz Kacprzyk   Systems Research Institute, Polish Academy of Sciences, Poland
Sadaaki Miyamoto   University of Tsukuba, Japan
Pierangela Samarati   Università degli Studi di Milano, Italy
Sandra Sandri   Instituto Nacional de Pesquisas Espaciais, Brazil
Michio Sugeno   Tokyo Institute of Technology, Japan
Ronald R. Yager   Iona College, USA

Program Committee

Kayode S. Adewole   Umeå University, Sweden
Laya Aliahmadipour   Shahid Bahonar University of Kerman, Iran
Cláudia Antunes   Universidade de Lisboa, Portugal
Eva Armengol   IIIA-CSIC, Spain
Edurne Barrenechea   Universidad Pública de Navarra, Spain
Gloria Bordogna   Consiglio Nazionale delle Ricerche, Italy
Humberto Bustince   Universidad Pública de Navarra, Spain
Alina Campan   North Kentucky University, USA
Francisco Chiclana   De Montfort University, UK
Susana Díaz   Universidad de Oviedo, Spain
Josep Domingo-Ferrer   Universitat Rovira i Virgili, Spain
Yasunori Endo   University of Tsukuba, Japan

Julian Salas	Universitat Oberta de Catalunya, Spain
H. Joe Steinhauer	University of Skövde, Sweden
László Szilágyi	Sapientia Hungarian University of Transylvania, Hungary
Aida Valls	Universitat Rovira i Virgili, Spain
Paolo Viappiani	Université Paris Dauphine-PSL, France
Zeshui Xu	Southeast University, China

Local Organizing Committee Chair

| Núria Agell | ESADE, Universitat Ramon Llull, Spain |

Additional Referees

Ashneet Khandpur Singh
Sergio Martinez Lluis
Fabio Stella
Rami Haffar
Najeeb Moharram Salim Jebreel

Supporting Institutions

ESADE Institute for Data-Driven Decisions
European Society for Fuzzy Logic and Technology (EUSFLAT)
Catalan Association for Artificial Intelligence (ACIA)
Japan Society for Fuzzy Theory and Intelligent Informatics (SOFT)
UNESCO Chair in Data Privacy

Invited Talks

Mathematical Modeling of COVID-19 from a Complex Systems Perspective

Clara Granell

University Rovira i Virgili

Abstract. The study of complex systems revolves around the idea of studying a system from the point of view of the interactions between its components, rather than focusing on the individual features of each of its parts. This general vision allows us to observe behaviors that would not be easily observed by studying the individual components alone. The human brain, human social networks, biological systems or transportation networks are examples of complex systems. Another example is the spreading of contagious diseases, where only the study of the whole system will allow us to understand what is the possible outcome of an epidemic. In this talk, I will introduce the mathematical models of epidemic spreading we have been developing in the past decade. We'll start with simple, compartmental models that allow us to gain a general understanding of how epidemics work. Then we will adapt these simple models to more realistic scenarios that are able to predict the evolution of COVID-19 in Spain.

Explaining Black Box Classifiers by Exploiting Auto-Encoders

Anna Monreale

Università di Pisa

Abstract. Artificial Intelligence is nowadays one of the most important scientific and technological areas, with a tremendous socio-economic impact and a pervasive adoption in every field of the modern society. Many applications in different fields, such as credit score assessment, medical diagnosis, autonomous vehicles, and spam filtering are based on Artificial Intelligence (AI) decision systems. Unfortunately, these systems often reach their impressive performance through obscure machine learning models that "hide" the logic of their internal decision processes to humans because not humanly understandable. For this reason this models are called black box models, i.e., models used by AI to accomplish a task for which either the logic of the decision process is not accessible, or it is accessible but not human-understandable.

Examples of machine learning black box models adopted by AI systems include Neural Networks, Deep Neural Networks, Ensemble classifiers, and so on.

The missing of interpretability of black box models is a crucial issue for ethics and a limitation to AI adoption in socially sensitive and safety-critical contexts such as healthcare and law. As a consequence, the research in eXplainable AI (XAI) has recently caught much attention and there has been an ever growing interest in this research area to provide explanations on the behavior of black box models.

A promising line of research in XAI exploits local explainers also supported by auto-encoders in case it is necessary to explain black box classifiers working on non-tabular data (e.g., images, time series and texts).

The ability of autoencoders to compress any data in a low-dimensional tabular representation, and then reconstruct it with negligible loss, provides the great opportunity to work in the latent space for the extraction of meaningful explanations, for example through the generation of new synthetic samples, consistent with the input data, that can be fed to a black-box to understand where its decision boundary lies.

In this presentation we discuss recent XAI solutions based on local explainers and autoencoders that enable the extraction of meaningful explanations composed by factual and counterfactual rules, and by exemplar and counter-exemplar samples, offering a deep understanding of the local decision of the black box.

The Labor Impacts of Algorithmic Management

Anna Ginès Fabrellas

Esade, Universitat Ramon Llull

Abstract. Although it seems taken from one of the best science fiction novels, the use of algorithms and artificial intelligence for work management is already a reality. Many companies are using these systems to make decisions on the selection of people, distribution of tasks or even dismissal. The use of algorithms and artificial intelligence to adopt automated decisions in people management generates benefits. By automating some decision processes, companies can make organizational decisions quickly and efficiently, thus improving their productivity and competitiveness. In addition, the use of artificial intelligence and algorithms is often presented as an opportunity to adopt mathematically objective decisions based entirely on merit. However, contrary to this aura of objectivity, certainty and precision that surrounds artificial intelligence, the truth is that it presents important challenges and risks for workers' fundamental rights. As the European Parliament maintains in its resolution of March 2017, one of the most relevant risks posed by the use of artificial intelligence and big data today is its impact on workers' fundamental rights to privacy, data protection and non-discrimination. In this sense, the aim of the panel is to analyze the potential risks that algorithmic management poses on workers' fundamental rights, as well as new legal, technological and ethical challenges that it poses.

Contents

Decision Making and Uncertainty

Optimality Analysis for Stochastic LP Problems

Zhenzhong Gao[✉] and Masahiro Inuiguchi

Osaka University, Osaka 560-8531, Japan
zhenzhong@inulab.sys.es.osaka-u.ac.jp, inuiguti@sys.es.osaka-u.ac.jp

Abstract. When a linear programming (LP) problem includes uncertain parameters, a decision-maker will be interested in the robustness of a candidate solution. Under strict uncertainty, researchers often use a hyper-box to represent the possible region of parameters due to the lack of information about the occurrence and realisations. However, when more information, such as expert knowledge and historical data, is available, the hyper-box representation becomes too weak to model the uncertainty. In this paper, we study an approach to an optimality analysis for stochastic linear programming problems. We assume that the constraints of the problems are deterministic, although the objective function coefficients obey a multivariate normal distribution. To such problems, we investigate the optimality degree of a non-degenerate basic feasible (NBF) solution. Namely, we focus on the probability of the NBF solution being optimal. Such problems are known as distribution problems in stochastic programming. The area of objective coefficient vectors where an NBF solution becomes optimal is called the optimality assurance cone of the solution, which is expressed by a system of linear inequalities. We show that the numerical analysis is practical and functional with mathematical programming tools. To make our analysis more useful, we apply the proposed optimality analysis to multiple NBF solutions. It enables the decision-maker to make a better decision with the overall view of candidate solutions.

Keywords: Stochastic LP problems · Random variable · Optimality analysis · Multivariate normal distribution

1 Introduction

In real-world optimisation problems, the coefficients may become uncertain due to noise, measurement restriction or insufficient knowledge. In this paper, we focus on the uncertainty in linear programming (LP) problems.

Sensitivity analysis [1] is one of the conventional methods for evaluating the influence of uncertainty in linear programming (LP) problems. It studies to what extent the optimal solution and optimal value change by the small perturbation in the coefficient of an LP problem. The analysis is carried out simply by using the shadow price. It can treat the uncertainty existing anywhere.

© The Author(s), under exclusive license to Springer Nature Switzerland AG 2022
V. Torra and Y. Narukawa (Eds.): MDAI 2022, LNAI 13408, pp. 3–14, 2022.
https://doi.org/10.1007/978-3-031-13448-7_1

However, its main drawback is that it can treat only a single coefficient. The method of *100% rules* [1] overcomes the drawback by constructing a convex cone of the coefficient vectors for a basic solution within which its optimality is ensured. This approach gives the foundation for succeeding approaches. For example, the *tolerance approach* [3,14,15] provides a straightforward calculation of independent fluctuation ranges of objective function coefficients preserving the optimality of the solution.

When the possible ranges are known and bounded, Inuiguchi and Sakawa [11] proposed concepts called *possible and necessary optimality* for LP problems with uncertain objective function coefficients. The possibly optimal solution is the solution optimal for a possible realisation of the uncertain objective function coefficient vector. On the other hand, the necessarily optimal solution is the solution optimal for all possible realisations of the uncertain objective function coefficient vector. The necessarily optimal solution is ideal, but it does not exist in many cases. To mitigate this shortcoming of the necessarily optimal solution, Inuiguchi et al. [10,11] introduce fuzzy numbers to represent the multiple possible range estimations of uncertain coefficients from the widest to the narrowest.

On the other hand, when information such as a specific probability distribution or the historical data is available, a more detailed analysis could be carried out by formulating a stochastic linear programming problem. Researchers have theoretically studied the probability distribution of optimal solutions and optimal values in the stochastic model [12,13]. However, the calculations are too complex.

To address the computational complexity, Curry et al. [2] built an approach for random variables obeying multivariate normal distributions theoretically and practically. Moreover, Gao and Inuiguchi [4] concentrated on utilising numerical analysis by computer programming to avoid being trapped in the calculation process. They updated the conventional analysis to the candidate solution's optimality with *optimality analysis*. However, the drawback is apparent since both methods can only analyse one candidate solution. If the probability of the solution being optimal is not sufficiently large, the decision-maker cannot accept the solution with no other choice.

We propose an approach to stochastic LP problems. We assume that the constraints of the problems are deterministic, although the objective function coefficients obey a multivariate normal distribution. The contribution of the proposed approach is twofold. One is the update of numerical calculation in evaluating the probability of a candidate solution being optimal. The other is to obtain multiple candidate solutions with the probability degrees to be optimal. We show that the proposed approach gives a reasonable outcome with a series of results, which enables the decision-maker to make a choice by referring to the probability distribution of optimal solutions.

This paper is organised as follows. Section 2 briefly explains LP problems and the optimality analysis. We look into the drawbacks in the previous analysis and propose our approach based on the probability theory and LP techniques. Section 3 illustrates the proposed approach and compare it with a conventional approach, and Sect. 4 gives some numerical examples. In Sect. 5, we conclude our study and indicate further research topics.

2 LP Problems and Robust Optimality Analysis

In this paper, the LP problem we address is in the following form:

$$\text{maximize } c^T x, \text{ subject to } Ax = b, \; x \geq 0, \tag{1}$$

where $x \in \mathbb{R}^n$ denotes the decision variable vector. $A \in \mathbb{R}^{m \times n}$, $b \in \mathbb{R}^m$ and $c \in \mathbb{R}^n$ are the coefficient matrix, the right-hand-side vector and the objective function coefficient vector, respectively.

By the simplex method [1], an *optimal basic feasible* solution x^* can be separated into basic sub-vector $x_B^* \in \mathbb{R}^m$ and non-basic sub-vector $x_N^* \in \mathbb{R}^{n-m}$ by an index set $\mathbb{I}_B(x^*) \subseteq \{1, 2, \ldots, n\}$ satisfying $\text{Card}(\mathbb{I}_B(x^*)) = m$. Consequently, matrix A is separated by $\mathbb{I}_B(x^*)$, where $A_B \in \mathbb{R}^{m \times m}$ is formed by the columns of A indexed by $\mathbb{I}_B(x^*)$ and $A_N \in \mathbb{R}^{(n-m) \times m}$ by the remaining. Vector c is also done similarly with $c_B \in \mathbb{R}^m$ and $c_N \in \mathbb{R}^{n-m}$.

Since A_B should always be non-singular, we have the following proposition about the necessary and sufficient condition for the optimality of a basic feasible solution.

Proposition 1. *Given an LP problem (1), a basic feasible solution x^* is optimal if and only if the following two conditions are valid:*

$$c_N - A_N^T A_B^{-T} c_B \leq 0 \; \text{(i)} \; and \; A_B^{-1} b \geq 0 \; \text{(ii)}, \tag{2}$$

where $A_B^{-T} = (A_B^{-1})^T$. The value of x^* is with $x_B^* = A_B^{-1} b$ and $x_N^* = 0$, and optimised value is $c_B^T A_B^{-1} b$. The first condition (i) shows the optimality and the second one (ii) shows the feasibility of x^*.

When treating an LP problem under uncertainty, we assume the feasible set formed by A and b are constant. Namely, we assume only the objective coefficient vector c contains uncertain coefficients. In this section, we assume that the possible range of the objective coefficient vector c is known as a set $\Phi \subseteq \mathbb{R}^n$. Moreover, we assume the feasible solution is *non-degenerate* and *basic*, called the *non-degenerate basic feasible* (NBF) solution. Although a basic feasible solution is degenerate, we obtain similar results to those described in this paper by considering all bases associated with the solution.

As a result, Inuiguchi et al. [10] proposed *optimality assurance cone* concept, which is derived from *100% rules* [1]:

Definition 1 (Optimality Assurance Cone). *Let x^* be an NBF solution to Problem (1). The optimality assurance cone $\mathscr{M}(x^*)$ is obtained as*

$$\mathscr{M}(x^*) = \left\{ c \in \mathbb{R}^n : c_N - A_N^T A_B^{-T} c_B \leq 0 \right\}, \tag{3}$$

where for simplification, we reformulate it as $\mathscr{M}(x^*) = \{c \in \mathbb{R}^n : M(x^*)c \leq 0\}$.

For the *degenerate* situation, Hladík [6], Gao and Inuiguchi [5] proposed approaches to obtain the optimality assurance cone with the same property. By Definition 1, we can use *possible and necessary optimality* [11] concept, defined by the following proposition [10]:

Proposition 2. *Let $\Phi \subseteq \mathbb{R}^n$ denote the set enclosing all uncertain objective coefficient vectors $\mathbf{c}$. Then an NBF solution $\mathbf{x}^*$ is*

▶ *possibly optimal if and only if $\Phi \cap \mathcal{M}(\mathbf{x}^*) \neq \emptyset$, or*
▶ *necessarily optimal if and only if $\Phi \subseteq \mathcal{M}(\mathbf{x}^*)$.*

Proposition 2 gives a direct way to analyse the optimality of an NBF solution. For the comparison with our proposed approach, we introduce the conventional tolerance approach with a numerical example.

2.1   LP Problems with Uncetainties in Intervals

The *interval linear programming* [7] studies the LP problem where uncertain coefficients are assumed to be in an interval hyper-box. Here we only introduce the theorem by Inuiguchi et al. [10]:

Theorem 1. *For Problem (1), let $\mathbf{c}$ be in an interval hyper-box $[\mathbf{c}^{\mathrm{L}}, \mathbf{c}^{\mathrm{R}}]$, where $\mathbf{c}^{\mathrm{L}} = [c_1^{\mathrm{L}}, c_2^{\mathrm{L}}, \ldots, c_n^{\mathrm{L}}]^{\mathrm{T}}$ and $\mathbf{c}^{\mathrm{R}} = [c_1^{\mathrm{R}}, c_2^{\mathrm{R}}, \ldots, c_n^{\mathrm{R}}]^{\mathrm{T}}$ denote the lower and upper bounds, respectively. Furthermore, let $\mathbf{c}^{\mathrm{C}} := (\mathbf{c}^{\mathrm{R}} + \mathbf{c}^{\mathrm{L}})/2$, $\mathbf{c}^{\mathrm{S}} := (\mathbf{c}^{\mathrm{R}} - \mathbf{c}^{\mathrm{L}})/2$ and $\mathbf{x}^*$ be an NBF solution obtained by $\mathbf{c}^{\mathrm{C}}$. For $k = 1, 2, \ldots, n - m$, let τ_k be defined as*

$$
\tau_k = \begin{cases} -\dfrac{\sum_{j=1}^{n} M_{kj}(\hat{\mathbf{x}}) c_j^{\mathrm{C}}}{\sum_{j=1}^{n} |M_{kj}(\hat{\mathbf{x}})| c_j^{\mathrm{S}}}, & \text{if } \sum_{j=1}^{n} |M_{kj}(\hat{\mathbf{x}})| c_j^{\mathrm{S}} > 0, \\ 0, & \text{otherwise}, \end{cases} \tag{4}
$$

where $\tau^{\min}$ is defined by

$$
\tau^{\min} = \min_{\substack{k=1,2,\ldots,n-m \\ \sum_{j=1}^{n} |M_{kj}(\mathbf{x}^*)| c_j^{\mathrm{S}} > 0}} \tau_k, \tag{5}
$$

and $|\cdot|$ denotes the entry-wise absolute operator. Then $\mathbf{x}^*$ is necessarily optimal to Problem (1) if and only if $\tau^{\min} \geq 1$.

We give a numerical example to illustrate Theorem 1:

Example 1. Let an LP problem be given as follows:

$$
\begin{aligned}
\text{maximize} \quad & c_1 x_1 + c_2 x_2, \\
\text{subject to} \quad & 3x_1 + 4x_2 \leq 42, \\
& 3x_1 + x_2 \leq 24, \\
& 0 \leq x_2 \leq 9, \ x_1 \geq 0,
\end{aligned}
$$

where c_1 and c_2 are uncertain coefficients satisfying $c_1 \in [12, 24]$ and $c_2 \in [13, 19]$. Check if there exists a necessarily optimal solution. If not, analyse the optimality of the obtained solution.

To solve the problem in the form of Problem (1), we add non-negative slack variable x_3, x_4 and x_5 at first. Then we can obtain an NBF solution $\hat{x}^* = (6, 6, 0, 0, 3)^T$ by $\hat{c}^C = (18, 16, 0, 0, 0)^T$, which gives the optimality assurance cone as

$$\mathscr{M}(\hat{x}^*) = \left\{ (c_1, c_2, c_3, c_4, c_5)^T \ \middle| \ \begin{array}{l} \frac{1}{9}c_1 - \frac{1}{3}c_2 + c_3 + \frac{1}{3}c_5 \leq 0 \\ -\frac{4}{9}c_1 + \frac{1}{3}c_2 + c_4 - \frac{1}{3}c_5 \leq 0 \end{array} \right\}.$$

Since x_3, x_4 and x_5 are slack variables, we remove them with $x^* = (6, 6)^T$ and

$$\mathscr{M}(x^*) = \left\{ (c_1, c_2)^T \ \middle| \ \begin{array}{l} \frac{1}{9}c_1 - \frac{1}{3}c_2 \leq 0 \\ -\frac{4}{9}c_1 + \frac{1}{3}c_2 \leq 0 \end{array} \right\}.$$

By Theorem 1, it is not difficult to obtain $\tau_1 = 2 > 1$ and $\tau_2 = 8/11 < 1$ by $c^C = (18, 16)^T$ and $c^S = (6, 3)^T$. Hence $x^* = (6, 6)^T$ is not necessarily optimal due to $\tau^{\min} = 8/11$.

Figure 1 shows the result in a c_1-c_2 coordinate with the origin at $x^* = (6, 6)^T$, where it is easy to find that vertex $(12, 19)^T$ is not in $\mathscr{M}(x^*)$. Hence, $(6, 6)^T$ is not necessarily optimal.

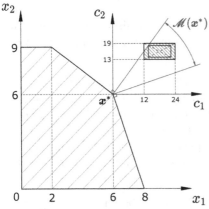

Fig. 1. The analysis in Example 1

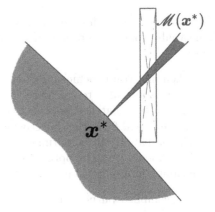

Fig. 2. When $\mathscr{M}(x^*)$ is too narrow

3   Stochastic Linear Programming

In the previous section, we described a conventional method for interval LP problems based on the tolerance approach. This approach has been extended to a case where the possible regions of coefficients are fuzzy numbers. However, we may face several limitations:

(i) The necessary optimality can be tested only for a single NBF solution obtained as an optimal solution to the LP problem whose objective coefficients are determined by the centres of intervals. Moreover the analysis assumes that the fluctuation of coefficients are symmetric to the centres and independent (see Inuiguchi et al. [10]). Although the possible optimality analysis is developed for treating all potentially optimal basic solutions (see Inuiguchi [9]), the concept of possible optimality is rather weak. Furthermore, those methods are not very useful when the possible range of objective function coefficient vector is a crisp set and the optimality assurance cone of some basic solution is too small (see Fig. 2).

(ii) The optimality analysis is sometimes too rough to satisfy the requirement. Let us review Example 1 for the illustration. Since $x^* = (6, 6)^{\mathrm{T}}$ is not necessarily optimal due to $\tau^{\min} = 8/11 < 1$, we can still assert that x^* has the *optimality degree* with 8/11, as Hladík [8] and Inuiguchi et al. [10] did. However, such a definition may lack a realistic meaning in applications. For example, if we are conscious of the size of area, the result of Example 1 saying *optimality degree* with 8/11 does not fit well to our feeling because the area ensuring the optimality of x^*, the result is $(8/11)^2 = 64/121$, which is much smaller than 8/11. The sense of impropriety would be larger as the blue hatched area of Fig. 1 is not counted.

To address these shortcomings, we regard the uncertain coefficients as random variables obeying a probability distribution considering the following advantages:

(i) When uncertain coefficients obey a multivariate probability distribution, it becomes available to calculate the probability to be optimal for a solution, e.g. the blue hatched area in Fig. 1, by integrating the *probability density function (p.d.f.)* of the objective coefficients.

(ii) The probability to be optimal can be applied to any NBF solution.

(iii) The probability to be optimal for an NBF solution can give a more realistic meaning in applications.

To accomplish purpose, the key is to obtain the probability to be optimal, i.e., the integration of the random variable's *p.d.f.* with high accuracy. Hence, we discuss this key first in the following content first.

3.1   The Optimality Degree of an NBF Solution

The utilisation of the probability distribution enables us to compensate for the shortcoming of the conventional approaches. However, we should deal with several difficulties to accomplish this purpose. The most considerable trouble is that the calculation process of the probability is complex. As the calculation of multivariate integration over a convex cone is complex, the theoretical calculation would be too difficult. Some previous literature [2, 12] gave a few theoretical results, which, however, make the merit of stochastic approach in vain. Then, we use a *numerical analysis* to achieve our goal.

As described above, we modify the definition of *optimality degree* from the original one defined by Hladík [8], as well as Gao and Inuiguchi [4]. The optimal degree is defined by the probability to be optimal as follows:

Definition 2 (Optimality Degree). *Let x^* be an NBF solution to Problem (1) and c be a random variable coefficient vector. Then the optimality degree of x^* corresponding to c is evaluated as*

$$\mathscr{D}(x^*) = \Pr\Big(C \in \mathscr{M}(x^*)\Big), \tag{6}$$

where C represents the scenario event of c.

When C obeys continuous distributions, such as the normal distribution and the uniform distribution, Eq. (6) in Definition 2 is rewritten as the following equation:

$$\mathscr{D}(x^*) = \int \cdots \int_{c \in \mathscr{M}(x^*)} f(c_1, c_2, \ldots, c_n) \mathrm{d}c_1 \mathrm{d}c_2 \ldots \mathrm{d}c_n, \tag{7}$$

where $f(\cdot) : \mathbb{R}^n \to \mathbb{R}$ denotes the continuous *p.d.f* of c in Problem (1) and $c = (c_1, c_2, \ldots, c_n)^{\mathrm{T}}$.

Equation (7) provides the way to theoretically calculate the optimality degree of a given NBF solution, which, as we have already mentioned, can only give the result in rare situations. For example, even if $f(\cdot)$ obeys independent multivariate normal distribution and $\mathscr{M}(x^*)$ is decomposable, we still need to refer to the *standard normal table* for the result.

Therefore, instead of being trapped in a theoretical result, a numerical one may be better if the error can be assessed and bounded by a sufficiently small number. For our purpose, the multivariate integration function in the programming library has to satisfy at least following two requirements:

▶ It can treat any multivariate *p.d.f.* of c.
▶ It can accept any integration range.

The first requirement is fulfilled with most of multivariate integration libraries (see Gao and Inuiguchi [4]). However, the second requirement is rather strong. The conventional multivariate integration principle makes it essential to decompose the variables (see *Fubini's Theorem*). However, general situations do not always support the decomposition, especially when the integration region is a convex cone. Even when decomposable, such as in $\mathbb{R}^2$, we still have to do the process manually with extra trouble. Hence, it is necessary to find an integration library satisfying the second requirement.

Fortunately, the NIntegrate function in Mathematica supports the second requirement, which only needs a series of inequalities defining the convex cone. Hence, we can avoid the trap and calculate the result.

3.2 Generation of Multiple NBF Solutions

After proposing the method for calculating the optimality degree of a given NBF solution, we start considering the generation of multiple candidate solutions.

The most straightforward way is to list all vertices of the feasible set and evaluate their respective optimality degree. However, listing all vertices of a polyhedral convex set costs enormous computational efforts. Moreover, it is not essential in most situations. Hence, in this paper, we only consider the neighbour vertices of the one obtained by the $p.d.f.$'s centre of c, where the number should be at most $(n + 1)$ in $\mathbb{R}^n$ space.

Since obtaining the neighbour of a vertex (basic solution) on a polyhedral convex set can be accomplished by *tabular pivoting* [1], we can obtain them with the respective optimality assurance cone. It enables us to evaluate the respective optimality degree by numerical calculation by Eq. (7). Since the process itself is studied extensively, we do not give more illustration on this subject.

3.3 Algorithm

We propose the overall algorithm by combining the evaluation of a candidate solution's optimality degree and the generation of multiple candidate solutions. Since we need to obtain an initial candidate solution, we must first determine an objective coefficient vector.

As we have mentioned at the beginning of this paper, the uncertainty is usually caused by noise, measurement restrictions or insufficient knowledge. Therefore, the distribution function is assumed to be a normal distribution, where the corresponding $p.d.f.$ is a concave function with a limited maximum at a limited extent. Hence, choosing the one at the maximal value of the $p.d.f.$ is a preferred option, referred to as c^C in general. Moreover, in uniform distributions, we can pick the centre of the interval as c^C.

Hence, the proposed algorithm is obtained as follows:

Algorithm of Optimality Analysis

$\Diamond$ Solve the conventional LP problem with c^C. Let x^0 denote the optimal NBF solution, obtain the corresponding optimality assurance cone $\mathscr{M}(x^0)$ by Eq. (3).

$\Diamond$ Calculate $\mathscr{D}(x^0)$ by Eq. (7) and record it.

$\Diamond$ Obtain all neighbour of x^0 by tabular pivoting and denote them as $\{x^i : i = 1, 2, \ldots\}$. (Assume every x^i is also an NBF solution.)

$\Diamond$ For each x^i in $\{x^i\}$:

   $\circ$ Obtain $\mathscr{M}(x^i)$ by Eq. (3).

   $\circ$ Calculate $\mathscr{D}(x^i)$ by Eq. (7) and record it.

$\Diamond$ Output the list containing the result of x^i and $\mathscr{D}(x^i)$.

We note that our approach does not provide the best choice with giving a unique solution output. Instead, we only help decision-maker(s) make their decision with a list of solutions with associated optimality degrees. If the solution with the largest optimality degree is preferred, they can directly choose it. If they want to consider extra aspects of the solutions, the given list of the solutions may help them to find good candidates.

4   Numerical Examples

To validate our proposed algorithm, we use Example 1 again. First, we assume objective coefficient vector c is the vector composed of random variables obeying a multivariate normal distribution.

Example 2. Let the problem given the same as Example 1, where $c = (c_1, c_2)^T$ denote random variables obeying a multivariate normal distribution $N(c|\mu, \Sigma^2)$ with *p.d.f.* $f : \mathbf{R}^2 \to [0, 1]$. Assume $\mu = (5, 5)^T$ and $\Sigma^2 = (4^2, 0; 0, 4^2)$. Then, solve the problem and analyse the optimality of obtained solutions.

According to the proposed algorithm, we first use the mean vector of the distribution $f(c|\mu, \Sigma^2)$, i.e. $c^C = (5, 5)^T$, as the objective coefficient vector for obtaining the initial solution. The result is the same as Example 1, which is $x^0 = (6, 6)^T$ (It is noted that we still ignore the slack variables, where the original solution should be $\hat{x}^0 = (6, 6, 0, 0, 3)^T$) with $\mathscr{M}(x^0)$. Therefore, by Eq. (7), it is not hard to calculate the optimality degree as $\mathscr{D}(x^0) = 0.387988$.

Then we search the neighbour NBF solutions of x^0 by pivoting the simplex tabular. We find two NBF solutions $x^1 = (2, 9)^T$ ($\hat{x}^1 = (2, 9, 0, 9, 0)^T$) and $x^2 = (8, 0)^T$ ($\hat{x}^2 = (8, 0, 18, 0, 9)^T$). The corresponding optimality assurance cones are:

$$\mathscr{M}(x^1) = \left\{ (c_1, c_2)^T \;\middle|\; \begin{array}{c} -\frac{1}{3}c_1 \leq 0 \\ \frac{4}{3}c_1 - c_2 \leq 0 \end{array} \right\},$$

$$\mathscr{M}(x^2) = \left\{ (c_1, c_2)^T \;\middle|\; \begin{array}{c} -\frac{1}{3}c_1 + c_2 \leq 0 \\ -\frac{1}{3}c_1 \leq 0 \end{array} \right\}.$$

In the same way, we obtain $\mathscr{D}(x^1) = 0.300345$ and $\mathscr{D}(x^2) = 0.206016$. Therefore, we list the solutions as in Table 1.

Table 1. The result of Example 2

x	$\hat{x}$	$\mathscr{D}(x)$
$(6, 6)^T$	$(6, 6, 0, 0, 3)^T$	0.387988
$(2, 9)^T$	$(2, 9, 0, 9, 0)^T$	0.300345
$(8, 0)^T$	$(8, 0, 18, 0, 9)^T$	0.206016

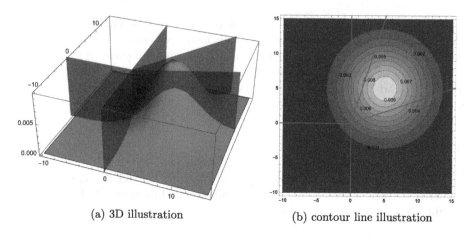

(a) 3D illustration   (b) contour line illustration

Fig. 3. The result of Example 2

Figure 3 illustrate our result of Example 2, where Sub-Fig. (3a) shows the 3D illustration and Sub-Fig. (3b) shows the corresponding contour line of Sub-Fig. (3a).

We can see that there are five optimality assurance cones, which correspond to five vertices (solutions) on the feasible set. We use the upper-left one (containing the smallest circle in Sub-Fig. (3b) for initialisation and calculate its optimality degree. Then we obtain two neighbours of it and do the process again. Hence, we can analyse three solutions, covering the half-right region and occupying most optimality degrees.

After having the general result of the normal distribution, we consider comparing our approach with the result in interval linear programming. We re-use Example 1 but convert the interval hyper-box into the random variables obeying a multivariate uniform distribution.

Example 3. Let the problem given the same as Example 1, where $c = (c_1, c_2)^{\mathrm{T}}$ denotes the random variables obeying a multivariate uniform distribution on the interval hyper-box $([12, 24], [13, 19])^{\mathrm{T}}$. Solve the problem and analyse the optimality of the obtained solutions.

Since the process is the same as Example 2, we only give our result as below:

We can see that we still have three evaluations, though one of the results is 0. Moreover, the geometrical result in Example 1 is $64/121 \approx 52.89\%$. However, our approach evaluates the result as 95.31%, which is much larger.

If we prefer obtaining the theoretical result by area calculation, it is not hard to compute the triangular area in $\mathscr{M}(x^1)$, which turns out to be $\frac{1}{2} \cdot 3 \cdot \frac{9}{4} = 27/8$. Since whole area is $12 \cdot 6 = 72$, the theoretical result should be $\mathscr{D}(x^1) = \frac{3}{64} = 0.046875$, which corresponds the result from our proposed approach. Hence, we can assert that the proposed approach can obtain more precise results than conventional ones (Table 2).

Table 2. The result of Example 3

$\boldsymbol{x}$	$\hat{\boldsymbol{x}}$	$\mathscr{D}(\boldsymbol{x})$
$(6,6)^{\mathrm{T}}$	$(6,6,0,0,3)^{\mathrm{T}}$	0.953125
$(2,9)^{\mathrm{T}}$	$(2,9,0,9,0)^{\mathrm{T}}$	0.046875
$(8,0)^{\mathrm{T}}$	$(8,0,18,0,9)^{\mathrm{T}}$	0

5 Conclusions

We proposed an optimality analysis of multiple NBF solutions to an LP problem with random objective function coefficients obeying a multivariate normal distribution. The proposed approach evaluates the optimality degrees of multiple NBF solutions. Previous approaches that evaluate the optimality degree of a single NBF solution may provide insufficient information when the optimality degree is too small. In comparison, our proposed analysis using multiple NBF solutions guarantees to provide sufficiently valuable information.

To avoid the trap of formidable difficulties of exact computation, we focused on a numerical result with high precision. We utilised the integration function in mathematical programming tools for calculating the probability of an NBF solution to be optimal. Moreover, the analysis of multiple NBF solutions can be performed seamlessly by pivoting techniques. We gave numerical examples to demonstrate the advantage over the previous approach.

There remain some issues to be improved and developed. Exploring multiple NBF solutions is not very efficient as we generate all adjacent NBF solutions from a visited optimal NBF with a certain probability. We may restrict the exploration to only possibly optimal NBF solutions with a technique proposed in Inuiguchi [9]. The study on this restricted exploration is one of the future topics.

References

1. Bradley, S.P., Hax, A.C., Magnanti, T.L.: Applied Mathematical Programming. Addison-Wesley Publishing Company, Boston (1977)
2. Curry, S., Lee, I., Ma, S., Serban, N.: Global sensitivity analysis via a statistical tolerance approach. Eur. J. Oper. Res. **296**(1), 44–59 (2022)
3. Filippi, C.: A fresh view on the tolerance approach to sensitivity analysis in linear programming. Eur. J. Oper. Res. **167**(1), 1–19 (2005)
4. Gao, Z., Inuiguchi, M.: Estimating the optimal probability of a candidate basic solution in stochastic linear programming. In: 2021 60th Annual Conference of the Society of Instrument and Control Engineers of Japan (SICE), pp. 640–643. IEEE (2021)
5. Gao, Z., Inuiguchi, M.: An analysis to treat the degeneracy of a basic feasible solution in interval linear programming. In: Honda, K., Entani, T., Ubukata, S., Huynh, V.N., Inuiguchi, M. (Eds.) Integrated Uncertainty in Knowledge Modelling and Decision Making. IUKM 2022. Lecture Notes in Computer Science. LNCS. vol.

13199, pp. 130–142.. Springer, Cham (2022). https://doi.org/10.1007/978-3-030-98018-4_11

6. Hladík, M.: Multiparametric linear programming: support set and optimal partition invariancy. Eur. J. Oper. Res. **202**(1), 25–31 (2010)

7. Hladík, M.: Tolerance analysis in linear systems and linear programming. Optim. Methods Softw. **26**(3), 381–396 (2011)

8. Hladík, M.: Robust optimal solutions in interval linear programming with forall-exists quantifiers. Eur. J. Oper. Res. **254**(3), 705–714 (2016)

9. Inuiguchi, M.: Enumeration of all possibly optimal vertices with possible optimality degrees in linear programming problems with a possibilistic objective function. Fuzzy Optim. Decis. Making **3**, 311–326 (2004)

10. Inuiguchi, M., Gao, Z., Henriques, C.O.: Robust optimality analysis of non-degenerate basic feasible solutions in linear programming problems with fuzzy objective coefficients. Fuzzy Optim. Decis. Making. 1–29 (2022). https://doi.org/10.1007/s10700-022-09383-2

11. Inuiguchi, M., Sakawa, M.: Possible and necessary optimality tests in possibilistic linear programming problems. Fuzzy Sets Syst. **67**(1), 29–46 (1994)

12. Kall, P., Mayer, J., et al.: Stochastic Linear Programming, vol. 7. Springer, New York (1976). https://doi.org/10.1007/b105472

13. Madansky, A.M.: Inequalities for stochastic linear programming problemÅc. Manag. Sci. **6**, 197–204 (1960)

14. Wendell, R.E.: The tolerance approach to sensitivity analysis in linear programming. Manag. Sci. **31**(5), 564–578 (1985)

15. Wondolowski, F.R., Jr.: A generalization of Wendell's tolerance approach to sensitivity analysis in linear programming. Decis. Sci. **22**(4), 792–811 (1991)

A Multi-perceptual-Based Approach for Group Decision Aiding

Olga Porro[1], Núria Agell[1], Mónica Sánchez[2], and Francisco J. Ruiz[2(✉)]

[1] Esade, Barcelona, Spain
[2] BarcelonaTech, Barcelona, Spain
francisco.javier.ruiz@upc.edu

Abstract. This paper presents a multi-perceptual framework for multi-criteria group decision aiding based on unbalanced hesitant linguistic information. The concept of a perceptual map is introduced to break the uniformity among the set of basic labels considered in linguistic term sets. Projected perceptual maps are considered to provide multi-perceptual frameworks for group decision aiding. This approach enables decision-makers to use sets of labels or different meanings for the same set of labels (since not all decision-makers feel comfortable using the same linguistic term set when expressing their judgements). Distances and measures of centrality and agreement or consensus are revised based on the concept of a perceptual map and a projected perceptual map that enables us to merge information from decision makers.

Keywords: Perceptual map · Projected perceptual maps · Hesitant fuzzy linguistic terms set

1 Introduction

Multi-criteria decision aiding (MCDA) is a research field in which a wide variety of models are proposed to assess and aggregate criteria on the preferences of decision makers (DMs) for choice, ranking, and sorting problems. Experts or DMs in group decision aiding environments often feel uneasy using numerical values to express their judgements, and feel more comfortable using linguistic terms (i.e., words) since they have already formed a specific meaning for those linguistic terms. Natural language governs uncertain human cognitive processes and is more appropriate for expressing uncertain assessments whose nature is vague, imprecise, or incomplete [2, 3]. The introduction of hesitant fuzzy linguistic term sets (HFLTSs) has recently attracted significant attention from researchers. Many practical applications have used HFLTSs to deal with the linguistic information involved in MCDA problems. A state of the art and list of applications can be found in [4]. Additionally, recent publications have also operated with this hesitant fuzzy linguistic approach to solve complex MCDA problems [6]. Since its introduction, many contributions on HFLTS properties and theory can be found in the literature (for example, in relation to aggregation operators [4, 7], comparison methods

V. Torra and Y. Narukawa (Eds.): MDAI 2022, LNAI 13408, pp. 15–25, 2022.
https://doi.org/10.1007/978-3-031-13448-7_2

[7], correlation coefficients of HFLTSs [2], similarities and distance measures between HFLTSs [5], and consensus degrees [10]).

Most of the group decision aiding applications found in the literature (which are framed as multi-criteria decision aiding problems with linguistic assessments modelled using HFLTSs) are assumed to be built over a uniform and symmetrically distributed linguistic term set – as in analytical hierarchy processes such as ELECTRE or TOPSIS applications [4]. This seems to be appropriate for cases where the semantics of each term have a proportional uncertainty and are usually equally placed around a central label. However, there are many situations in which attributes relate to qualitative characteristics that need to be assessed by linguistic terms represented by unsymmetrical or not uniformly distributed linguistic terms sets [10]. Similarly, it is also common to find that DMs have different backgrounds or knowledge, and this also needs to be modelled by unbalanced linguistic term sets [1, 12]. Moreover, some consensus measures and consensus reaching processes have been adapted to flexibly handle problems with unbalanced HFLTSs [1, 11]. Note that unbalanced linguistic information may arise from the nature and characteristics of some linguistic variables – such as those involved in a grading system. In the literature, several methods were proposed to deal with unbalanced linguistic term sets. Some models are built on the linguistic hierarchy and a 2-tuple fuzzy linguistic model – while other approaches use generalized absolute orders of magnitude qualitative spaces or asymmetric sigmoid semantics [2, 3, 9]. As with the initial 2-tuple linguistic models, HFLTSs originated with the assumption of linguistic terms with equidistant labels [3, 9]. Regarding HFLTS modeling, several linguistic computational models have recently been developed to handle unbalanced linguistic term sets [4, 6]. For instance, in [15], a framework containing several algorithms for implementing attitudinal HFLTS possibility distribution generation is developed that is based on the similarity measure of linguistic terms. This method is used in combination with several aggregation algorithms for solving real business MCDA problems, such as the selection of professional third-party reverse logistic providers or the prioritization of factors affecting in-cabin passenger comfort on high-speed rail in China. Other works also focalize on obtaining the semantics of linguistic information using optimization models [19].

Nonetheless, even if all these approaches can effectively deal with unbalanced HFLTSs, few can simultaneously deal with multi-granularity and unbalanced hesitant linguistic information. Multi-granularity refers to the use of different set of labels or different meanings for the same set of labels by different DMs. In a multi-criteria group decision situation, not all DMs might feel comfortable using the same linguistic term set when expressing their judgements. It might happen that some attributes or criteria are better evaluated using a different linguistic term set (for instance, some might be more appropriately evaluated with a linguistic term set with greater granularity). Multi-granularity is a logical step after unbalancedness. If a separate meaning is given to each linguistic label (related to uncertainty), it is conceivable that each DM may have his or her own manner of expressing these meanings. Managing information assessed in different linguistic term sets has always represented another challenge for collective performance evaluations [11, 15]. Some methodologies were introduced to deal with multi-granular linguistic term sets in a multi-criteria decision aiding problem based on the concept of linguistic hierarchy and the use of fuzzy sets with membership functions or fuzzy preference relations [4, 9]. An extensive range of methods is proposed for uniform and aggregation of multi-granular linguistic information without loss of information. [3, 16]. Recently, several approaches [17] have been developed to handle multi-granularity in HFLTSs modeling, but most methods that focus on multi-granularity lack treatment for unbalanced linguistic terms sets.

An example of a decision aiding framework that can focus simultaneously on modeling unbalanced and multi-granular DM linguistic information by means of HFLTSs can be found in [10]. In this paper, the authors introduced a signed distance measure between HFLTSs based on the ordinal semantics of linguistic terms and the possibility distribution method. With respect to consensus measures in GDM, various linguistic models have been adapted to deal with unbalanced linguistic information [1, 10–12]. Nonetheless, consensus measures modeled by means of unbalanced HFLTSs are limited. Some references can be found in [1, 4, 12]. For instance, Hao and Chiclana defined the concept of attitude linguistic quantifiers and associated it with the subjective preference of an expert [12]. The authors developed an attitude quantifier deriving method as the basis for generating possibility distribution in the HFLTS framework that extends the previous works of Wu and Xu [13] and Chen et al. [14]. But again, in these previous studies, DMs are limited to using the same unbalanced linguistic term set and the proposed measures fail to capture the complete heterogeneity of DMs. Therefore, the development of consensus measures that deal with multi-granular unbalanced linguistic term sets by means of HFLTSs are necessary. In this paper, a new linguistic representation methodology for group decision-aiding problems that simultaneously deals with hesitant unbalanced and multi-granular linguistic information is developed. The modelling is based on the algebraic structure of the extended lattice of HFLTSs [5] and the measures developed on it. There are some differences when compared with previous linguistic frameworks modelled by HFLTSs and these include: (1) subscript independence; (2) basic labels can be freely distributed without uniformity nor symmetry; (3) flexibility for different degrees of uncertainty and granularity for the experts.

In this paper we present a powerful framework for developing a multi-criteria group decision analysis that considers unbalance and multi-granularity. We present the concept of a perceptual map that gives an extended meaning to each basic label of the linguistic term set. When each DM has his or her own perceptual map, the projected perceptual map enables us to merge all this information to obtain the measures of central tendency and degree of consensus.

In the next section, all the new tools and structures needed for the method are developed. The third section introduces the perceptual map. Distances and measures of centrality and agreement or consensus are revised based on the concept of a perceptual map. Section 4 generalizes the concepts introduced in the previous section using the projected perceptual map. Finally, the conclusion summarizes the major points and suggests directions for future work.

2 Hesitant Fuzzy Linguistic Term Sets for Decision Aiding

This section provides the preliminary theoretical framework on the specific fuzzy linguistic approach used in this paper to model expert assessments, i.e., *hesitant fuzzy linguistic term sets.* In addition, a brief review on distances and consensus measures specifically developed for this fuzzy linguistic modeling is provided.

The concept of HFLTS was introduced by Rodriguez et al. in [3]. The concept is based on notions of fuzzy linguistic approach and hesitant fuzzy sets [8] and provides a linguistic and computational basis to increase the richness of linguistic elicitation. The use of HFLTSs enables experts to choose from among several linguistic terms and use richer and more complex linguistic expressions to assess an indicator, alternative, or variable. For instance, HFLTSs can represent expressions such as *"more than moderate"*, *"less than appropriate"* or *"between good and extremely good"*. A state-of-the-art survey on HFLTSs and its applications in decision-aiding can be found in [4].

2.1 The Lattice of HFLTS

Definition 1. [3] Let S be a totally ordered set of linguistic terms (or basic labels), $S = \{s_1, \ldots, s_n\}$, with $s_1 < \ldots < s_n$. A *hesitant fuzzy linguistic term set* (HFLTS) over S is a subset of consecutive linguistic terms of S, i.e., $\{x \in S | s_i \leq x \leq s_j\}$, for some i, $j \in \{1, \ldots, n\}$ with $i \leq j$. We call $[s_i, s_j]$ to this HFLTS, or $\{s_i\} \equiv [s_i, s_i]$ if $i = j$.

The set of all non-empty HFLTSs over S is denoted by $\mathcal{H}_S$. It is easy to prove that $card(\mathcal{H}_S) = \frac{n \cdot (n+1)}{2}$.

In $\mathcal{H}_S$, the *intersection* $\cap$ and the *connected union* $\bigsqcup$ are defined as follows:

Definition 2. Let $[s_i, s_j] \in \mathcal{H}_S$ and $[s_k, s_l] \in \mathcal{H}_s$,

- $[s_i, s_j] \cap [s_k, s_l] = [s_{\max\{i,k\}}, s_{\min\{j,l\}}]$ if this HFLTS exists or $\varnothing$ otherwise.
- $[s_i, s_j] \bigsqcup [s_k, s_l] = [s_{\min\{i,k\}}, s_{\max\{j,l\}}]$.

Note that intersection and connected union are closed binary operations defined on $\mathcal{H} \cup \{\varnothing\}$. It is not difficult to prove that the set $\mathcal{H}_S \cup \{\varnothing\}$, jointly with the two-binary operation intersection and connected union, form a *lattice* [5].

2.2 Concordance and Distance Between HFLTSs

If $H_1, H_2 \in \mathcal{H}_S$, a common distance defined in $\mathcal{H}_s$ is $d(H_1, H_2) = card(H_1 \bigsqcup H_2) - card(H_1 \cap H_2)$. However, this distance does not enable distinguishing all the possibilities between two HFLTS that have an equal connected union and empty intersection. For instance, $d([s_1, s_2], [s_4, s_5]) = d([s_1, s_2], [s_3, s_5])$ seems counterintuitive. This happens because this distance does not consider the length of the gap between the two disjointed HFLTSs. A new distance is defined using the concept of *concordance* to overcome this problem.

Definition 3. $H_1, H_2 \in \mathcal{H}_S$, the *concordance* of H_1 and H_2 is defined as:

$$
\mathcal{C}(H_1, H_2) = \begin{cases} card(H_1 \cap H_2) & \text{if } H_1 \cap H_2 \neq \varnothing \\ -card\left((H_1 \bigsqcup H_2) \cap \overline{H_1} \cap \overline{H_2}\right) & \text{if } H_1 \cap H_2 = \varnothing \end{cases} \tag{1}
$$

That is, the concordance of two non-disjointed HFLTSs is the number of basic labels in common; and the concordance of two disjointed HFLTSs is the opposite of the number of basic labels of the gap between the two HFLTSs. Note that the concordance can be positive or negative depending on whether the HFSTSs are disjointed or not. The concordance is 0 if the two HFLTSs are disjointed but with an empty gap (consecutive HFLTS).

Definition 4. $H_1, H_2 \in \mathcal{H}_S$, the *distance* between H_1 and H_2 is defined as:

$$d(H_1, H_2) = card\left(H_1 \bigsqcup H_2\right) - C(H_1, H_2) \tag{2}$$

Note that this distance can be also expressed as:

$$d(H_1, H_2) = 2 \cdot card\left(H_1 \bigsqcup H_2\right) - card(H_1) - card(H_2) \tag{3}$$

3 The Perceptual Map on the Structure of the Lattice $\mathcal{H}_S$

The previous definition of distance does not distinguish between different basic labels, and only considers the number of them. For instance, it considers that the distance between consecutive basic labels $d(\{s_i\}$ *and* $\{s_{i+1}\})$ is always 2, independently of i, and this is not reasonable in many cases. To overcome this situation, the concept of *perceptual map* is introduced. This concept enables us to give an extended meaning to each basic label and to each HFLTS.

Definition 5. Let S be a totally ordered finite set $S = \{s_1, \ldots, s_n\}$ and then a *basic perceptual map* is a pair (S, μ), where μ is a measure over S, that is, $\mu : S \to R^+ = (0, +\infty)$. If $s_i \in S$, we call $\mu(s_i) \equiv \mu_i$ the *width* of the basic label s_i.

This measure over S can easily be extended to $\mathcal{H}_S$ using that the *width* of the HFLTS $\left[s_i, s_j\right]$ is $\mu\left(\left[s_i, s_j\right]\right) = \sum_{k=i}^{j}\mu_k$. We use the expression *perceptual map* for the pair $(\mathcal{H}_S, \mu)$ that we also note as $\mathcal{H}_{(S,\mu)}$.

Considering the perceptual map $\mathcal{H}_{(s,\mu)}$, the concepts of concordance and distance are redefined as follows:

Definition 6. $H_1, H_2 \in \mathcal{H}_{(S,\mu)}$, the *concordance* of H_1 and H_2 is defined as:

$$C(H_1, H_2) = \begin{cases} width(H_1 \cap H_2) & if \ H_1 \cap H_2 \neq \emptyset \\ -width\left((H_1 \bigsqcup H_2) \cap \overline{H_1} \cap \overline{H_2}\right) & if \ H_1 \cap H_2 = \emptyset \end{cases} \tag{4}$$

Definition 7. $H_1, H_2 \in \mathcal{H}_{(S,\mu)}$, the *distance* of H_1 and H_2 is defined as:

$$d(H_1, H_2) = width\left(H_1 \bigsqcup H_2\right) - C(H_1, H_2) \tag{5}$$

Note that this distance can also be expressed as:

$$d(H_1, H_2) = 2 \cdot width\left(H_1 \bigsqcup H_2\right) - width(H_1) - width(H_2) \tag{6}$$

The difference between the original definition of HFLTSs and the perceptual map is shown in Fig. 1. On the right, the lattice $\mathcal{H}_{(s,\mu)}$ is not balanced, i.e., the width of each basic label is different.

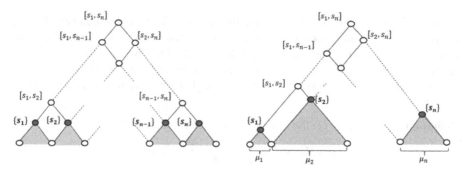

Fig. 1. Difference between the original definition of HFLTSs ($\mathcal{H}_S$) (on the left) and the perceptual map ($\mathcal{H}_{(S,\mu)}$) (on the right)

3.1 Centroid and Degree of Consensus

Definition 9. Given a group of k DMs, $G = \{d_1, \ldots, d_k\}$ with each providing an assessment $H_i \in \mathcal{H}_{(S,\mu)}$ over one alternative, then the *centroid* of the group, denoted as H^C, is defined as:

$$H^C = \arg \min_{H \in \mathcal{H}_{(S,\mu)}} \sum_{j=1}^{k} d\left(H, H_j\right) \tag{7}$$

This centroid represents the central tendency of all assessments given by the DM group G.

The following proposition proves that the centroid can be calculated using the two medians of the two sets of indexes.

Proposition. If $H_i = \left[s_i^L, s_i^R\right] \in \mathcal{H}_{(S,\mu)} \ \forall i \in \{1, \ldots, k\}$ then the centroid is calculated as:

$$H^C = \{[s_L, s_R] \in \mathcal{H}_{(S,\mu)} | L \in \mathbb{M}\left(s_1^L, \ldots, s_1^L\right), R \in \mathbb{M}\left(s_1^R, \ldots, s_1^R\right)\} \tag{8}$$

where $\mathbb{M}$ is the set that contains just the median if k is odd, or two central values and any integer number between them if k is even. The proof of this proposition can be found in [1].

From the previous proposition, it follows that when the number of DMs is odd, the centroid is unique. However, when the number of DMs is even, the centroid is not unique.

The value $\sum_{j=1}^{k} d\left(H^C, H_j\right)$ can be considered a measure of *disagreement* among the DMs. This sum has a minimum value of 0 if $H_i = H_j \forall ij$ and is upper bounded by $\zeta = \lfloor k/2 \rfloor \cdot \left(2 \cdot \sum_i \mu_i - \mu_1 - \mu_n\right)$. This bounding enables us to define the *degree of agreement or consensus* of G as:

$$\delta(G) = 1 - \frac{\sum_{j=1}^{k} d\left(H^C, H_j\right)}{\zeta} \in [0, 1] \tag{9}$$

4   A Transformation Function for Multi-perceptual GDM

In this section, we seek to establish the basis for modelling multiple perceptual maps or multi-granularity. Multi-granularity refers to the use of different set of labels or different meanings for the same set of labels by different DMs, that is, from now on we associate a different perceptual map for each DM. To aggregate all this information from the group of DMs, we develop a perceptual-based transformation function to project linguistic assessments built over different perceptual maps onto a projected linguistic structure. This approach is inspired by some of the ideas developed for linguistic hierarchies [4, 9], multi-granular contexts [9, 10], and the extension of a discrete linguistic term set [18]. In the following paragraphs, G is assumed to be a set of DMs, $G = \{d_1, \ldots, d_k\}$. Each d_j expresses his or her opinion based on his or her own perceptual map $(\mathcal{H}_{S_j}, \mu^j)$ over his or her appropriate linguistic term set $S_j = \left\{ s_1^j, \ldots, s_{n_j}^j \right\} j \in \{1, \ldots, k\}$ of cardinality n_j.

Given that a basic linguistic perceptual map (S, μ) can be considered as a partition of some real interval of length $L = \sum_i \mu_i$, we consider k different basic perceptual maps (S_j, μ^j) such as $\sum_i \mu_i^j = L \forall j \in \{1, \ldots, k\}$. This last equality simply expresses a normalization that enables the comparison of different perceptual maps.

Given k basic perceptual maps (S_j, μ^j), we can consider a *basic projected perceptual map* (S^P, π) such as $N \equiv Card(S^P) \leq \sum n_j - 1$ and where $\pi_1 = \min_j \mu_1^j$ and $\pi_N = \min_j \mu_{n_j}^j$. This projected perceptual map forms a refinement of the partitions where all the HFLTSs from any DM have equivalence in this basic projected perceptual map. From the set S^P and the measure π, the *projected perceptual map* $\mathcal{H}_{(S^P, \pi)}$ is obtained as usual (see Fig. 2).

If $H_j \in \mathcal{H}_{(S_j, \mu^j)}$ is the assessment of DM j using the perceptual map $\mathcal{H}_{(S_j, \mu^j)}$, this HFLTS has an equivalent $H_j^* \in \mathcal{H}_{(S^P, \pi)}$. For instance, in the example shown in Fig. 2:

- $H_1 = [s_1, s_2]$ defined over the perceptual map $\mathcal{H}_{(S_1, \{\mu_1^1, \mu_2^1, \mu_3^1\})}$ has an equivalent in $\mathcal{H}_{(S^P, \pi)}$ that is $H_1^* = [s_1^*, s_5^*]$.
- $H_2 = \{s_2\}$ defined over the perceptual map $\mathcal{H}_{(S_2, \{\mu_1^2, \mu_2^2, \mu_3^2, \mu_4^2\})}$ has an equivalent in $\mathcal{H}_{(S^P, \pi)}$ that is $H_2^* = [s_3^*, s_4^*]$.
- $H_3 = \{s_1\}$ defined over the perceptual map $\mathcal{H}_{(S_3, \{\mu_1^3, \mu_2^3\})}$ has an equivalent in $\mathcal{H}_{(S^P, \pi)}$ that is $H_2^* = [s_1^*, s_3^*]$.

The *centroid* can now be considered using the projected perceptual map and its associated distance:

$$H^C = \arg \min_{H \in \mathcal{H}_{(S^P, \pi)}} \sum_{j=1}^k d_{\mathcal{H}_{(S^P, \pi)}} \left(H, H_j^* \right) \tag{10}$$

where $d_{\mathcal{H}_{(S^P, \pi)}}$ is the distance in the perceptual map $\mathcal{H}_{(S^P, \pi)}$ and H_j^* is the projection of H_j onto this projected perceptual map.

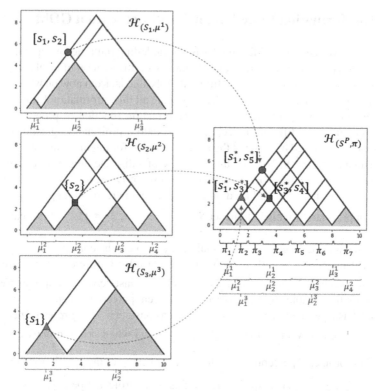

Fig. 2. Example of projected perceptual map π from perceptual maps μ^1, μ^2 and μ^3.

Again, the sum $\sum_{j=1}^{k} d_{\mathcal{H}_{(S^P,\pi)}}\left(H, H_j^*\right)$ is upper bounded by $\zeta = \lfloor k/2 \rfloor \cdot \left(2 \cdot \sum_i \pi_i - \pi_1 - \pi_n\right)$ and this enables defining the *degree of consensus* as:

$$\delta(G) = 1 - \frac{\sum_{j=1}^{k} d_{\mathcal{H}_{(S^P,\pi)}}(H^C, H_j^*)}{\zeta} \tag{11}$$

To illustrate this calculus let's find the centroid and the degree of consensus in the example in Fig. 2. Let's suppose the perceptual maps:

- $\left(S_1, \mu^1\right)$ where $\mu_1^1 = 1$, $\mu_2^1 = 5$, $\mu_3^1 = 4$.
- $\left(S_2, \mu^2\right)$ where $\mu_1^2 = 2$, $\mu_2^2 = 3$, $\mu_3^2 = 3$, $\mu_4^2 = 2$.
- $\left(S_3, \mu^3\right)$ where $\mu_1^3 = 3$, $\mu_2^3 = 7$.
- $\left(S^P, \pi\right)$ where $\pi_1 = 1$, $\pi_2 = 1$, $\pi_3 = 1$, $\pi_4 = 2$, $\pi_5 = 1$, $\pi_6 = 2$, $\pi_7 = 2$.

The assessment of the three DMs are:

- $H_1 = [s_1, s_2]$, that is $H_1^* = \left[s_1^*, s_5^*\right]$.
- $H_2 = \{s_2\}$, that is $H_2^* = \left[s_3^*, s_4^*\right]$.

- $H_3 = \{s_1\}$, that is $H_3^* = [s_1^*, s_3^*]$.

Therefore, the centroid is:

$$H^C = \left\{ [s_L^*, s_R^*] \in \mathcal{H}_{(S,\mu)} \,\middle|\, L \in \mathbb{M}(s_1^*, s_3^*, s_1^*), R \in \mathbb{M}(s_5^*, s_4^*, s_3^*) \right\} = [s_1^*, s_4^*]$$

The distances between the centroid and each assessment are:

- $d_{\mathcal{H}_{(SP,\pi)}}(H^C, H_1^*) = d_{\mathcal{H}_{(SP,\pi)}}([s_1^*, s_4^*], [s_1^*, s_5^*]) = \pi_5$
- $d_{\mathcal{H}_{(SP,\pi)}}(H^C, H_2^*) = d_{\mathcal{H}_{(SP,\pi)}}([s_1^*, s_4^*], [s_3^*, s_4^*]) = \pi_1 + \pi_2$
- $d_{\mathcal{H}_{(SP,\pi)}}(H^C, H_3^*) = d_{\mathcal{H}_{(SP,\pi)}}([s_1^*, s_4^*], [s_1^*, s_3^*]) = \pi_3$

and the degree of consensus is:

$$\delta(G) = 1 - \frac{d_{\mathcal{H}_{(SP,\pi)}}(H^C, H_1^*) + d_{\mathcal{H}_{(SP,\pi)}}(H^C, H_2^*) + d_{\mathcal{H}_{(SP,\pi)}}(H^C, H_3^*)}{\zeta} = 1 - \frac{\pi_5 + \pi_1 + \pi_2 + \pi_3}{(2 \cdot L - \pi_1 - \pi_7)} = \frac{13}{17}.$$

that is, a degree of consensus of approximately 76.5%.

This last example clearly illustrates all steps in the calculus of the degree of consensus when different perceptual maps are taken into account, that is, in a multi-perceptual GDM scenario.

5   Conclusion and Future Work

This paper presents a multi-perceptual framework for multi-criteria group decision aiding based on unbalanced hesitant linguistic information. The framework presented enables DMs to use their own perception maps, that is, their own linguistic labels with their own meanings. This contribution represents a step forward with respect to the existing methods for MCDA in which DMs with different backgrounds or knowledge and may feel more comfortable using their own linguistic term sets when expressing judgements. Even the same linguistic term can have different meanings depending on the DM who uses it because each DM may have acquired a specific meaning for a term as a result of his or her experience.

The multi-perceptual framework is based on the projected perceptual map, a hyper-perceptual map where all HFLTSs from each of the perceptual maps from all DMs have equivalences. The concepts of distance, centroid, and degree of consensus can be interpreted directly in this projected perceptual map. An illustrative example is provided to demonstrate the overall approach.

Compared with previous linguistic frameworks with HFLTSs in the literature, the main contribution of this work is found in three aspects. Firstly, basic labels can be freely distributed and there is no need for uniformity nor symmetry. Secondly, the meaning of basic linguistic terms does not only depend on their position, but also on their measures. Finally, the proposed framework enables flexibility for different degrees of uncertainty and granularity among the experts.

Future research is oriented in various directions. Firstly, analyzing how to translate hesitancy among different perceptual maps without increasing granularity. Secondly, analyzing the evolution of the degree of consensus when a new DM joins the decision group. Thirdly, capturing the perceptual map associated with each DM from previous assessments through machine learning techniques. Finally, all of these directions will revert positively in common-sense reasoning understanding and contribute to improving human-machine interaction.

Acknowledgements. This research has been partially supported by the PERCEPTIONS Research Project (PID2020-114247GB-I00), funded by the Spanish Ministry of Science and Information Technology.

References

1. Porro, O., Agell, N. Sánchez, M., Ruiz, F.J.: A multi-attribute group decision model based on unbalanced and multi-granular linguistic information: An application to assess entrepreneurial competencies in secondary schools. Appl. Soft Comput. **111** (2021)
2. Liao, H., et al.: Qualitative decision making with correlation coefficients of hesitant fuzzy linguistic term sets. Knowl. Based Syst. **76**, 127–138 (2015)
3. Rodriguez, R.M., Martinez, L., Herrera, F.: Hesitant fuzzy linguistic term sets for decision making. IEEE Trans. Fuzzy Syst. **20**, 109–119 (2012)
4. Liao, H., et al.: Hesitant fuzzy linguistic term set and its application in decision making: a state-of-the-art survey. Int. J. Fuzzy Syst. **20**(7), 2084–2110 (2018)
5. Montserrat-Adell, J., et al.: Modeling group assessments by means of hesitant fuzzy linguistic term sets. J. Appl. Log. **23**, 40–50 (2017)
6. Chen, Z.-S., et al.: Third-party reverse logistics provider selection: a computational semantic analysis-based multi-perspective multi-attribute decision making approach. Expert Syst. Appl. **166**, 114051 (2021)
7. Wei, C., Zhao, N., Tang, X.: Operators and comparisons of hesitant fuzzy linguistic term sets. IEEE Trans. Fuzzy Syst. **22**(3), 575–585 (2013)
8. Torra, V.: Hesitant fuzzy sets. Int. J. Intell. Syst. **25.6**, 529–539 (2010)
9. Herrera, F., Martínez, L.: A model based on linguistic 2-tuples for dealing with multigranular hierarchical linguistic contexts in multi-expert decision-making. IEEE Trans. Syst. Man Cybern. Part B (Cybernetics) **31.2**, 227–234 (2001)
10. Tian, Z., et al.: Signed distance-based consensus in multi-criteria group decision-making with multi-granular hesitant unbalanced linguistic information. Comput. Ind. Eng. **124**, 125–138 (2018)
11. Cabrerizo, F.J., Al-Hmouz, R., Morfeq, A., Balamash, A.S., Martínez, M.A., Herrera-Viedma, E.: Soft consensus measures in group decision making using unbalanced fuzzy linguistic information. Soft. Comput. **21**(11), 3037–3050 (2015). https://doi.org/10.1007/s00500-015-1989-6
12. Hao, J., Chiclana, F.: Attitude quantifier based possibility distribution generation method for hesitant fuzzy linguistic group decision making. Inf. Sci. **518**, 341–360 (2020)
13. Wu, Z., Xu, J.: Possibility distribution-based approach for MAGDM with hesitant fuzzy linguistic information. IEEE Trans. Cybern. **46**(3), 694–705 (2015)
14. Chen, Z.S., et al.: Proportional hesitant fuzzy linguistic term set for multiple criteria group decision making. Inf. Sci. **357**, 61–87 (2016)
15. Chen, Z.S., et al.: Customizing semantics for individuals with attitudinal HFLTS possibility distributions. IEEE Trans. Fuzzy Syst. **26**(6), 3452–3466 (2018)

16. Roselló, L., et al.: Using consensus and distances between generalized multi-attribute linguistic assessments for group decision-making. Inf. Fus. **17**, 83–92 (2014)
17. Zhang, Z., Chen, S.M., Wang, C.: Group decision making based on multiplicative consistency and consensus of fuzzy linguistic preference relations. Inf. Sci. **509**, 71–86 (2020)
18. Xu, Z.: Group decision making based on multiple types of linguistic preference relations. Inf. Sci. **178**(2), 452–467 (2008)
19. Le, H., et al.: Deriving the personalized individual semantics of linguistic information from flexible linguistic preference relations. Inf. Fus. **81**, 154–170 (2022)

Probabilistic Judgement Aggregation by Opinion Update

Magdalena Ivanovska[1]([⊠])(iD) and Marija Slavkovik[2](iD)

[1] BI Norwegian Business School, Oslo, Norway
`magdalena.ivanovska@bi.no`
[2] University of Bergen, Bergen, Norway
`marija.slavkovik@uib.no`

Abstract. We consider a situation where agents are updating their probabilistic opinions on a set of issues with respect to the confidence they have in each other's judgements. We adapt the framework for reaching a consensus introduced in [2] and modified in [1] to our case of uncertain probabilistic judgements on logically related issues. We discuss possible alternative solutions for the instances where the requirements for reaching a consensus are not satisfied.

Keywords: Judgement aggregation · Probabilistic logic · Markov chains

1 Introduction

Judgement aggregation (JA) is concerned with aggregating categorical judgements about the truth values of logically related issues (propositions) [4,7]. An example is given in Table 1, where the rows contain judgements of agents over the issues p, q, and $p \wedge q$. As observed from the example, pooling the truth valuations on each issue does not always lead to a consistent set of collective judgements. JA designs and studies aggregators that produce a consistent outcome.

Table 1. An example of a judgement aggregation using the simple majority rule.

	p	q	$p \wedge q$
Agent 1	True	True	True
Agent 2	True	False	False
Agent 3	False	True	False
Majority	True	True	False

Aggregation problems, however, are not always Boolean, since the judgements on whether an issue is true or false are not always certain. In order to deal with this kind of uncertainty, in [6] we define a framework that aims at aggregating judgements about the probabilities of issues, as in the example given in Table 2.

V. Torra and Y. Narukawa (Eds.): MDAI 2022, LNAI 13408, pp. 26–37, 2022.
https://doi.org/10.1007/978-3-031-13448-7_3

Table 2. An example of probabilistic judgement aggregation with a threshold majority rule. The numbers in each row represent the probabilities of the issues being true according to the corresponding agent.

	p	q	$p \wedge q$
Agent 1	0.7	0.8	0.7
Agent 2	0.6	0.7	0.5
Agent 3	0.2	0.8	0.2
Majority$_{\geq 0.6}$	True	True	False

One way of aggregating judgements into a consistent collective opinion would be to modify (update) some of the individual judgements until the chosen aggregation rule produces a consistent judgement. This idea is obviously more applicable to probabilistic judgements than to categorical ones, since the modification there amounts to adjusting a probability value rather than completely changing the attitude about the truth of an issue. As can be observed in the example in Table 2, a small modification of an individual opinion (in this case agent 2's judgement on $p \wedge q$) could result in obtaining a consistent collective judgement.

In this paper we consider a setting where agents update their individual opinions to align with each other and eventually converge to a consensual opinion. We adopt the model for reaching a consensus over probability distributions described in [2] and show that it is applicable to the case of probabilistic opinions on logically related issues as well. The model presumes a confidence matrix representing the trust the agents have in each other's opinions. The opinion updating is performed based on the confidence matrix. In the cases where the repeated updates converge to a consensus, the aggregated opinion is obtained from the individual opinions through a linear function, and some desirable properties follow by definition. We discuss possible solutions to the cases where this repeated update will not lead to a consensus due to the properties of the confidence matrix and the particular opinions that are to be aggregated.

2   Framework

We use a slightly modified version of the framework defined in [6] which we include for self-sufficiency.

2.1   Probabilistic Judgement Profiles

Let $\mathcal{L}$ be a set of propositional logic formulas. An *agenda* is a finite set $\Phi \subset \mathcal{L}$,

$$\Phi = \{\varphi_1, \ldots, \varphi_m\}, \tag{1}$$

s.t. φ_i is neither a tautology nor a contradiction. We call the elements of the agenda *issues*. For example, in Table 1, we have $\Phi = \{p, q, p \wedge q\}$. We are interested in aggregating a collection of judgements on the agenda issues coming from a group of *information sources* (we will also call them *agents*) into a collective judgement representative for the group. Let $\Phi^{\cup} = \Phi \cup \{\neg\varphi \mid \varphi \in \Phi\}$. We model the information sources as sets of likelihood judgements on $\Phi^{\cup}$.

A *likelihood judgement* on the issue $\varphi \in \Phi^{\cup}$ is a simple likelihood formula of the type:

$$\ell(\varphi) \geq a, \tag{2}$$

where $a \in [0, 1]$. The likelihood judgement $\ell(\varphi) \geq a$ expresses that the likelihood (probability)[1] of the statement φ being true is at least a. The formula (2) is an instance of the logic of likelihood (see [3] and [5]), the language of which consists of Boolean combinations of linear likelihood formulas of the type

$$a_1\ell(\varphi_1) + \ldots + a_n\ell(\varphi_n) \geq b, \tag{3}$$

where a_i, b are real numbers, and φ_i are pure propositional formulas.[2] The likelihood formulas are interpreted in probability spaces $M = (W, F, \mu)$, where W is a set of possible worlds, F is a σ-algebra on W, and $\mu : F \to [0, 1]$ is a probability measure. The propositional formulas are given possible world semantics in the standard way:

$$\varphi^M = \{w \in W \mid w \models \varphi\}, \tag{4}$$

and the term $\ell(\varphi)$ is interpreted as $\mu(\varphi^M)$[3], i.e. as the probability of the set of worlds at which φ is true. This leads to the following interpretation of (3):

$$a_1\mu(\varphi_1^M) + \ldots + a_n\mu(\varphi_n^M) \geq b, \tag{5}$$

i.e. (3) is true in M if and only if (5) holds. The interpretation of Boolean combinations of formulas of type (3) is defined in the standard way.

The axiomatic system for the logic of likelihood consists of axioms for propositional reasoning, reasoning about inequalities, and reasoning about probabilities. In particular, for every propositions φ and ψ, and every likelihood formulas f and g, the following are axioms:

- (Prop) All substitution instances of tautologies in propositional logic,
- (MP) From f and $f \to g$, infer g,
- (Inq) All substitution instances of valid linear inequality formulas,
- (L1) $\ell(\varphi) \geq 0$,
- (L2) $\ell(\top) = 1$,
- (L3) $\ell(\varphi) = \ell(\varphi \wedge \psi) + \ell(\varphi \wedge \neg\psi)$,
- (L4) From $\varphi \leftrightarrow \psi$ infer $\ell(\varphi) = \ell(\psi)$.

The above set of axioms is shown to be sound and complete with respect to the above interpretation [3].

---

[1] In this paper we interpret likelihood as probability and we use the two terms interchangeably. Note that, however, likelihood can also be interpreted as another measure of belief, see [5].

[2] Expressions containing all the other types of inequalities or equality can be defined as abbreviations.

[3] To ensure that every φ^M is measurable, we may take $F = 2^W$.

Each of the information sources is represented as a *set of likelihood judgements* $\hat{J}$. The set $\hat{J}$ has one likelihood judgement on each of the issues in $\Phi^\cup$:

$$\hat{J} = \{\ell(\varphi) \geq a(\varphi) \mid \varphi \in \Phi^\cup\}, \tag{6}$$

where $a(\varphi) \in [0,1]$ is called a *judgement coefficient* of φ.

From a given judgement set $\hat{J}$ as defined in (6), using the above axioms, we can derive $\ell(\varphi) \leq 1 - a(\neg\varphi)$. This means that providing likelihood formulas for both φ and $\neg\varphi$ in the judgement set $\hat{J}$ is equivalent to providing intervals for the likelihood of φ. In the cases where $a(\varphi) + a(\neg\varphi) = 1$, these intervals collapse to a point, i.e. we obtain precise likelihood judgement. Judgements in $\hat{J}$ can also be Boolean, since we can represent by $\ell(\varphi) \geq 1$ that φ is true, and by $\ell(\neg\varphi) \geq 1$ that φ is false.

Given a set of n agents $N = \{1, \ldots, n\}$, a *likelihood profile*:

$$\hat{P} = (\hat{J}_1, \ldots, \hat{J}_n), \tag{7}$$

is a collection of sets of likelihood judgements for an agenda Φ, each representing one agent $k \in N$. We slightly abuse notation and write $\hat{J}_k \in \hat{P}$ to denote that $\hat{J}_k$ is the k-th likelihood judgement set in $\hat{P}$:

$$\hat{J}_k = \{\ell(\varphi) \geq a_k(\varphi) \mid \varphi \in \Phi^\cup\}, \tag{8}$$

where $a_k(\varphi) \in [0,1]$ are the judgement coefficients of the k-th agent, $k = 1, \ldots, n$. An example of a likelihood profile is given in Table 3.

Table 3. An example of a likelihood profile over the agenda $\Phi = \{p, q, p \wedge q\}$. The set of likelihood judgements of agent 1 is $J_1 = \{\ell(p) \geq 0.7, \ell(\neg p) \geq 0.2, \ell(q) \geq 0.8, \ell(\neg q) \geq 0.1, \ell(p \wedge q) \geq 0.7, \ell(\neg(p \wedge q)) \geq 0.2\}$. Similarly, for J_2 and J_3.

	p	$\neg p$	q	$\neg q$	$p \wedge q$	$\neg(p \wedge q)$
Agent 1	≥ 0.7	≥ 0.2	≥ 0.8	≥ 0.1	≥ 0.7	≥ 0.2
Agent 2	≥ 0.6	≥ 0.2	≥ 0.7	≥ 0.3	≥ 0.5	≥ 0.5
Agent 3	≥ 0.2	≥ 0.2	≥ 0.8	≥ 0.2	≥ 0.2	≥ 0.4

The example in Table 2 is a special case of a likelihood profile for the agenda $\Phi = \{p, q, p \wedge q\}$, where each row represents a judgement set with precise likelihood judgements. For example, 0.6 in the row of agent 2 stands for $\ell(p) = 0.6$, or, equivalently, $\ell(p) \geq 0.6$ and $\ell(\neg p) \geq 0.4$.

2.2 Rationality of Probabilistic Judgement Sets

We require that the sets of likelihood judgements in the profile are *rational*. We now define what are rational likelihood judgements sets.

A probabilistic judgement set is *consistent* if it is a consistent set of formulas in the logic of likelihood. A probabilistic judgement set is not always consistent. Consider, for example, the agenda $\Phi = \{p_1 \wedge p_2, p_1 \wedge \neg p_2\}$ and a set $\hat{J}$ containing the judgements $\ell(p_1 \wedge p_2) \geq 0.4$ and $\ell(p_1 \wedge \neg p_2) \geq 0.7$. The set $\hat{J}$ is an inconsistent set of formulas, because it implies $\ell(p_1) \geq 1.1$ by axiom (L3). Furthermore, note that for a judgement set $\hat{J}$ defined as in (6) to be consistent, it has to satisfy $a(\varphi) + a(\neg\varphi) \leq 1$, for every $\varphi \in \Phi$.

A set of likelihood judgements is always *complete* in the sense that it contains a likelihood judgement for each of the issues. This assumption does not limit the freedom of not having a specific likelihood estimate for a given issue φ. To represent the absence of a specific likelihood or an "abstention" on an issue φ, we can use the tautologies $\ell(\varphi) \geq 0$ and $\ell(\neg\varphi) \geq 0$.

In classical judgement aggregation, a judgement set is rational if it is consistent and complete, which means it provides a truth value for each of the issues in the agenda, and these values are consistent. In the probabilistic case, consistency and completeness are not enough of conditions for rationality. For example, $\hat{J} = \{\ell(p_1) \geq 0.3, \ell(\neg p_1) \geq 0.5, \ell(p_1 \wedge p_2) \geq 0.4, \ell(\neg(p_1 \wedge p_2)) \geq 0.5\}$ is a consistent set. However, if we use the axioms, we can easily derive $\ell(p_1) \geq 0.4$, which is stronger than the existing $\ell(p_1) \geq 0.3$ and, as such, is a more valuable judgement. In general, we say that $\ell(\varphi) \geq a$ is a *stronger judgement* than $\ell(\varphi) \geq b$ iff $a > b$. To ensure that we always have the strongest possible judgements in the consistent judgement sets, we introduce the notion of a *final judgement*. A consistent probabilistic judgement set is *final* if it does not imply stronger judgements than the ones it contains, i.e. a judgement set $\hat{J}$ as defined by (6) is final iff $\hat{J} \vdash \ell(\varphi) \geq c$ implies $c \leq a(\varphi)$, for every $\varphi \in \Phi^{\cup}$. We say that the probabilistic judgement set $\hat{J}$ is *rational* if it is consistent and final. A profile is rational if all the judgement sets in it are rational.

3   Updating Probabilistic Judgements

One can imagine there are many different ways the agents can update their judgements, depending on the kind of information the update is based upon. Here, we handle the situation where there is no new factual information that the agents receive, but they are able to observe each other's judgements and update their own judgement sets based on this observation. Similarly as in [2], we assume that each agent has certain degrees of confidence in the other agents' opinions and in her own, and updates her probabilistic judgements upon observing the judgements of others based on these confidence degrees. More formally, let

$$t_k = (t_{k1}, \ldots, t_{kn}), \tag{9}$$

where $t_{kr} \in [0, 1]$, for every r, and $\sum_{r=1}^{n} t_{kr} = 1$, be the confidence distribution of the k-th agent, $k = 1, \ldots, n$. t_{kr} is interpreted as the degree of confidence the agent k assigns to the agent r, $r = 1, \ldots, n$. We call the matrix $T = [t_{kr}]_{n \times n}$, where each row represents a confidence distribution of the corresponding agent, a *confidence matrix*.

Given a likelihood profile $\hat{P} = (\hat{J}_1, \ldots, \hat{J}_n)$, we assume that the agent k is updating her judgements by calculating new judgement coefficients as weighted average of everyone's judgement coefficients wrt. her confidence distribution t_k:

$$\hat{J}_k^1 = \{\ell(\varphi) \geq \sum_{r=1}^{n} t_{kr} a_r(\varphi) \mid \varphi \in \Phi^{\cup}\}. \tag{10}$$

The updating process can iterate several times, and the result of each iteration is defined recursively:

$$\hat{J}_k^i = \{\ell(\varphi) \geq a_k^i(\varphi) \mid \varphi \in \Phi^\cup\}, \tag{11}$$

where the judgement coefficients are determined by

$$a_k^i(\varphi) = \sum_{r=1}^{n} t_{kr} a_r^{i-1}(\varphi), \tag{12}$$

for $k = 1, \ldots, n$, where $a_r^0(\varphi) = a_r(\varphi)$. $\hat{P}^i = (\hat{J}_1^i, \ldots, \hat{J}_n^i)$ is the i-th update of the profile $\hat{P} = (\hat{J}_1, \ldots, \hat{J}_n)$, for $i \in \mathbb{N}$.

Theorem 1. *Let $\hat{P} = (\hat{J}_1, \ldots, \hat{J}_n)$ be a rational profile and $T = [t_{kr}]_{n \times n}$ be a confidence matrix. Then $\hat{P}^i = (\hat{J}_1^i, \ldots, \hat{J}_n^i)$ is a rational profile, for every $i \in \mathbb{N}$.*

The proof of the above theorem follows directly from the following proposition.

Proposition 1. *Let $\hat{P} = (\hat{J}_1, \ldots, \hat{J}_n)$ be a rational profile and $t = (t_1, \ldots, t_n)$ be a vector of coefficients such that $t_k \in [0, 1]$, for every $k = 1, \ldots, n$, and $\sum_{k=1}^{n} t_k = 1$. Then the judgement set $\hat{J} = \{\ell(\varphi) \geq \sum_{k=1}^{n} t_k a_k(\varphi) \mid \varphi \in \Phi^\cup\}$ is rational.*

Proof. Consistency: Let W be a set of possible worlds and let $F = 2^W$ be the σ-algebra of all the subsets of W. Since the profile $\hat{P}$ is rational, the set $\hat{J}_k = \{\ell(\varphi) \geq a_k(\varphi) \mid \varphi \in \Phi^\cup\}$ is a consistent set of formulas, for every $k = 1, \ldots, n$. This means that there exist probability measures on (W, F), $\mu_k : F \to [0, 1]$, $k = 1, \ldots, n$, such that the inequalities in the sets $\{\mu_k(\varphi^M) \geq a_k(\varphi) \mid \varphi \in \Phi^\cup\}$ hold. Then the linear function of these measures with the components of the vector t as coefficients, $\mu = \sum_k t_k \mu_k$, is a probability measure on (W, F) for which the set of inequalities $\{\mu(\varphi^M) \geq \sum_k t_k a_k(\varphi) \mid \varphi \in \Phi^\cup\}$ holds. The last implies consistency of the judgement set $\hat{J} = \{\ell(\varphi) \geq \sum_k t_k a_k(\varphi) \mid \varphi \in \Phi^\cup\}$.

Finality: Let us denote by $a(\varphi) = \sum_k t_k a_k(\varphi)$ the likelihood coefficients of the set $\hat{J}$. Suppose that the set $\hat{J}$ is not final. This means that there exists $\varphi_i \in \Phi^\cup$, and $c > a(\varphi_i)$, such that $\hat{J} \vdash \ell(\varphi_i) \geq c$, i.e. that using the formulas in $\hat{J}$ and the axioms of the logic, one can derive $\ell(\varphi_i) \geq c$. Since $c > a(\varphi_i)$, this derivation needs to include axioms (L3), (L4) and some of the likelihood judgements of $\hat{J}$ referring to issues other than φ_i. In particular, φ_i must "include" some of the other issues, i.e. there must exist issues $\varphi_{i_1}, \ldots, \varphi_{i_r} \in \Phi^\cup$, other than φ_i, such that

$$\vdash \ell(\varphi_i) \geq \ell(\varphi_{i_1}) + \cdots + \ell(\varphi_{i_r}), \tag{13}$$

and their judgement coefficients are such that:

$$a(\varphi_{i_1}) + \cdots + a(\varphi_{i_r}) \geq c. \tag{14}$$

Now, from (13) and the consistency of $\hat{J}_k$, for every k, we will have

$$\hat{J}_k \vdash \ell(\varphi_i) \geq a_k(\varphi_{i_1}) + \cdots + a_k(\varphi_{i_r}). \tag{15}$$

From this and the finality of $\hat{J}_k$, we obtain

$$a_k(\varphi_i) \geq a_k(\varphi_{i_1}) + \cdots + a_k(\varphi_{i_r}), \tag{16}$$

for every k. But then,

$$\sum_k t_k a_k(\varphi_i) \geq \sum_k t_k a_k(\varphi_{i_1}) + \cdots + \sum_k t_k a_k(\varphi_{i_r}), \tag{17}$$

which with the shortened notation becomes

$$a(\varphi_i) \geq a(\varphi_{i_1}) + \cdots + a(\varphi_{i_r}) \tag{18}$$

The last, together with (14), implies $a(\varphi_i) \geq c$, which is in contradiction with the initial assumption.

4   Convergence to a Consensus

Let us denote $a_{kj} = a_k(\varphi_j)$, for $\varphi_j \in \Phi^\cup$, and $k = 1, \ldots, n$. Then $A = [a_{kj}]_{n \times 2m}$ is a matrix consisting of the judgement coefficients of the n agents on the set of propositions $\Phi^\cup$, with each row corresponding to one agent, and each column corresponding to one issue of the extended agenda $\Phi^\cup$. We call it a *judgement matrix* of the profile $\hat{P} = (\hat{J}_1, \ldots, \hat{J}_n)$. For example, the likelihood profile given in Table 3 is represented by the judgement matrix given in Fig. 1.

$$A = \begin{bmatrix} 0.7 \ 0.2 \ 0.8 \ 0.1 \ 0.7 \ 0.2 \\ 0.6 \ 0.2 \ 0.7 \ 0.3 \ 0.5 \ 0.5 \\ 0.2 \ 0.2 \ 0.8 \ 0.2 \ 0.2 \ 0.4 \end{bmatrix}$$

Fig. 1. An example of a judgement matrix of three agents on the extended agenda $\Phi^\cup = \{p, \neg p, q, \neg q, p \wedge q, \neg(p \wedge q)\}$.

If A is a judgement matrix of the profile $\hat{P}$ and T is a confidence matrix, then the matrix

$$A^1 = TA$$

will be the judgement matrix of the profile $\hat{P}^1$, we denote it by $A^1 = [a^1_{kj}]$. For example, if T is defined as:

$$T = \begin{bmatrix} 1/2 \ 1/2 \ 0 \\ 1/4 \ 3/4 \ 0 \\ 1/3 \ 1/3 \ 1/3 \end{bmatrix}$$

then the judgement matrix given in Fig. 1 will be updated as follows:

$$A^1 = \begin{bmatrix} 0.650000 & 0.200000 & 0.750000 & 0.200000 & 0.600000 & 0.350000 \\ 0.625000 & 0.200000 & 0.725000 & 0.250000 & 0.550000 & 0.425000 \\ 0.500000 & 0.200000 & 0.766667 & 0.200000 & 0.466667 & 0.366667 \end{bmatrix}$$

In general, if we denote $A^0 = A$, from Eq. (12) we will have

$$A^i = TA^{i-1}, \tag{19}$$

for $i \in \mathbb{N}$, where the matrices $A^i = [a^i_{kj}]$ and $A^{i-1} = [a^{i-1}_{kj}]$ are the judgement matrices of the profiles $\hat{P}^i$ and $\hat{P}^{i-1}$, correspondingly. Applying the associativity of matrix multiplication at Eq. (19), we obtain:

$$A^i = T^i A, \tag{20}$$

which means that for every $i \in \mathbb{N}$, the matrix of the profile $\hat{P}^i$ can be obtained from the matrix of the initial profile $\hat{P}$ and the i-th power of the confidence matrix T.

Let us assume that the agents continue to update their judgement sets, i.e. iterations continue indefinitely, or until for some i, we obtain $A^{i+1} = A^i$, which would mean that the opinions are no longer being updated. During this updating process, we assume that a *consensus is reached* if the opinions of the agents converge to the same judgement set, i.e. there exists a judgement set $\hat{J}^*$, such that

$$\lim_{i \to \infty} \hat{J}^i_k = \hat{J}^*, \tag{21}$$

for every $k = 1, \ldots, n$. This amounts to all the rows of the matrix A^i, we denote them by A^i_k, converging to the same row vector, i.e. *convergence to a consensus* presumes existence of a vector $a^* = (a^*_1, \ldots, a^*_{2m})$, such that:

$$\lim_{i \to \infty} A^i_k = a^*, \tag{22}$$

for every $k = 1, \ldots, n$, and equivalently, due to Eq. (20):

$$\lim_{i \to \infty} T^i_k A = a^*, \tag{23}$$

for every $k = 1, \ldots, n$, where T^i_k is the k-th row of the matrix T^i.

Now, from Eq. (23) we can observe the following: If the rows of T^i converge to the same row vector i.e., if there exists a vector $\pi = (\pi_1, \ldots, \pi_n)$ such that:

$$\lim_{i \to \infty} T^i_k = \pi, \tag{24}$$

for every $k = 1, \ldots, n$, then the matrix product in Eq. (23) will converge to πA, hence this product will determine a vector a^* with the above requirements. Now, having the vector a^* defined as:

$$a^* = \pi A, \tag{25}$$

the corresponding consensual judgement set will be given by:

$$\hat{J}^* = \{\ell(\varphi_j) \geq a_j^* \mid j = 1, \ldots, 2m\}, \tag{26}$$

or, in terms of the input judgement sets and the notation in Sect. 2:

$$\hat{J}^* = \{\ell(\varphi) \geq \sum_{r=1}^{n} \pi_r a_r(\varphi) \mid \varphi \in \Phi^{\cup}\} . \tag{27}$$

5 A Necessary and Sufficient Condition for Reaching a Consensus

According to the discussion in the previous section, the existence of a vector π such that Eq. (24) holds is a *sufficient* condition for reaching a concensus and the consensual solution in the case this condition is satisfied is obtained by mutiplying the initial opinion matrix A by π. It is worth noticing that, if such a vector $\pi = (\pi_1, \ldots, \pi_n)$ exists, then its components are non-negative and $\sum_{r=1}^{n} \pi_r = 1$. Let us now see when such π exists.

Observe that the matrix T is a row stochastic matrix (the sum of each row is 1). This means that it can be regarded as the transition probability matrix of a time-homogeneous Markov chain with n states. With this interpretation of T, the condition in Eq. (24) means that π is the limiting distribution of T, which (since T is time-homogeneous) is also a stationary distribution, i.e. satisfies the equation $\pi T = \pi$. Hence, if a solution π to the last equation exists, then a consensus is reached, and the vector π provides the coefficients for the linear combination of individual judgements that gives the consensual solution a^*, i.e. $a^* = \pi A$.

In the example of a confidence matrix of three agents given in the previous section, the corresponding stationary solution will be:

$$\pi = (1/3, 2/3, 0),$$

and the corresponding consensual vector $a^* = \pi A$, where A is the judgement matrix given in Fig. 1, will be the following:

$$a^* = (0.633333, 0.200000, 0.733333, 0.233333, 0.566667, 0.400000) .$$

Now, the existence of a limiting distribution is equivalent to the Markov chain being irreducible and aperiodic. This means that all the agents need to form one closed communicating aperiodic class for a global consensus to be reached. In cases where T is block-diagonal, like the one in Fig. 2, i.e. there are smaller groups of agents that only give positive confidence to members of their own group, a global consensus will not be reached in the way described above, that is through the stationary distribution of the confidence matrix. Here, a possible solution would be to determine the consensual opinions of each of the groups and then aggregate them, for example, by taking an average.

However, as observed in [1], it is not hard to imagine a case where a consensus obviously exists no matter of the matrix T (and the existence of a stationary distribution). For example, in the trivial case where all the agents have the same probabilistic

$$
\begin{bmatrix}
1/3 & 2/3 & 0 & 0 \\
1/2 & 1/2 & 0 & 0 \\
0 & 0 & 1/4 & 3/4 \\
0 & 0 & 1/2 & 1/2
\end{bmatrix}
$$

Fig. 2. A confidence matrix of a group of four agents. Each row is a distribution of trust that an agent has in the opinions of the other agents. Agents 1 and 2 "listen" to each other and form one closed reccurent group of agents that will reach a consensus between themselves. Similarly, agents 3 and 4 communicate between each other and will reach a consensus.

judgement set $\hat{J}$, the consensus is the set $\hat{J}$ itself, no matter of the confidence matrix T. The authors of [1] proceed further with the above observation and derive a *necessary and sufficient condition* for a consensus to be reached that applies to any possible choice of T and A: For each reccurent class of agents, they construct a certain linear combination of the agents' probability distributions, and show that the consensus exists if and only if all of these linear combinations lead to the same probability distribution. For example, for the confidence matrix given in Fig. 3, they calculate that the consensus is reached if and only if $\frac{3}{8}p_1 + \frac{3}{11}p_2 + \frac{4}{11}p_3 = \frac{11}{25}p_4 + \frac{14}{25}p_5 = \frac{9}{25}p_6 + \frac{16}{25}p_7$ holds for the probability distributions $p_1, \ldots, p_8$ of the agents. We refer the reader to Theorem 2 in [1] for the latter result as stating it properly here would require introducing terminology and notation that is beyond the scope of this paper.

$$
\begin{bmatrix}
1/2 & 1/4 & 1/4 & 0 & 0 & 0 & 0 & 0 \\
1/3 & 1/3 & 1/3 & 0 & 0 & 0 & 0 & 0 \\
1/4 & 1/4 & 1/2 & 0 & 0 & 0 & 0 & 0 \\
0 & 0 & 0 & 0 & 0 & 1/2 & 1/2 & 0 \\
0 & 0 & 0 & 0 & 0 & 1/4 & 3/4 & 0 \\
0 & 0 & 0 & 1/3 & 2/3 & 0 & 0 & 0 \\
0 & 0 & 0 & 1/2 & 1/2 & 0 & 0 & 0 \\
1/3 & 0 & 0 & 1/3 & 0 & 0 & 0 & 1/3
\end{bmatrix}
$$

Fig. 3. A confidence matrix of a group of eight agents.

The work in both [2] and [1] considers the case where the opinions of the agents are expressed in terms of (precise) probability distributions over a set of mutually exclusive propositions, while in our case, the opinions of the agents are effectively expressed as probability intervals over logically related issues. While the result of [2] applies directly to our case as it depends solely on the matrix T, it is not immediately clear how to apply the result of [1] to our case. One way to proceed would be to form a system of equations based on the linear combinations of distributions as defined in Theorem 2 in [1] and the initial intervals for each probability value, and try to find a solution in terms of imprecise probabilities over the issues (probabilistic judgement set). Another idea would be to look at the intersection of the sets of all possible probability distributions of each agent (if non-empty) determined by the initial probabilistic profile and try to find those probability distributions among them that satisfy the requirement for convergence given in [1]. Exploring these ideas is a future work.

There will still be many cases of a periodic or reccurent confidence matrix not satisfying the necessary and sufficient conditions for reaching a consensus as given in [1], even in the case of imprecise probabilities. A possible general solution would then be to require a modification of the confidence matrix T to an aperiodic irreducible matrix that will have a stationary solution. In practice, this means the agents to be required to redistribute their confidence degrees in a certain way that enables the resulting confidence matrix to have a stationary solution. Finding out how exactly this should be done is also a part of our future work.

6   Conclusions

In this paper we refine our framework for probabilistic judgement aggregation defined in [6] and we propose a new method for aggregating probabilistic judgement of agents based on the method for aggregating probability distributions described in [2]. In order to apply the method from [2] to our case, we prove that any linear combination of the judgements of all the agents leads to a rational judgement if the individual judgements are rational, which we consider a central result of the paper.

By defining the judgement coefficients of the collective judgement as a linear combination of the judgement coefficients of the individual judgements, we satisfy certain aggregation properties by definition: *Universal domain* will certainly hold, as J^* in Eq. (27) is well-defined for every choice of $a_r(\varphi)$, by construction. Proposition 1 proves the property of *rationality*. If all the individual judgements assign a probability estimate larger than $c \in [0, 1]$, then the linear combination of these estimates will also be larger than c, hence *unanimity* will as well be satisfied. If the matrix T has a column k that contains only 1's (while all the other elements are 0), then $\hat{J}^* = \hat{J}_k$ and the aggregation is *dictatorial*.

According to [2], the convergence to a consensus relies on the properties of the confidence matrix which can be regarded as a transition probability matrix of a time-homogeneous Markov chain with n states and hence, according to the theory of Markov chains and their properties, a consensus exists whenever this matrix has a stationary solution. However, as observed in [1], the existence of a stationary vector for the matrix T is just a sufficient, but not a necessary condition for a consensus to be reached, and we discuss how a consensual solution could be reached in cases when the properties of the matrix T do not guarantee one.

There exist other works on aggregating opinions on logically related issues by convergence to a consensus using the DeGroot framework [8]. However, the way these works express and deal with the logical relatedness of the issues is different than ours, namely, they express the opinions of agents as subjective degrees of pair-wise logical relatedness of the issues. In our case, the logical relatedness of the issues is predetermined (by an agenda setter, for example) and formalized in their representation as propositional formulas, while the opinions of the agents are probabilistic estimates of the truth of the issues.

References

1. Berger, R.: A necessary and sufficient condition for reaching a consensus using DeGroot's method. J. Am. Statist. Assoc. **76**, 415–418 (1981)
2. DeGroot, M.H.: Reaching a consensus. J. Am. Statist. Assoc. **69**, 118–121 (1974)
3. Fagin, R., Halpern, J.Y., Megiddo, N.: A logic for reasoning about probabilities. Inf. Comput. **87**, 78–128 (1990). https://doi.org/10.1016/0890-5401(90)90060-U
4. Grossi, D., Pigozzi, G.: Judgment Aggregation: A Primer. Morgan and Claypool Publishers, San Rafael, CA, USA (2014). https://doi.org/10.2200/S00559ED1V01Y201312AIM027
5. Halpern, J.Y.: Reasoning About Uncertainty. MIT Press, Cambridge (2005). https://mitpress.mit.edu/books/reasoning-about-uncertainty-second-edition
6. Ivanovska, M., Slavkovik, M.: Aggregating probabilistic judgments. In: Moss, L.S. (ed.) Proceedings Seventeenth Conference on Theoretical Aspects of Rationality and Knowledge, TARK 2019. EPTCS, vol. 297, pp. 273–292 (2019). https://doi.org/10.4204/EPTCS.297.18, https://doi.org/10.4204/EPTCS.297.18
7. List, C., Puppe, C.: Judgment aggregation: a survey. In: Anand, P., Puppe, C., Pattanaik, P. (eds.) The Handbook of Rational and Social Choice. Oxford University Press, UK (2009). https://doi.org/10.1093/acprof:oso/9780199290420.003.0020
8. Parsegov, S.E., Proskurnikov, A.V., Tempo, R., Friedkin, N.E.: Novel multidimensional models of opinion dynamics in social networks. IEEE Trans. Autom. Control **62**, 2270–2285 (2017). https://doi.org/10.1109/TAC.2016.2613905

Semiring-Valued Fuzzy Rough Sets and Colour Segmentation

Jiří Močkoř$^{(\boxtimes)}$ and Petr Hurtik

Institute for Research and Applications of Fuzzy Modeling,
Centre of Excellence IT4Innovations, University of Ostrava,
30. dubna 22, 701 03 Ostrava 1, Czech Republic
Jiri.Mockor@osu.cz
http://irafm.osu.cz/

Abstract. Many of the new fuzzy structures with complete MV-algebras as value sets, such as hesitant, intuitionistic, neutrosophic, or fuzzy soft sets, can be transformed into one common type of fuzzy sets with values in special semirings. We use this transformation of fuzzy structures to unify the theory of $(\mathcal{R}, \mathcal{R}^*)$-fuzzy rough sets with these new fuzzy structures. For this purpose, we use the $(\mathcal{R}_2, \mathcal{R}_2^*)$-fuzzy rough set defined for fuzzy soft sets and $(\mathcal{R}_1, \mathcal{R}_1^*)$-fuzzy rough sets defined for intuitionistic fuzzy sets. We also show how this general theory can be used to determine the upper and lower approximations of a colour segment corresponding to a particular colour.

1 Introduction

Over time, many generalizations and modifications of lattice-valued fuzzy sets have appeared, such as intuitionistic fuzzy sets [1,2], hesitant fuzzy sets [17,20], neutrosophis fuzzy sets [10], or fuzzy soft sets [11], and their mutual combinations. As expected, new variants of rough set theory appeared soon, making it possible to approximate the concepts expressed using these new fuzzy structures. For example, intuitionistic fuzzy rough set [23,24], soft rough fuzzy sets [13], hesitant fuzzy rough sets [22], or rough neutrosophic sets [4] and many other variants of these hybrid structures. Given the way these hybrid structures were created, it is not surprising that in many cases there are several variants that define these structures; see [13] and [19]. On the other hand, in some of these new fuzzy structures, rough variants are not yet introduced.

In our previous paper [15], we tried to unify the theories of certain classes of new fuzzy structures, that is, fuzzy structures with the complete MV-algebra as a set of values. The principle of this unification was that these fuzzy structures can be transformed into special fuzzy sets with values in special partially ordered semirings, called $(\mathcal{R}, \mathcal{R}^*)$-fuzzy sets. In this way, intuitionistic, neutrosophic, hesitant, or fuzzy soft sets with values in the complete MV-algebra, or their

This work was partly supported from ERDF/ESF project CZ.02.1.01/0.0/0.0/17-049/0008414.

V. Torra and Y. Narukawa (Eds.): MDAI 2022, LNAI 13408, pp. 38–50, 2022.
https://doi.org/10.1007/978-3-031-13448-7_4

mutual combinations, were transformed. This transformation makes it possible to use general methods of $(\mathcal{R}, \mathcal{R}^*)$-fuzzy sets to unify the theories of these new fuzzy structures or to create new theories if this theory has not yet been created in the given fuzzy structure.

The contribution of the paper is two-fold. First, we unify the notion of rough fuzzy structures using the term of $(\mathcal{R}, \mathcal{R}^*)$-fuzzy sets. Secondly, we define the notion of the approximation space (X, Q) consisting of a set X and a $(\mathcal{R}, \mathcal{R}^*)$-fuzzy relation Q in X and for arbitrary $(\mathcal{R}, \mathcal{R}^*)$-fuzzy set s we define the notion of the rough $(\mathcal{R}, \mathcal{R}^*)$-fuzzy sets of s in the approximation space (X, Q). The benefits are that the notion of rough $(\mathcal{R}, \mathcal{R}^*)$-fuzzy sets can be universally applied to any fuzzy structure that is transformable to $(\mathcal{R}, \mathcal{R}^*)$-fuzzy sets and that the properties of rough $(\mathcal{R}, \mathcal{R}^*)$-fuzzy sets can be directly transferred to the analogous properties of these new rough fuzzy structures without new proofs. In this paper, we will also show how these $(\mathcal{R}, \mathcal{R}^*)$-fuzzy rough structures can be used to determine the upper and lower approximations of a colour segment corresponding to a particular colour in a colour image.

2   Semiring-Valued Fuzzy Sets

Here, using [3,8,15], we recall the notion of a $(\mathcal{R}, \mathcal{R}^*)$-fuzzy set based on the adjoint pair $(\mathcal{R}, \mathcal{R}^*)$ of partially ordered semirings.

Definition 1 ([3,8]). A partially preordered (or ordered) idempotent commutative semiring $\mathcal{R} = (R, \leq_R, +, \times, 0_R, 1_R)$ (or, shortly, *po*-semiring) is an algebraic structure with the following properties:

1. $(R, +, 0_R)$ is an idempotent commutative monoid,
2. $(R, \times, 1_R)$ is a commutative monoid,
3. $x \times (y + z) = x \times y + x \times z$ holds for all $x, y, z \in R$,
4. $0_R \times x = 0_R$ holds for all $x \in R$.
5. $(R, \leq_R)$ is a partially preordered (or ordered) set such that for all $a, b, c \in R$ the following hold: $a \leq_R b \Rightarrow a +_R c \leq_R b +_R c, \quad a \times_R c \leq_R b \times_R c, \quad a \geq_R 0_R.$

If a semiring $\mathcal{R}$ is such that for any subset $S \subseteq R$ there exists the sum of elements $r \in S$, then $\mathcal{R}$ is called a complete semiring. The sum of elements $x \in S$ is denoted by $\sum_{r \in S}^{\mathcal{R}} r$. The notion of a *po-semiring homomorphism* is defined as a standardly defined homomorphism between algebraic structures, that is, a *po*-semiring homomorphism $\Phi : \mathcal{R} \to \mathcal{S}$ is a mapping $\Phi : R \to S$ between the underlying sets of these semirings such that Φ is a homomorphism of semirings and it is order-preserving.

The basic value set structure we use is the so-called adjoint pair of complete *po*-semirings $(\mathcal{R}, \mathcal{R}^*)$ which was introduced in [15].

Definition 2 ([15]). Let $\mathcal{R} = (R, \leq, +, \times, 0, 1)$ and $\mathcal{R}^* = (R, \leq^*, +^*, \times^*, 0^*, 1^*)$ be complete *po*-semirings with the same underlying set R. The pair $(\mathcal{R}, \mathcal{R}^*)$ is called the adjoint pair of *po*-semirings if there exists a *po*-semiring isomorphism $\Phi : \mathcal{R} \to \mathcal{R}^*$ and the following statements hold:

1. Φ is self-inverse, i.e., $\Phi.\Phi = id_R$,
2. $\forall a, b \in R$, $a \leq b \Leftrightarrow a \geq^* b$,
3. $\forall a, b_i \in R, i \in I$, $\quad a \times^* \sum_i^{\mathcal{R}} b_i = \sum_i^{\mathcal{R}} (a \times^* b_i)$,
4. $\forall a, b_i \in R, i \in I$, $\quad a + \sum_i^{\mathcal{R}^*} b_i = \sum_i^{\mathcal{R}^*} (a + b_i)$,
5. $\forall a, b \in R$, $\quad a +^* b \leq a + b$.

The basic structure with which we will work with is the $(\mathcal{R}, \mathcal{R}^*)$-fuzzy set. As we showed in our previous paper [15], many of the new variants of fuzzy structures, such as intuitionistic, hesitant, neutrosophis, or fuzzy soft sets with values in complete MV-algebras, can be transformed into $(\mathcal{R}, \mathcal{R}^*)$-fuzzy sets for appropriate po-semirings $\mathcal{R}$. We repeat the basic definition of this structure and operations on $(\mathcal{R}, \mathcal{R}^*)$-fuzzy sets.

Definition 3 ([15])**.** Let $(\mathcal{R}, \mathcal{R}^*)$ be the adjoint pair of po-semirings with the common underlying set R and isomorphism Φ. Let X be a set.

1. A mapping $s : X \to R$ is called the $(\mathcal{R}, \mathcal{R}^*)$-fuzzy set in X. The set of all $(\mathcal{R}, \mathcal{R}^*)$-fuzzy sets in X is denoted by $(\mathcal{R}, \mathcal{R}^*)^X$.
2. Operations on $(\mathcal{R}, \mathcal{R}^*)$-fuzzy sets and external operation with elements of R are defined for arbitrary $s, t \in (\mathcal{R}, \mathcal{R}^*)^X$ and $a \in R$ by
   (a) The intersection $s \sqcap t$ is defined by $(s \sqcap t)(x) = s(x) +^* t(x)$, $x \in X$,
   (b) The union $s \sqcup t$ is defined by $(s \sqcup t)(x) = s(x) + t(x)$, $x \in X$,
   (c) The complement $\neg s$ is defined by $(\neg s)(x) = \Phi(s(x))$.

For the illustration of the transformations of new fuzzy structures to $(\mathcal{R}, \mathcal{R}^*)$-fuzzy sets, we present two examples of adjoint pairs of po-semirings, which represent intuitionistic fuzzy sets and fuzzy soft sets with values in a complete MV-algebra, respectively. In these examples, $\mathcal{L} = (L, \oplus, \neg, 0_L)$ is a complete MV-algebra, where we standardly set

$$x \otimes y = \neg(\neg x \oplus \neg y), \quad x \vee y = (x \oplus \neg y) \otimes y, \quad x \wedge y = (x \otimes \neg y) \oplus y, \quad x \leq y \Leftrightarrow x \vee y = y.$$

Example 1. [15]

1. The po-semiring $\mathcal{R}_1 = (R_1, \leq_1, +_1, \times_1, 0_1, 1_1)$ is defined by
   (a) $R_1 = \{(\alpha, \beta) \in L^2 : \neg\alpha \geq \beta\} \subseteq L^2$,
   (b) $(\alpha, \beta) +_1 (\alpha_1, \beta_1) := (\alpha \vee \alpha_1, \beta \wedge \beta_1)$,
   (c) $(\alpha, \beta) \times_1 (\alpha_1, \beta_1) := (\alpha \otimes \alpha_1, \beta \oplus \beta_1)$,
   (d) $0_1 = (0_L, 1_L)$, $\quad 1_1 = (1_L, 0_L)$,
   (e) $(\alpha, \beta) \leq_1 (\alpha', \beta') \Leftrightarrow \alpha \leq \alpha', \beta \geq \beta'$.
2. The po-semiring $\mathcal{R}_1^* = (R, \leq^*, +^*, \times^*, 0^*, 1^*)$ is defined by
   (a) $(\alpha, \beta) +_1^* (\alpha_1, \beta_1) := (\alpha \wedge \alpha_1, \beta \vee \beta_1)$,
   (b) $(\alpha, \beta) \times_1^* (\alpha_1, \beta_1) := (\alpha \oplus \alpha_1, \beta \otimes \beta_1)$,
   (c) $0_1^* = (1_L, 0_L)$, $\quad 1_1^* = (0_L, 1_L)$,
   (d) $(\alpha, \beta) \leq_1^* (\alpha', \beta') \Leftrightarrow (\alpha, \beta) \geq_1 (\alpha', \beta')$.

Let $\Phi_1 : \mathcal{R}_1 \to \mathcal{R}_1^*$ be defined by $\Phi_1(\alpha, \beta) = (\beta, \alpha)$, for $(\alpha, \beta) \in R_2$. Then $(\mathcal{R}_1, \mathcal{R}_1^*)$ is the adjoint pair of po-semirings and Φ_1 is the adjoint po-semiring isomorphism.   □

Example 2. [15]

1. Let K be the fixed set of criteria. The po-semiring $\mathcal{R}_2 = (R_2, \leq_2, +_2, \times_2, 0_2, 1_2)$ is defined by
   (a) $R_2 = \{(E, \psi) : E \subseteq K, \psi \in L^K\} \subseteq L^K$, where $(E, \psi) \in L^K$ is defined by

   $$k \in K, \quad (E, \psi)(k) = \begin{cases} \psi(k), & k \in E, \\ 0_L, & k \notin E \end{cases}.$$

   (b) $(E, \varphi), (F, \psi) \in R_2$, $(E, \varphi) +_2 (F, \psi) := (E \cap F, \varphi \vee \psi)$, where $\varphi \vee \psi$ is the supremum in L^K,
   (c) $(E, \varphi), (F, \psi) \in R_2$, $(E, \varphi) \times_2 F, \psi) = (E \cap F, \varphi \times \psi)$, where $\varphi \times \psi \in L^K$ is defined by $\varphi \times \psi(k) = \varphi(k) \otimes \psi(k)$,
   (d) $0_2 = (K, \underline{0}_L)$, $1_2 = (K, \underline{1}_L)$, where $\underline{\alpha}(k) = \alpha$ for arbitrarily $k \in K$, $\alpha \in L$,
   (e) $(E, \varphi) \leq_2 (F, \psi) \Leftrightarrow (E, \varphi)(k) \leq (F, \psi)(k), \forall k \in E \cap F$.
2. The po-semiring $\mathcal{R}_2^* = (R_2, \leq_2^*, +_2^*, \times_2^*, 0_2^*, 1_2^*)$ is defined by
   (a) $(E, \varphi), (F, \psi) \in R_2$, $(E, \varphi) +_2^* (F, \psi) := (E \cap F, \varphi \wedge \psi)$, where $\varphi \wedge \psi$ is the infimum in L^K,
   (b) $(E, \varphi), (F, \psi) \in R_2$, $(E, \varphi) \times_2^* (F, \psi) = (E \cap F, \varphi \oplus \psi)$, where $\oplus$ in L^K is defined component-wise.
   (c) $0_2^* = (K, \underline{1}_L)$, $1_2^* = (K, \underline{0}_L)$, where $\underline{\alpha}(k) = \alpha$ for arbitrary $k \in K$, $\alpha \in L$,
   (d) $(E, \varphi) \leq_2^* (F, \psi) \Leftrightarrow (E, \varphi) \geq_2 (F, \psi)$.

Let $\Phi : \mathcal{R}_2 \to \mathcal{R}_2^*$ be defined by $\Phi(E, \psi) = (E, \neg\psi)$, for $(E, \psi) \in R_2$, where $\neg\psi$ is defined component-wise. Then $(\mathcal{R}_2, \mathcal{R}_2^*)$ is the adjoint pair of po-semirings and Φ_2 is the adjoint po-semiring isomorphism.   □

The basic relationship between the $(\mathcal{R}, \mathcal{R}^*)$-fuzzy sets of these two examples and intuitionistic fuzzy sets or fuzzy soft sets is described as follows.

Example 3. [15] Let $\mathcal{L}$ be the complete MV-algebra.

1. The algebraic structure $(J(X), \cup, \cap, \neg, \leq)$ of all intuitionistic $\mathcal{L}$-fuzzy sets is isomorphic to the structure $((\mathcal{R}_1, \mathcal{R}_1^*)^X, \sqcup, \sqcap, \neg, \subseteq)$,
2. The algebraic structure $(S(X), \cup, \cap, \neg, \leq)$ of all $\mathcal{L}$-fuzzy soft sets in X is isomorphic to the structure $((\mathcal{R}_2, \mathcal{R}_2^*)^X, \sqcup, \sqcap, \neg, \subseteq)$.   □

As was proven in [15], an analogous result holds for some other of the new fuzzy structures.

3   Rough $(\mathcal{R}, \mathcal{R}^*)$-Fuzzy Sets

As we mentioned in the introduction, our goal in this paper is to define the theory of rough $(\mathcal{R}, \mathcal{R}^*)$-fuzzy sets, so that the existing rough fuzzy sets of the mentioned fuzzy structures will be special examples of this theory.

As with classical rough fuzzy sets, this unifying theory of rough $(\mathcal{R}, \mathcal{R}^*)$-fuzzy sets will be based on the notion of the $(\mathcal{R}, \mathcal{R}^*)$-fuzzy relation, which we define in the following definition. In what follows, by the po-semirings from $(\mathcal{R}, \mathcal{R}^*)$ we understand $\mathcal{R} = (R, \leq, +, \times, 0, 1)$ and $\mathcal{R}^* = (R, \leq^*, +^*, \times^*, 0^*, 1^*)$.

Definition 4. Let $(\mathcal{R}, \mathcal{R}^*)$ be the adjoint pair of po-semirings with the adjoint isomorphism Φ and let X be a set. By $(\mathcal{R}, \mathcal{R}^*)$-relation in a set X we understand a $(\mathcal{R}, \mathcal{R}^*)$-fuzzy set $Q : X \times X \to R$ in the Cartesian product $X \times X$.

Analogously as for classical fuzzy relations, we can define operations for $(\mathcal{R}, \mathcal{R}^*)$-relations.

Definition 5. Let S, T be $(\mathcal{R}, \mathcal{R}^*)$-relations in a set X as follows.

1. The composition $T \circ S$ of S and T is the $(\mathcal{R}, \mathcal{R}^*)$-relation $T \circ S(x, z) = \sum_{y \in X}^{\mathcal{R}} S(x, y) \times T(y, z)$ for arbitrarily $x, z \in X$.
2. The dual composition of S and T is defined by $T \circ^* S(x, z) = \sum_{y \in X}^{\mathcal{R}^*} S(x, y) \times^* T(y, z)$.
3. The negation $\neg T$ of T is defined by $(\neg T)(x, y) = \Phi(T(x, y))$,
4. $S \preceq T$ iff $\forall x, y \in X, S(x, y) \leq T(x, y)$ and $S \preceq^* T$ iff $\forall x, y \in X, S(x, y) \leq^* T(x, y)$ hold.

Because our main goal is to show the possibility of using the theory of $(\mathcal{R}, \mathcal{R}^*)$-fuzzy rough sets in other fuzzy structures, $(\mathcal{R}, \mathcal{R}^*)$-fuzzy relations must comprise the existing fuzzy relations in these new fuzzy structures. It should be mentioned that for some fuzzy structures, there exist several variants of definitions of relations. An example of this situation can be fuzzy soft sets, where there are several variants of the definition of fuzzy soft relations. For example, Definition 3.1 in [12], where the fuzzy soft relation is defined between two fuzzy soft sets (E, s) and (F, t) in a fuzzy soft space (K, X); and Definition 6 in [18], where the fuzzy soft relation is defined between two fuzzy soft spaces (K, X) and (K, Y).

For the illustration of relationships between $\mathcal{L}$-fuzzy relations in new fuzzy structures and $(\mathcal{R}, \mathcal{R}^*)$-relations, we show that $(\mathcal{R}_2, \mathcal{R}_2^*)$-fuzzy relations in a set X are isomorphic to $\mathcal{L}$-fuzzy soft relations in a soft space (K, X) defined by [18] and $(\mathcal{R}_1, \mathcal{R}_1^*)$-fuzzy relations are identical to intuitionistic $\mathcal{L}$-fuzzy relations with composition defined in [5, 16].

Proposition 1. 1. Let $(\mathcal{S}(X \times X), \boxtimes)$ be the monoid of all $\mathcal{L}$-fuzzy soft relations in a set X with the standard composition $\boxtimes$ of fuzzy soft set relations and let $((\mathcal{R}_2, \mathcal{R}_2^*)^{X \times X}, \circ)$ be the monoid of all $(\mathcal{R}_2, \mathcal{R}_2^*)$-fuzzy relations in X with the composition $\circ$. Then these monoids are isomorphic, i.e.,

$$(\mathcal{S}(X \times X), \boxtimes) \cong ((\mathcal{R}_2, \mathcal{R}_2^*)^{X \times X}, \circ).$$

2. Let $(\mathcal{J}(X \times X), \boxtimes)$ be the monoid of all intuitionistic $\mathcal{L}$-fuzzy relations in a set X with the composition $\boxtimes$ of fuzzy soft set relations defined in [16] and let $(((\mathcal{R}_1, \mathcal{R}_1^*)^{X \times X}, \circ))$ be the monoid of all $(\mathcal{R}_1, \mathcal{R}_1^*)$-fuzzy relations in X with the composition $\circ$. Then we have

$$(\mathcal{J}(X \times X), \boxtimes) = ((\mathcal{R}_1, \mathcal{R}_1^*)^{X \times X}, \circ).$$

For a set X and a $(\mathcal{R}, \mathcal{R}^*)$-fuzzy relation T in X, the pair (X, T) is called the $(\mathcal{R}, \mathcal{R}^*)$-*approximation space*. In the following definition, we introduce the notion of upper and lower approximations of $(\mathcal{R}, \mathcal{R}^*)$-fuzzy sets defined by the $(\mathcal{R}, \mathcal{R}^*)$-approximation space.

Definition 6. Let $(\mathcal{R}, \mathcal{R}^*)$ be the adjoint pair of *po*-semirigs with the adjoint isomorphism Φ and let (X, T) be an $(\mathcal{R}, \mathcal{R}^*)$-approximation space.

1. The upper $(\mathcal{R}, \mathcal{R}^*)$-approximation defined by T is a mapping $T^\uparrow : R^X \to R^X$ defined by

$$s \in R^X, x \in X, \quad T^\uparrow(s)(x) = \sum_{z \in X}^{\mathcal{R}} T(x, z) \times s(z).$$

2. The lower $(\mathcal{R}, \mathcal{R}^*)$-approximation defined by T is a mapping $T^\downarrow : R^X \to R^X$ defined by

$$s \in R^X, x \in X, \quad T^\downarrow(s)(x) = \sum_{z \in X}^{\mathcal{R}^*} \Phi(T(x, z)) \times^* s(z).$$

3. The pair $(T^\downarrow(s), T^\uparrow(s))$ is called the $(\mathcal{R}, \mathcal{R}^*)$-fuzzy rough set of s with respect to (X, T).

The Definition 6 allows us to introduce the concept of a rough fuzzy structure for all types of new fuzzy structures that can be transformed into $(\mathcal{R}, \mathcal{R}^*)$-fuzzy sets. To illustrate the application of Definition 6 to the new fuzzy structures, the upper and lower approximations will be specified according to Definition 6 for two examples of fuzzy structures. Namely, we show that the existing definitions of the rough intuitionistic $\mathcal{L}$-fuzzy set and the rough $\mathcal{L}$-fuzzy soft set given in [5,18] are identical to the rough fuzzy structures according to Definition 6.

Example 4. Let S be the intuitionistic $\mathcal{L}$-fuzzy relation in X and let f be an intuitionistic $\mathcal{L}$-fuzzy set in X. The *rough intuitionistic fuzzy set* $(\underline{S}(f), \overline{S}(f))$ of f is defined by

$$\overline{S}(f)(x) = (\bigvee_{y \in X} T(S_1(x, y), f_1(y)), \bigwedge_{y \in X} I(S_2(x, y), f_2(y))),$$
$$\underline{S}(f)(x) = (\bigwedge_{y \in X} I(\neg(S_2(x, y)), f_1(y)), \bigvee_{y \in X} T(S_1(x, y), f_2(y))),$$

where for arbitrary $(x, x') \in X \times X$, $S(x, x') = (S_1(x, x'), S_2(x, x'))$ and $f(x) = (f_1(x), f_2(x))$, T is a t-norm and I is an implicator (see [24]).

From Proposition 1 it follows that S is also $(\mathcal{R}_1, \mathcal{R}_1^*)$-relation, i.e., $S : X \times X \to R_1$ and if we set

$$T(a, b) = a \otimes b, \quad I(a, b) = \neg a \oplus b$$

for $a, b \in \mathcal{L}$, we obtain $S^\uparrow(f)(x) = \overline{S}(f)(x)$ and $S^\downarrow(f)(x) = \underline{S}(f)(x)$. Therefore, if $\mathcal{L}$ is the MV-algebra, the intuitionistic $\mathcal{L}$-fuzzy rough sets are $(\mathcal{R}_1, \mathcal{R}_1^*)$-fuzzy rough sets.   □

In the next example, we focus on *rough fuzzy soft sets*, for which there are a number of variants of this notion, including possible variants of names (see, e.g., [7,9,21]). It follows that rough fuzzy soft sets defined by fuzzy soft relations have not been systematically introduced so far. In the next example, we show how we can explicitly define this notion using Definition 6 and Proposition 1. According to Example 3, a fuzzy soft set in X can be identified with the mapping $X \to R_2$ and a fuzzy soft relation in X is identified with the mapping $X \times X \to R_2$.

Example 5. Let K be a fixed set of criteria, and let X be a set, and let $(\mathcal{R}_2, \mathcal{R}_2^*)$ be an adjoint pair of *po*-semirings from Example 3. Let $f : X \to R_2$ be a $(\mathcal{R}_2, \mathcal{R}_2^*)$-fuzzy set (i.e., the fuzzy soft set), such that $f(x) = (F_x, f_x) \in R_2$, where $F_x \subseteq K$, $f_x : K \to L$ and $(F_x, f_x) : K \to L$ is such that

$$(F_x, f_x)(k) = \begin{cases} f_x(k), & k \in F_x, \\ 0_L, & k \in K \setminus F_x. \end{cases}$$

Let $\mathcal{T} : X \times X \to R_2$ be the $(\mathcal{R}_2, \mathcal{R}_2^*)$-relation in X. Hence, for $(x, x') \in X \times X$ we have

$$\mathcal{T}(x, x') = (E_{xx'}, \psi_{xx'}) \in R_2,$$

$$k \in K, \quad (E, \psi_{xx'})(k) = \begin{cases} \psi_{xx'}(k), & k \in E_{xx'}, \\ 0_L, & k \in K \setminus E_{xx'}. \end{cases}$$

Therefore, according to Definition 6, the rough $(\mathcal{R}_2, \mathcal{R}_2^*)$-fuzzy soft set $(\mathcal{T}^\downarrow(f), \mathcal{T}^\uparrow(f))$ is for $x \in X, k \in K$ defined by

$$\mathcal{T}^\uparrow(f)(x)(k) = \left(\sum_{z \in X}^{\mathcal{R}_2} \mathcal{T}(x, z) \times_2 f(z) \right)(k) = \left(\sum_{z \in X}^{\mathcal{R}_2} (E_{xz}, \psi_{xz}) \times_2 (F_z, f_z) \right)(k) =$$

$$\begin{cases} \bigvee_{z \in X} \psi_{xz}(k) \otimes f_z(k), & k \in E_{xz} \cap F_z, \\ 0_L, & k \in K \setminus E_{xz} \cap F_z, \end{cases}$$

$$\mathcal{T}^\downarrow(f)(x)(k) = \left(\sum_{z \in X}^{\mathcal{R}_2^*} \neg(\mathcal{T}(x, z)) \times_2^* f(z) \right)(k) = \left(\sum_{z \in X}^{\mathcal{R}_2^*} \neg(E_{xz}, \psi_{xz}) \times_2^* (F_z, f_z) \right)(k) =$$

$$\begin{cases} \bigwedge_{z \in X} \Phi_2(\psi_{xz}(k)) \oplus f_z(k), & k \in E_{xz} \cap F_z, \\ 0_L, & k \in K \setminus E_{xz} \cap F_x. \end{cases}$$

It can be proven that the $(\mathcal{R}_2, \mathcal{R}_2^*)$-fuzzy rought set $(\mathcal{T}^\downarrow(f), \mathcal{T}^\uparrow(f))$ can be identified with the rough fuzzy soft set defined in [18].

4   Examples of Applications

In this section, we show two examples of possible applications of fuzzy rough structures created using the theory of $(\mathcal{R}, \mathcal{R}^*)$-fuzzy rough sets. For this purpose, we will use the $(\mathcal{R}_2, \mathcal{R}_2^*)$-fuzzy rough set defined for the fuzzy soft set in Example 5 and $(\mathcal{R}_1, \mathcal{R}_1^*)$-fuzzy rough sets defined for intuitionistic fuzzy sets in Example 4. In both cases, we show how these fuzzy rough structures can be used to determine the upper and lower approximations of a colour segment corresponding to a particular colour k in a colour image. Because we use the same default conditions in these examples, it allows us to compare how fuzzy soft sets and intuitionistic fuzzy sets solve this problem.

We suppose that a colour image consists of pixels of the set X and that for each pixel $x \in X$ a value $S(x)$ represents the colour of a pixel x. The colour is given by a triplet $S(x) = [h_x, s_x, v_x]$, where h_x represents the hue of the colour, s_x represents a saturation dimension, and v_x represents the value dimension similar to the mixture of these paints with varying amounts of black or white paint in the pixel x. Furthermore, let K be the set of all possible colours.

In the next part, we suppose that $\mathcal{L} = ([0,1], \otimes, \oplus, \neg)$ is the Łukasiewicz algebra with the bi-residuum $\leftrightarrow$ defined by $a \leftrightarrow b = (a \to b) \wedge (b \to a)$.

4.1 $(\mathcal{R}_2, \mathcal{R}_2^*)$-Fuzzy Rough Sets

To illustrate the possible applications of rough $(\mathcal{R}_2, \mathcal{R}_2^*)$-fuzzy sets from the soft space (K, X), we present a method for approximations of a colour segment in an image. Unlike Examples 10 and 11 from [14], for these approximations, we use different $(\mathcal{R}_2, \mathcal{R}_2^*)$-relations $\mathcal{T}$.

Let $E = S(X) \subseteq K$ and consider the $(\mathcal{R}_2, \mathcal{R}_2^*)$-fuzzy set $f : X \to R_2^K$ defined by

$$x \in X, \quad f(x) = (E, f_x), \quad k \in K, \tag{1}$$

$$f_x(k) := \frac{\sum_{z \in X} \rho(x,z) \cdot \sigma(S(z), k)}{\sum_{z \in X} \rho(x,z)} \in [0,1], \tag{2}$$

where $\sigma(k, k') \in [0,1]$ represents a similarity degree of two colours in K and the fuzzy similarity relation $\rho : X \times X \to [0,1]$ expresses the fact that pixels x and z are close to each other. For example, we can set

$$(x,y) \in X \times X, \quad \rho(x,y) = \begin{cases} \frac{1}{d(x,y)^\omega}, & d(x,y) \neq 0, \\ 1, & d(x,y) = 0, \end{cases}$$

where $\omega \in \mathbb{R}^+$. Similarly, the similarity relation σ can be defined by

$$k = [h_k, s_k, v_k], m = [h_m, s_m, v_m] \in K, \quad \sigma(k,m) := 1 - \frac{|h_k - h_m| + |s_k - s_m| + |v_k - v_m|}{3},$$

where $h, s, v \in [0,1]$. In that case, the $(\mathcal{R}_2, \mathcal{R}_2^*)$-fuzzy set f represents the concept describing segments corresponding to the colours $k \in E$.

The lower and upper approximations of the segment f are defined as the $(\mathcal{R}_2, \mathcal{R}_2^*)$-rough set $(T^{\downarrow}(f), T^{\uparrow}(f))$ of f with respect to the $(\mathcal{R}_2, \mathcal{R}_2^*)$-relation $T : X \times X \rightarrow R_2$, defined by

$$(x, x') \in X \times X, \quad T(x, x') = (E, \psi_{xx'}) \in R_2, \quad k \in K, \tag{3}$$
$$\psi_{xx'}(k) = \sigma(S(x), k) \leftrightarrow \sigma(S(x'), k) \in [0,1]. \tag{4}$$

According to Example 5, the rough $(\mathcal{R}_2, \mathcal{R}_2^*)$-fuzzy set $(T^{\downarrow}(f), T^{\uparrow}(f))$ is defined by

$$T^{\downarrow}(f)(x)(k) = \begin{cases} \bigwedge_{z \in X} \neg \psi_{xz}(k) \oplus f_z(k), & k \in \cap F, \\ 0_L, & k \in E \setminus E \cap F \end{cases}$$
$$T^{\uparrow}(f)(x)(k) = \begin{cases} \bigvee_{z \in X} \psi_{xz}(k) \otimes f_z(k), & k \in E \cap F, \\ 0_L, & k \in K \setminus E \cap F. \end{cases}$$

These upper and lower approximations of the colour segment f corresponding to the colour $k \in K$ can be approximated by the α-cuts, i.e., by subsets

$$T^{\downarrow}(f)(k)_\alpha = \{x \in X : T^{\downarrow}(f)(x)(k) \geq \alpha\},$$
$$T^{\uparrow}(f)(k)_\alpha = \{x \in X : T^{\uparrow}(f)(x)(k) \geq \alpha\},$$

where $\alpha \in \mathcal{L}$.

4.2 $(\mathcal{R}_1, \mathcal{R}_1^*)$-Fuzzy Rough Sets

We illustrate how the same problem of the colour segment approximation can be solved by rough $(\mathcal{R}_1, \mathcal{R}_1^*)$-fuzzy sets. For this, we use some notation from Sect. 4.1.

To define the $(\mathcal{R}_1, \mathcal{R}_1^*)$-fuzzy sets, which represents the concept describing a color segment, we use the same function (2) and transform it into the $(\mathcal{R}_1, \mathcal{R}_1^*)$-fuzzy set $X \rightarrow R_1$. For this purpose, we use the so-called intuitionistic fuzzy generators defined in [6].

Definition 7 ([6]). A function $\varphi : [0,1] \rightarrow [0,1]$ is called an intuitionistic fuzzy generator, if $\varphi(x) \leq 1 - x$ for all $x \in [0,1]$.

Using the intuitionistic fuzzy generator φ, the $(\mathcal{R}_1, \mathcal{R}_1^*)$-fuzzy set $w_{k,\phi}$ is defined by

$$x \in X, \quad w_{k,\varphi}(x) = \left(f_x(k), \frac{1 - f_x(k)}{1 + \lambda f_x(k)} \right) \in \mathcal{R}_1,$$

which represents the intuitionistic concept describing the segment in the colour image corresponding to the colour $k \in E$. As in the previous example, using definition (4), the approximation of this intuitionistic concept $w_{k,\varphi}$ can be defined as the rough $(\mathcal{R}_1, \mathcal{R}_1^*)$-fuzzy set of $w_{k,\varphi}$ with respect to the $(\mathcal{R}_1, \mathcal{R}_1^*)$-fuzzy relation $\mathcal{T}_k : X \times X \to R_1$, such that

$$(x, x') \in X \times X, \quad \mathcal{T}_k(x, x') = (\psi_{xx'}(k), \varphi(\psi_{xx'}(k))) \in R_1,$$

where we use the same intuitionistic fuzzy generator φ. According to Example 1 and Definition 6, the upper and lower approximations of the intuitionistic colour segment $w_{k,\varphi}$ corresponding to the colour k are defined for $x \in X$ by

$$\mathcal{T}_k^\uparrow(w_{k,\varphi})(x) = \left(\bigvee_{y \in X} \psi_{xy}(k) \otimes w_k(y), \bigwedge_{y \in Y} \varphi(\psi_{xy}(k))) \oplus \varphi(w_k(y)) \right),$$

$$\mathcal{T}_k^\downarrow(w_{k,\varphi})(x) = \left(\bigwedge_{y \in Y} \varphi(\psi_{xy}(k)) \oplus w_k(y), \bigvee_{y \in Y} \psi_{xy} \otimes \varphi(w_k(y)) \right).$$

To be able to visualize these upper and lower intuitionistic approximations of $w_{k,\varphi}$, we must first transform according to fuzzy sets into classical fuzzy sets. According to the procedure presented in [1], we use the transformation of elements $(\gamma, \delta) \in R_1$ into the classical $\mathcal{L}$-value of a fuzzy set defined by

$$(\gamma, \delta) \in \mathcal{R}_1 \mapsto \frac{1}{2}(1 + \gamma - \delta) \in \mathcal{L}.$$

In that way, from $(\mathcal{R}_1, \mathcal{R}_1^*)$-fuzzy sets $T^\uparrow(w_{k,\varphi})$ and $T^\downarrow(w_{k,\varphi})$ we obtain the standard $\mathcal{L}$-fuzzy sets $W_k^\uparrow(w_{k,\varphi})$ and $W_k^\downarrow(w_{k,\varphi})$, and, analogously to the previous example, these fuzzy sets can be approximated by α-cuts $W_k^\uparrow(w_{k,\varphi})_\alpha$ and $W_k^\downarrow(w_{k,\varphi})_\alpha$.

4.3   Visualisation and Colour Segmentation

Rough $(\mathcal{R}_1, \mathcal{R}_1^*)$ and $(\mathcal{R}_2, \mathcal{R}_2^*)$-fuzzy sets can be applied to arbitrary-dimensional data; here, we will demonstrate the visualization using 2D image data and a colour image segmentation problem. On contrary to semantic segmentation that is well-solved by deep neural networks, colour image segmentation is ill-solved due to the fact there exist multiple correct solutions to one input image, depending on the choice of target colour. Note that the standard raster image uses 16.5M unique colours. Here, the colour of pixels $x \in T^\uparrow(f)(k)_\alpha$ or $x \in T^\downarrow(f)(k)_\alpha$ for $(\mathcal{R}_2, \mathcal{R}_2^*)$-fuzzy rough sets and $W_k^\uparrow(w_{k,\varphi})_\alpha$ or $W_k^\downarrow(w_{k,\varphi})_\alpha$ for $(\mathcal{R}_1, \mathcal{R}_1^*)$- fuzzy rough sets will be $S(x)$ and the colour of other pixels will be transformed to the colour in the black and white scale, i.e., the saturation of these pixels will be reduced to zero, see Fig. 1.

From the theoretical point of view, it allows us to visually confirm the following.

1. $|T^\downarrow(f)(k)_\alpha| \leq |T^\uparrow(f)(k)_\alpha|$ for $(\mathcal{R}_2, \mathcal{R}_2^*)$-fuzzy rough sets,
2. $|W_k^\downarrow(w_{k,\varphi})_\alpha| \leq |W_k^\uparrow(w_{k,\varphi})_\alpha|$ for $(\mathcal{R}_1, \mathcal{R}_1^*)$-fuzzy rough sets,

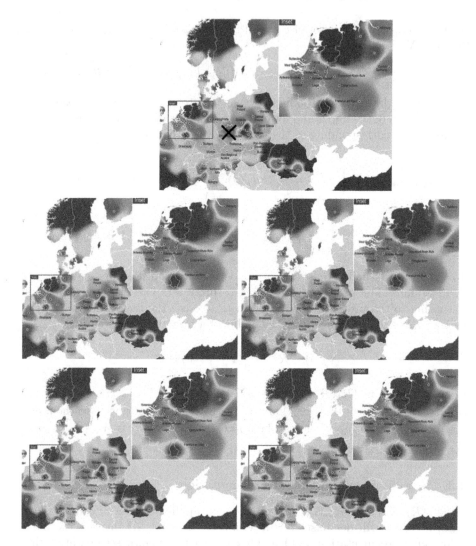

Fig. 1. Image 'Europe'. The original image credit: Prologis research (https://www.prologis.com). The black cross in the top (original) image denotes the position of selected colour k. Middle row shows colour segments for $W_k{}^{\downarrow}(w_k, \varphi)_\alpha$ and $W_k{}^{\uparrow}(w_k, \varphi)_\alpha$ of $(\mathcal{R}_1, \mathcal{R}_1^*)$-fuzzy rough set. Bottom rows shows colour segments $\mathcal{T}^{\downarrow}(f)(k)_\alpha$ and $\mathcal{T}^{\uparrow}(f)(k)_\alpha$ of $(\mathcal{R}_2, \mathcal{R}_2^*)$-fuzzy rough set. To create the colour segments, we set $\alpha = 0.84$ and preserved only colours in the α-cuts.

3. $|\mathcal{T}^{\downarrow}(f)(k)_\alpha| \leq |W_k{}^{\downarrow}(w_{k,\varphi})_\alpha|$,
4. $|\mathcal{T}^{\uparrow}(f)(k)_\alpha| \leq |W_k{}^{\uparrow}(w_{k,\varphi})_\alpha|$.

From a practical point of view, the figure demonstrates that by selecting a proper rough set and switching between upper and lower approximations, we can control the similarity between the selected colour and the other colours, that is, the size of segmented area. The visualization also shows that we can involve even discontinuous areas, which differs from other local methods used for colour image segmentation. The output can be used for creating selectively coloured images to highlight the important information or for measuring the size of affected area in, e.g., biological images (namely plant stress measurement), where it is essential to control the similarity and handle discontinuities.

5   Conclusions

The main contribution of the paper is the introduction of a unified theory of rough semi-ring-valued fuzzy sets and the subsequent possibility of applying this theory to most new MV-valued fuzzy structures. Although this theory has a purely theoretical basis, it also has a wide practical application in individual new fuzzy structures, as shown in the example of fuzzy soft sets and intuitionistic fuzzy sets. A partial limitation of the applicability of this theory for new fuzzy structures is that it requires a complete MV-algebra as a valued set.

References

1. Atanassov, K.T.: Intuitionistic Fuzzy Sets: Theory and Applications. Springer, Heidelberg (1999). https://doi.org/10.1007/978-3-7908-1870-3
2. Atanassov, K.T.: Intuitionistic fuzzy relations. In: Atanassov, K.T. (ed.) On Intuitionistic Fuzzy Sets Theory, vol. 283, pp. 147–193. Springer, Heidelberg (2012). https://doi.org/10.1007/978-3-642-29127-2_8
3. Berstel, J., Perrin, D.: Theory of Codes. Academic Press, Cambridge (1985)
4. Broumi, S., Smarandache, F., Dhar, M.: Rough neutrosophic sets. Neutrosophic Sets Syst. **3**, 62–67 (2014)
5. Bustince, H., Burillo, P.: Structures on intuitionistic fuzzy relations. Fuzzy Sets Syst. **78**, 293–303 (1996)
6. Bustince, H., Kacprzyk, J., Mohedano, V.: Intuitionistic fuzzy generators application to intuitionistic fuzzy complementation. Fuzzy Sets Syst. **114**(3), 485–504 (2000)
7. Feng, F., Liu, X.V., Leoreanu-Fotes, V., Jun, Y.B.: Soft sets and soft rough sets. Inf. Sci. **181**, 1125–1137 (2011)
8. Gan, A.P., Jiang, Y.L.: On ordered ideals in ordered semirings. J. Math. Res. Exposition **31**(6), 989–996 (2011)
9. Chen, X.: Rough soft sets in fuzzy setting. In: Tan, Y., Shi, Y., Mo, H. (eds.) ICSI 2013. LNCS, vol. 7928, pp. 530–539. Springer, Heidelberg (2013). https://doi.org/10.1007/978-3-642-38703-6_62
10. James, J., Mathew, S.C.: Lattice valued neutrosophis sets. J. Math. Comput. Sci. **11**, 4695–4710 (2021)
11. Maji, P.K., et al.: Fuzzy soft-sets. J. Fuzzy Math. **9**(3), 589–602 (2001)
12. Mattam, A.S., Gopalan, S.: Rough approximate operators based on fuzzy soft relation. Italian J. Pure Appl. Math. **42**, 912–925 (2020)
13. Meng, D., Zhang, X., Qin, K.: Soft rough fuzzy sets and soft fuzzy rough sets. Comput. Math. Appl. **62**, 4635–4645 (2011)

14. Močkoř, J., Hurtik, P.: Fuzzy soft sets and image processing application. In: Aliev, R.A., Kacprzyk, J., Pedrycz, W., Jamshidi, M., Babanli, M., Sadikoglu, F.M. (eds.) ICAFS 2020. AISC, vol. 1306, pp. 47–54. Springer, Cham (2021). https://doi.org/10.1007/978-3-030-64058-3_6

15. Močkoř, J.: Semiring-valued fuzzy sets and f-transform. Mathematics **9**(23), 3107 (2021)

16. Pan, X., Xu, P.: An algebraic analysis for binary intuitionistic l-fuzzy relations. In: Sun, F., Li, T., Li, H. (eds.) Foundations and Applications of Intelligent Systems. AISC, vol. 213, pp. 11–20. Springer, Heidelberg (2014). https://doi.org/10.1007/978-3-642-37829-4_2

17. Rodríguez, R.M., et al.: Hesitant fuzzy sets: state of the art and future directions. Int. J. Intell. Syst. **29**(6), 495–524 (2014)

18. Sut, D.K.: An application of fuzzy soft set relation in decision making problems. Int. J. Math. Trends Technol. **3**(2), 50–53 (2012)

19. Sun, B., Ma, W.: Soft fuzzy rough sets and its application in decision making. Artif. Intell. Rev. **41**, 67–80 (2014)

20. Torra, V.: Hesitant fuzzy sets. Int. J. Intell. Syst. **25**(6), 529–539 (2010)

21. Wang, C.Y., Zhang, X., Wu, Y.: New results on single axioms for L-fuzzy rough approximation operators. Fuzzy Sets Syst. **380**, 131–149 (2020)

22. Yang, X., Song, X., Qi, Y., Yang, J.: Constructive and axiomatic approaches to hesitant fuzzy rough set. Soft. Comput. **18**(6), 1067–1077 (2013). https://doi.org/10.1007/s00500-013-1127-2

23. Zhang, Z.M.: Generalized intuitionistic fuzzy rough sets based on intuitionistic fuzzy coverings. Inf. Sci. **198**, 186–206 (2012)

24. Zhong, Y., Yan, C.-H.: Intuitionistic L-fuzzy rough sets, intuitionistic L-fuzzy pre-orders and intuitionistic L-fuzzy topologies. Fuzzy Inf. Eng. **8**(3), 255–279 (2016). https://doi.org/10.1016/j.fiae.2016.11.002

Data Privacy

Bistochastic Privacy

Nicolas Ruiz[⊠] and Josep Domingo-Ferrer

Departament d'Enginyeria Informàtica i Matemàtiques, Universitat Rovira i Virgili, Av. Països
Catalans 26, 43007 Tarragona, Catalonia
{nicolas.ruiz,josep.domingo}@urv.cat

Abstract. We introduce a new privacy model relying on bistochastic matrices,
that is, matrices whose components are nonnegative and sum to 1 both row-wise
and column-wise. This class of matrices is used to both define privacy guarantees
and a tool to apply protection on a data set. The bistochasticity assumption happens
to connect several fields of the privacy literature, including the two most popular
models, k-anonymity and differential privacy. Moreover, it establishes a bridge
with information theory, which simplifies the thorny issue of evaluating the utility
of a protected data set. Bistochastic privacy also clarifies the trade-off between
protection and utility by using bits, which can be viewed as a natural currency
to comprehend and operationalize this trade-off, in the same way than bits are
used in information theory to capture uncertainty. A discussion on the suitable
parameterization of bistochastic matrices to achieve the privacy guarantees of this
new model is also provided.

Keywords: Bistochastic matrices · Randomized response · Privacy model ·
Statistical disclosure control · Information theory

1 Introduction

In the clash between pervasive big data collection and exploratory big data analytics
on the one hand, and stronger data protection legislation on the other hand, anonymization stands out as a way to reconcile both sides. Indeed, the European General Data
Protection Regulation (GDPR, [8]), which can be viewed as an epitome of strong regulation, establishes that personally identifiable information (PII) is no longer personal after
anonymization. Hence, anonymized data fall outside the scope of privacy regulations
and can be freely stored and processed. For anonymization to provide effective privacy
protection, it has to prevent disclosure. Disclosure can occur if an intruder can determine the identity of the subject to whom a piece of anonymized data corresponds—re-
identification disclosure—, or can estimate the value of a subject's confidential attribute
after seeing the anonymized data—attribute disclosure.

The traditional approach to anonymization, still very dominant among statistical
agencies, can be called utility-first. It essentially consists of leveraging a repertoire of
masking methods collectively known as statistical disclosure control (SDC, [9]). An SDC
method with a heuristic parameter choice and suitable utility preservation properties is
run to anonymize the original data. Then the risk of disclosure is assessed empirically

(for example using record linkage between the original and the anonymized data) or analytically (using generic measures or measures tailored to a specific SDC method). If the remaining risk is deemed too high, the data protector tries an SDC method having more privacy-stringent parameters and generally more utility loss. This process is iterated until the risk is low enough.

The computer science approach to anonymization could be termed privacy-first, and it is based on privacy models. A privacy model is a privacy condition dependent on a parameter that guarantees an upper bound on the re-identification risk and perhaps on the attribute disclosure risk. Each privacy model can be enforced using one or several SDC methods. There are currently two main families of privacy models, one based on k-anonymity [14] and the other on ε-differential privacy [7]. As shown in [2], the two families are complementary and have their own merits.

A problem with the current state of the art in the literature is that it appears as a variegated collection of SDC methods and privacy models. Whereas the permutation model [4] has been proposed to give a conceptual connection among SDC methods, no encompassing framework exists for privacy models. The ambition of this paper is to break ground towards a framework that not only unifies the two main families of privacy models—differential privacy and k -anonymity—but also aligns anonymization with information theory, which in turn simplifies what is meant by utility for an anonymized data set. We introduce bistochastic privacy, a specific form of randomized response in which the anonymized data Y are obtained from the original data X using Markov transition matrices that are bistochastic, that is, whose components are nonnegative and sum to 1 both row-wise and column-wise.

Section 2 connects bistochastic matrices with differential privacy, k-anonymity and SDC. A new privacy model, aligning information theory and privacy is then presented in Sect. 3, while Sect. 4 discusses the parametrization of bistochastic matrices. Finally, conclusions and directions for future work are gathered in Sect. 5. The Appendix gives background on randomized response, the permutation model of SDC and information theory.

2 Connections Between SDC, Differential Privacy and k-Anonymity Through Bistochastic Matrices

To the best of our knowledge, this is the first time that bistochastic matrices are explicitly considered in the privacy literature. However, it happens that, without it being clearly stated, they have already been implicitly used. In what follows, we establish novel theoretical results showing that the bistochasticity assumption is a connector across SDC, differential privacy and k-anonymity.

2.1 Connection with SDC

We will assume a randomized response matrix P (see Expression (A.1) in the appendix) that fulfills the additional left stochasticity constraints that $\sum_{u=1}^{r} p_{uv} = 1 \; \forall v = 1, \ldots, r$. This makes P bistochastic (left stochasticity implies that any anonymized categories must come from the original categories). The following result then follows:

Theorem 1 (Birkhoff-Von Neumann [12]): *If an $r \times r$ matrix P is bistochastic, then there exist $\lambda_1, \ldots, \lambda_J \geq 0$ with $\sum_{j=1}^{J} \lambda_j = 1$ and $P_1, \ldots, P_J$ permutation matrices such that:*

$$P = \sum_{j=1}^{J} \lambda_j P_j \tag{1}$$

Theorem 1 states that any bistochastic matrix can always be expressed as a convex combination of permutation matrices. Note that while there are $r!$ possible permutations of r categories, every $r \times r$ doubly stochastic matrix can be represented as a convex combination, which may not be unique, of at most $r^2 - 2r + 2$ permutation matrices [12].

This result directly establishes a connection with SDC through the permutation model. In fact, SDC can be viewed as a specific case of a more general approach that uses bistochastic matrices to perform anonymization. The permutation model considers a crisp permutation within the data set domain: it yields values occurring in the data set, except perhaps for a small noise addition that does not alter ranks. In contrast, a bistochastic matrix is described by Theorem 1 as a probabilistic model of permutation within the domain of attributes:

- The bistochastic transition matrix maps true values in the original data set to reported values that can in general be any value in the domain of the attributes—perhaps very different from the attribute values occurring in the data set.
- Expression (1) can be viewed as a probabilistic permutation: each permutation matrix P_j has a probability λ_j of being actually used. Only if $\lambda_j = 1$ for some j in Expression (1), which describes the functioning of any SDC methods, is permutation P_j certain to occur.

2.2 Connection with Differential Privacy

Differential privacy (DP) is a privacy model that can be enforced using a variety of SDC techniques [13]. In what follows, we choose Randomized Response (RR) as a technique to enforce DP. This is a legitimate setting, as during the inception of differential privacy, randomized response was already considered as a method to produce differentially private data sets. Thus, the connection established can be viewed as reasonably general. It follows that differential privacy constraints on an RR scheme happen to enforce bistochasticity, as is shown by the following proposition, proven in [16]:

Proposition 1: *The $r \times r$ matrix P of an ε-differentially private randomized response scheme is of the form:*

$$p_{uv} = \begin{cases} \frac{e^{\varepsilon}}{r-1+e^{\varepsilon}} & \text{if } u = v \\ \frac{1}{r-1+e^{\varepsilon}} & \text{if } u \neq v \end{cases} \quad \text{with } \varepsilon \geq \ln \max_{u=1,\ldots,r} \frac{\max_{u=1,\ldots,K} p_{uv}}{\min_{u=1,\ldots,K} p_{uv}} \tag{2}$$

Expression (2) describes a bistochastic matrix, as both its rows and columns sum to 1. Note also that taking $\varepsilon = 0$ in this matrix yields perfect secrecy (see Appendix), as the probabilities within each column are identical.

More generally, this result sheds an alternative light on the functioning of differential privacy, at least when it is attained through RR. To see this, assume $r = 3$. In the extreme case of the strictest differential privacy, i.e. when $\varepsilon = 0$, Expression (2) implies that all components of P must be equal to 1/3. Following Theorem 1, the associated differentially private randomized response scheme can be expressed as the following combination of permutation matrices:

$$
P = \begin{pmatrix} 1/3 & 1/3 & 1/3 \\ 1/3 & 1/3 & 1/3 \\ 1/3 & 1/3 & 1/3 \end{pmatrix} = \frac{1}{3}\begin{pmatrix} 1 & 0 & 0 \\ 0 & 1 & 0 \\ 0 & 0 & 1 \end{pmatrix} + \frac{1}{3}\begin{pmatrix} 0 & 0 & 1 \\ 1 & 0 & 0 \\ 0 & 1 & 0 \end{pmatrix} + \frac{1}{3}\begin{pmatrix} 0 & 1 & 0 \\ 0 & 0 & 1 \\ 1 & 0 & 0 \end{pmatrix}.
$$

Clearly, with the strictest setting, no permutation pattern is favored. However, for $\varepsilon = 2$, one gets:

$$
P = \begin{pmatrix} \frac{e^2}{2+e^2} & \frac{1}{2+e^2} & \frac{1}{2+e^2} \\ \frac{1}{2+e^2} & \frac{e^2}{2+e^2} & \frac{1}{2+e^2} \\ \frac{1}{2+e^2} & \frac{1}{2+e^2} & \frac{e^2}{2+e^2} \end{pmatrix} = \frac{e^2}{2+e^2}\begin{pmatrix} 1 & 0 & 0 \\ 0 & 1 & 0 \\ 0 & 0 & 1 \end{pmatrix} + \frac{1}{2+e^2}\begin{pmatrix} 0 & 0 & 1 \\ 1 & 0 & 0 \\ 0 & 1 & 0 \end{pmatrix} + \frac{1}{2+e^2}\begin{pmatrix} 0 & 1 & 0 \\ 0 & 0 & 1 \\ 1 & 0 & 0 \end{pmatrix}.
$$

When the constraints imposed by differential privacy are relaxed, the probability of not altering the data (the identity matrix being a special case of permutation) is favored with a probability of $\frac{e^2}{2+e^2} = 0.78$, while other permutation patterns have a probability of 0.11 of being taken.

The usual notion of differential privacy is that the presence or absence of any given record in a data set cannot be noticed, up to $exp(\varepsilon)$, upon seeing anonymized outputs on the data set. When differential privacy is achieved via RR and is viewed through the lens of bistochastic matrix, it can be seen as ensuring blindness on how attribute categories are permuted. The strictest enforcement of differential privacy ($\varepsilon = 0$) amounts to random permutation and, as we saw, to perfect secrecy. With a laxer enforcement, some specific permutation patterns are more likely to occur. In Expression (2) we see that for $\varepsilon = 2$ not enough privacy is provided, because the chances of releasing the original data unaltered are 78%. Thus, *the privacy budget ε can also be seen as being proportional to the probability of not permuting the data.* Hence, too large a budget does not provide sufficient deniability. Conversely, the smaller the budget, the more credible is an individual who can deny that her reported category is her original category. Therefore, the smaller ε, the higher is plausible deniability.

2.3 Connection with k-Anonymity

A bistochastic matrix can also be parametrized to fulfill k-anonymity, more specifically its Anatomy variant [18]. Like standard k-anonymity, Anatomy relies on splitting the records in the data set into classes of at least k records. However, unlike standard k-anonymity, the quasi-identifier values within each class are not made equal. Instead, two tables are released for each class: one contains the projection of the original records of the class on the quasi-identifier attributes, and the other the projections of the original records on the rest of attributes. The correspondence between entries in the two tables of each class is not revealed: thus, if the class contains k records, there are $k!$ possible bijections between its quasi-identifier value combinations and its value combinations for the other attributes. In particular, given a quasi-identifier combination, the probability that an intruder finds the matching confidential attribute values is at most $1/k$, as in standard k-anonymity (note here that l-diversity is not guaranteed on the rest of attributes).

Let X be an original data set that is "anatomized" as follows:

- Compute k-anonymous classes of the records. Let the number of resulting classes be L and the number of different quasi-identifier combinations in the l-th class be n_l, for $l = 1,...,L$.
- For each class release two tables as in Anatomy, one table containing a random permutation of quasi-identifier combinations and the other table the projections of the records on the remaining attributes (those that are not quasi-identifiers). The set of the two tables for every class constitutes the anatomized data set Y.

The quasi-identifier tables of the anatomized k-anonymous data set Y can be viewed as having been obtained using the following transition matrix:

$$Q = \begin{pmatrix} Q_1 & 0 & \cdots & \cdots & 0 \\ 0 & Q_2 & 0 & \cdots & 0 \\ \vdots & 0 & \ddots & \ddots & \vdots \\ \vdots & \vdots & \ddots & \ddots & 0 \\ 0 & 0 & \cdots & 0 & Q_L \end{pmatrix} \tag{3}$$

with Q_l being the following $n_l \times n_l$ submatrix, for $l = 1,...,L$:

$$Q_l = \begin{pmatrix} 1/n_l & \cdots & 1/n_l \\ \vdots & \ddots & \vdots \\ 1/n_l & \cdots & 1/n_l \end{pmatrix}.$$

Each submatrix Q_l randomly permutes the quasi-identifier combinations within a class. If a combination of quasi-identifiers is repeated in two different classes i and j, it is permuted differently in each class, according to the respective submatrices Q_i and Q_j. That is, the combination has two different rows and two different columns in Q, specifically one row and one column in Q_i and one row and one column in Q_j. Finally, note that Q_l is bistochastic $\forall l = 1,...,L$, and that the overall Q is also bistochastic.

Thus, k-anonymity can be viewed as the application of a special parametrization of a bistochastic matrix. In fact, and as each submatrix Q_l achieves perfect secrecy, k-anonymity can be seen as a collection of perfect privacy blocks, which is exactly the original intuition behind k-anonymity, gathered into a block-diagonal, bistochastic matrix.

3   A Privacy Model Based on Bistochastic Matrices

At first sight, one could wonder about the necessity of imposing an additional constraint on RR and its ex-post version PRAM [11], some well-trodden approaches for anonymization that have proved their merits over the years. However, and beyond the appeal of the theoretical connections developed above, the interest in bistochasticity is justified by the following theorem (see Appendix A.3 for some background notion on majorization and the $\succ$ relationship):

Theorem 2 (Hardy, Littlewood, and Polya [12]): $p \succ q$ *if and only if* $q = P^T p$ *for some bistochastic matrix P.*

Theorem 2 states that a bistochastic matrix never decreases uncertainty and is the only class of matrices to do so. In fact, and when it is not a permutation matrix, it always increase uncertainty. When P is only right stochastic, as in the traditional approach to RR, no particular majorization relationship emerges and the resulting anonymized attribute cannot be qualified as more (or less) uncertain (in the sense of information theory) than the original attribute. However, when P is bistochastic but not a permutation matrix, the anonymized attribute will always be more uncertain, i.e. it will always contain more entropy. Here lies the fundamental functioning behind the privacy model proposed in this paper. The idea is to infuse a data set with uncertainty, which in fact provides protection but at the same time degrades information.

3.1   Univariate Bistochastic Privacy

We start by the simplest case where we seek to anonymize only one attribute to prevent disclosure. In what follows, we will assume that in Expression (1) $p_{uv} > 0 \forall u, v$. The transition matrix P has only strictly positive entries, meaning that any individual in any of the r categories can be reported in the anonymized attribute in any other of the r categories. As some of the transition probabilities can be made as small as desired, this is not really binding for the validity of the anonymized attribute. However, this additional constraint makes P the transition matrix of an ergodic Markov chain [3]. In turn, that implies that P has a unique stationary distribution, which, as P is bistochastic, is the uniform distribution [3].

The entropy rate of P is then given by the standard formula:

$$H(P) = - \sum_{u,v=1}^{r} \mu_u p_{uv} \log_2 p_{uv}, \tag{4}$$

where μ_u denotes the uniform distribution, i.e. $\mu_u = 1/r$.

The entropy rate of P is the average of the entropies of each row of P. Note that, in the case of perfect secrecy where all probabilities in P are equal, that we will denote hereafter by P^*, we have $H(P^*) = \log_2 r$, which is the maximum achievable entropy for an $r \times r$ bistochastic matrix. The definition of bistochastic privacy then follows:

Definition 1 (Univariate Bistochastic Privacy): *The anonymized version Y of an original attribute X is β-bistochastically private for $0 \leq \beta \leq 1$ if:*

i) $Y = P^T X$ with P bistochastic
ii) $\frac{H(P)}{H(P^*)} \geq \beta.$

An anonymized attribute satisfies β-bistochastic privacy if it is the product of a bistochastic matrix P and the original attribute, and if the entropy rate of P is at least 100 $\beta\%$ of the maximum achievable entropy. $H(P^*)$ represents the maximum "spending" that can be allocated to privacy, and because we defined entropy with logarithm to the base 2, this maximum amount is $\log_2 r$ bits. Thus, when $\beta = 1$, all the bits have been spent and the attribute has been infused with the maximum possible amount of uncertainty; in this case, perfect secrecy is achieved and it is clear that $Y = P^{*T} X$ returns the uniform distribution. The other extreme case $\beta = 0$ means that the attribute has been left untouched and no uncertainty has been injected, i.e. $H(P) = 0$. Thus, for $0 < \beta < 1$ there lies a continuum of cases where varying amount of uncertainty bits can be injected, which will guarantee a varying amount of protection.

Here, what we mean by protection can be illustrated by assuming that an attacker has been able to re-identify an individual through her quasi-identifiers (in whatever way those have been protected), and now wants to learn the value of her confidential attribute from the bistochastically private release of this attribute, Y. If the attribute is 1- bistochastically private, nothing can be learnt by virtue of perfect secrecy. The attacker is facing a uniform distribution and at best can only perform a random guess, and the strength of plausible deniability is maximal. An alternative way to illustrate the situation faced by an attacker is to consider the quantity $2^{H(Y)}$, which yields the number of equally probable outcome values that can be represented by Y. Since Y is the uniform distribution, this number is r. One way to think about this value is that, to learn about the value of the confidential attribute of the re-identified person, an attacker is facing an imaginary dice with r sides. The targeted individual can exactly claim that strength of plausible deniability.

In this example, the links between the confidential attribute and the quasi-identifiers have been completely broken, while the distribution of the former has been completely uniformized. Thus, information has been totally lost. In addition, and because P^* is singular, an estimate about the univariate distribution cannot be retrieved through the procedure described in the Appendix on randomized response. In that case, the price to pay for perfect secrecy in terms of information is maximal.

On the other hand, when $H(P) = 0$ the original information is left untouched and the data user gets the highest possible utility from the data. Consequently, moving β between 0 and 1 in bistochastic privacy is equivalent to operating a trade-off between information and protection. The more bits are injected in the attribute *via* a bistochastic matrix, the more information is taken away from the user and traded against protection.

Unlike other privacy models, bistochastic privacy makes the trade-off between privacy and information explicit. In fact, it can be considered as a privacy *and* utility-first approach. Moreover, it also offers the additional advantage of distorting the original information of the data *always* in the same direction. This is so because, following Theorem 2, only bistochastic matrices can increase entropy (in physics for example, it is well-known that bistochastic Markov chains are the only stochastic process satisfying the second law of thermodynamics, [10]). An additional consequence of this is that, unlike other privacy models that can be attained using several SDC techniques, bistochastic privacy must be achieved using bistochastic matrices. Whereas this might be viewed as limiting, at the same time it simplifies privacy implementation, as the same entities that are used to define the privacy guarantees of the model are also used to achieve them. In the case of differential privacy, it has been recently shown that the actual protection level offered by differentially private data sets generated through different methods can be very different, even if the same level of differential privacy guarantees is enforced at the onset [13].

By always increasing entropy, bistochastic privacy always produces anonymized data that are a coarsened version of the original data. Stated otherwise, bistochastically private data are always a compact version of the original data, where some details have been lost. This is in line with intuition, to the extent that detailed information is where privacy risks reside. A popular SDC method that also coarsens data is microaggregation, which is a common approach to achieve k-anonymity on a numerical attribute [9]. Microaggregation reports the centroids of clusters instead of individual values. It can be noted that if the matrix of Expression (3) is applied to a numerical attribute instead of a categorical one, the product of this matrix and the original attribute will produce a microaggregated version of the latter, with the centroids being the means of the clusters.

The fact of always coarsening data means that the evaluation of information loss for bistochastically private data is simplified as it can be systematically assessed trough this lens: any analytical needs to be performed on the data can be gauged through their behavior when data are coarsened. For example, the properties of standard econometric estimators on coarsened data are already established [17]. We believe this presents a clear advantage over other privacy models and SDC methods, for which the direction in which information is distorted is often unclear, and where one must rely on specific information loss metrics related to the analytical task to be performed.

3.2 Bistochastic Privacy at the Data Set Level

We now consider the case of several attributes. First, we start by noting that, following the remark on microaggregation just above, bistochastic matrices can be applied on both categorical and numerical attributes. In the categorical case, the original proportions of respondents whose values fall in each of the r categories will be changed, which will coarsen the distribution to deliver randomized proportions closer to the uniform distribution. In the latter case, it will tend to average the numerical values of respondents. In fact, if PRAM is used for randomization, then in a bistochastic randomized response scheme on a numerical attribute *the individuals are used as categories*. Moreover, and because *bistochastic matrices are mean-preserving*, the anonymized numerical attribute will have the same mean as the original numerical attribute (note that this would not be possible with a non-bistochastic Markov matrix, which is generally not mean-preserving).

Bistochastic randomized response scheme on a numerical attribute can be given additional intuition by considering Expression (1). As a bistochastic matrix can always be expressed as a convex combination of permutation matrices, applying a bistochastic matrix on a numerical attribute is equivalent to permuting individuals, albeit here this is done in a probabilistic way, unlike in typical permutation/swapping SDC methods.

Finally, one can note that, in the case where matrix P^* (with all probabilities in it being identical) is used, all the values of the anonymized numerical attribute Y are equal to the average of the original attribute X. This a rather extreme case of coarsening, which makes Y a k-anonymous version of X with only one cluster.

From now on, denote by X a data set comprised of K attributes $X_1,...,X_K$. Based on the discussion above, we will not precise if the attributes are numerical or categorical. As a result, n_k will denote either the number of categories if X_k is a categorical attribute, or the number of individuals N if X_k is a numerical attribute. Y, the anonymized version of X, is generated by injecting entropy in each attribute k through $n_k \times n_k$ bistochastic matrices P_k:

$$P_k = \begin{pmatrix} p_{11} & \cdots & p_{1n_k} \\ \vdots & \ddots & \vdots \\ p_{n_k1} & \cdots & p_{n_kn_k} \end{pmatrix} \tag{5}$$

where $p_{u_kv_k} = \Pr(Y_k = v_k|X_k = u_k)$ denotes the probability that the original response (or the original individual) u_k in X_k is reported as v_k in Y_k, for $u_k, v_k \in \{1, \dots, n_k\}$. Under this procedure, the following proposition holds:

Proposition 2: *The maximum number of bits that can be injected into a data set X is* $H^*(P_1^*, \dots, P_K^*) = \sum_{k=1}^{K} H(P_k^*)$.

This property stems from the fact that joint entropy is always subadditive, i.e. it always hold that $H(P_1, \dots, P_K) \leq \sum_{k=1}^{K} H(P_k)$ [3]. This leads to the following definition:

Definition 2 (Conservative multivariate bistochastic privacy): *The anonymized version Y of an original data set X is conservatively β-bistochastically private for $0 \leq \beta \leq 1$ if:*

i) $Y = (P_1^T X_1, \dots, P_K^T X_K)$ with P_k $\forall k = 1, \dots, K$ bistochastic

ii) $\dfrac{\sum_{k=1}^{K} H(P_k)}{\sum_{k=1}^{K} H(P_k^*)} \geq \beta$

Definition 2 has the merit of simplifying the implementation of bistochastic privacy on a whole data set. The fact that each attribute is dealt with separately keeps the computational cost relatively low [6]. Moreover, estimating the distribution of the frequencies of each attribute is easily achievable because the computational cost of inverting each bistochastic matrix is also low. However, the drawback is that, because entropy is subadditive, one injects more bits than in the case of dealing directly with the joint distribution. More protection is applied and, as result, more information is lost. In particular, the dependencies between attributes may end up getting more degraded than necessary. Unnecessary information loss is only avoided in the case where all the original attributes are independent.

A way to avoid information loss when attributes are dependent is to apply a bistochastic matrix P_J directly on the joint distribution $X_J = X_1 \times \cdots \times X_K$. This leads to the following definition:

Definition 3 (True Multivariate Bistochastic Privacy): *The anonymized version Y_J of a multivariate distribution X_J is β-bistochastically private for $0 \leq \beta \leq 1$ if:*

i) $Y_j = P_j^T X_J$ with P_J bistochastic

ii) $\frac{H(P_j)}{H(P_j^*)} \geq \beta$

While this definition of multivariate bistochastic privacy appears in principle the most appropriate one, its computational cost may however result in practical hurdles. To perform anonymization, matrix P_J may reach a very large size, in particular if the original data set contains many numerical attributes. Moreover, and while it will be still possible to retrieve an estimate of the true joint distribution using the procedure described in the Appendix on randomized response, the computational cost of inverting P_J grows exponentially with the number of attributes and the presence of numerical attributes. As a result, like other privacy models, bistochastic privacy is not immune to the curse of dimensionality. For this reason, Definition 2 remains more widely applicable than Definition 3.

4 Parameterization of Bistochastic Matrices

We discuss here how to achieve bistochastic privacy by the suitable parameterizations of matrices. We saw in Sect. 2 two possible cases that lead to differential privacy (Expression (2)) and k-anonymity (Expression (3)) guarantees. However, beyond popular privacy models more parameterizations are possible.

We start by noting that the diagonal of a bistochastic matrix is central in any construction. Indeed, the diagonal contains the probability, for an individual or a category, that the anonymized value is the true value, meaning that the diagonal values will indicate a certain level of "truthfulness" in the anonymized data. In fact, the level of truthfulness of a bistochastic matrix is related to its singularity:

Proposition 3: *If for a bistochastic matrix* $P_k = \begin{pmatrix} p_{11} & \cdots & p_{1n_k} \\ \vdots & \ddots & \vdots \\ p_{n_k 1} & \cdots & p_{n_k n_k} \end{pmatrix}$ $p_{u_k u_k} > 0.5 \forall u_k \in$

$\{1, \ldots, n_k\}$, *then* P_k *is non-singular.*

This proposition comes from the fact that a bistochastic matrix with its diagonal values superior to 0.5 is by definition a diagonally-dominant matrix, i.e. for every row of the matrix, the magnitude of the diagonal entry in a row is larger than or equal to the sum of the magnitudes of all the other (non-diagonal) entries in that row. By the Levy–Desplanques theorem [12], such matrix is always non-singular. For anonymization (and also data utility), this means that, if a bistochastic matrix is randomizing in such a way that more than half of the time the true values are reported in the anonymized data set, then the matrix is also invertible. An estimate of the univariate distribution can then always be retrieved following the procedure outlined in the Appendix on randomized response. The setting of diagonal values is thus pivotal for parameterization but it is in no way binding. One can still set an "untruthful" matrix with very small diagonal values, albeit the non-singularity of the matrix will not always be guaranteed.

A convenient way of building a bistochastic matrix is to use a special case of Toeplitz matrices, namely a circulant matrix:

$$P_k = \begin{pmatrix} p_{11} & p_{12} & p_{13} & \cdots & p_{1n_k} \\ p_{1n_k} & p_{11} & p_{12} & \cdots & p_{1(n_k-1)} \\ p_{1(n_k-1)} & p_{1n_k} & p_{11} & \cdots & p_{1(n_k-2)} \\ \vdots & \vdots & \vdots & \vdots & \vdots \\ p_{12} & p_{13} & p_{14} & \cdots & p_{11} \end{pmatrix} \qquad (6)$$

In that case, the first row of P_k determines all the elements of the matrix.

Another way is to consider symmetric tridiagonal matrices P_k of the following form (with $\alpha_{i-1} + \alpha_i \le 1, \forall i \in \{1, \ldots, n_k - 2\}$):

$$\begin{pmatrix} 1 - \alpha_1 & \alpha_1 & 0 & 0 & \cdots & 0 \\ \alpha_1 & 1 - \alpha_1 - \alpha_2 & \alpha_2 & 0 & \cdots & 0 \\ 0 & \alpha_2 & 1 - \alpha_2 - \alpha_3 & \alpha_3 & \cdots & 0 \\ \vdots & \vdots & \vdots & \vdots & \ddots & \vdots \\ 0 & 0 & 0 & \alpha_{n_k-1} & 1 - \alpha_{n_k-1} - \alpha_{n_k} & \alpha_{n_k} \\ 0 & 0 & \cdots & \cdots & \alpha_{n_k} & 1 - \alpha_{n_k} \end{pmatrix} \qquad (7)$$

Remark that in Expressions (7) and (3) the matrices contain zeros and thus strictly they are not describing an ergodic process. While one can always replace the zeros by an infinitesimal term $\gamma > 0$ and then adjust the other strictly positive remaining terms in order to get a strictly ergodic bistochastic matrix, a way to ease implementation is to *not* adjust the strictly positive terms to get what is called a super doubly stochastic matrix, where all rows and columns sums will be infinitesimally above one. In most cases, such matrices will behave almost like purely bistochastic ergodic matrices [10].

The latter way is the one we have followed in the examples of Table 1, where we give the number of bits of selected bistochastic matrices expressed as a percentage of the maximum possible number of bits achieved in the case of perfect secrecy, i.e. we report directly the β's. We consider 3 parameterizations for each type of bistochastic matrix considered: *i)* differential privacy following Expression (2) for $\varepsilon = 5, 3$ and 1, *ii)* k-anonymity following Expression (3) for $k = 2, 3$ and 6, *iii)* a tridiagonal matrix following Expression (7) with α_{i-1} and $\alpha_i = 0.1, 0.3$ and 0.4, and *iv)* a circulant matrix following Expression (6) with $p_{11}=0.9, 0.6$ and 0.2 (while the remaining probabilities in each row are all equal and add to $1 - p_{11}$). The cases are set to go each time in the direction of more entropy and less truthfulness. The matrices generated are *12 × 12* in size, thus meant to be applied on a numerical attribute with 12 individuals or on a categorical attribute with 12 categories.

In this example, the injection of $\log_2 12 = 3.6$ bits in the attribute achieves perfect secrecy, and one can see that the strictest parameter values of differential privacy and k-anonymity in Table 1 come relatively close to this amount. Moreover, as differential privacy via RR gives a circulant matrix (see Expression (2)), it is not surprising that our circulant matrix parameterization happens to mimic differential privacy quite closely.

Table 1. Example of bistochastic guarantees. Each column corresponds to a different parameter value.

Parametrization using:	Distance to perfect secrecy (β's)		
	1	2	3
Differential privacy	17%	60%	97%
K-anonymity	28%	56%	72%
Tridiagonal matrix	24%	35%	40%
Circulant matrix	21%	63%	93%

While a privacy model in itself, bistochastic privacy can ease the comparison of performances across privacy models, both in terms of privacy but also of information loss, through the β's values.

Note that to achieve bistochastic privacy, one just needs to select appropriate bistochastic matrices. To that end, the only information required on the data set to be anonymized is its size in terms of number of individuals and attributes and the number of categories for each categorical attribute. Therefore an agent, independent of the data controller, say a "data protector", can generate the appropriate matrices. The parameter β for those matrices will depend on the environment and the desired protection-utility trade-off.

5   Conclusions and Future Research

In this paper, we have proposed bistochastic privacy, a new model that aligns privacy with information theory and unifies the main privacy models in use, in addition to connecting with the permutation model that was shown to underlie all statistical disclosure control methods [4]. The functioning of this new model also clarifies and operationalizes the trade-off between protection and utility by expressing it in terms of bits, a natural unit of privacy and information loss.

This paper opens several lines for future research. One of them is to conduct further empirical work on real-life data sets. Another is to investigate if recent solutions developed to mitigate the dimensionality problem in RR can be adapted to the present model [6]. Yet another challenge is to extend bistochastic privacy to generate new privacy models that may be more suitable for data that are unstructured or dynamic.

Acknowledgements. Partial funding from the European Commission under project H2020–871042 "SoBigData++" is acknowledged. The second author is also partially funded by an ICREA Acadèmia Prize.

Appendix

A.1 Randomized Response

Let X denotes an original categorical attribute with $1, \ldots, r$ categories, and Y its anonymized version. Given a value $X = u$, randomized response (RR, [1]) computes a value $Y = v$ by using an $r \times r$ Markov transition matrix:

$$P = \begin{pmatrix} p_{11} & \cdots & p_{1r} \\ \vdots & \ddots & \vdots \\ p_{r1} & \cdots & p_{rr} \end{pmatrix} (A.1)$$

where $p_{uv} = \Pr(Y = v | X = u)$ denotes the probability that the original response u in X is reported as v in Y, for $u, v \in \{1, \ldots, r\}$. To be a proper Markov transition matrix, it must hold that $\sum_{v=1}^{r} p_{uv} = 1 \forall u = 1, \ldots, r$. P is thus right stochastic, meaning that any original category must be spread along the anonymized categories.

The usual setting in RR is that each subject computes her randomized response Y to be reported instead of her true response X. This is called the *ex-ante* or local anonymization mode. Nevertheless, it is also possible for a (trusted) data collector to gather the original responses from the subjects and randomize them in a centralized way. This *ex-post* mode corresponds to the Post-Randomization method (PRAM, [11]). Apart from who performs the anonymization, RR and PRAM operate the same way and make use of the same matrix P.

Let $\pi_1, \ldots, \pi_r$ be the proportions of respondents whose true values fall in each of the r categories of X; let $\lambda_v = \sum_{u=1}^{r} p_{uv} \pi_u$ for $v = 1, \ldots, r$ be the probability of the reported value Y being v. If we define by $\lambda = (\lambda_1, \ldots, \lambda_r)^T$ and $\pi = (\pi_1, \ldots, \pi_r)^T$, then we have $\lambda = P^T \pi$. Furthermore, if P is nonsingular, it is proven in [1] that an unbiased estimator $\hat{\pi}$ of π can be obtained as $\hat{\pi} = (P^T)^{-1} \lambda$. Thus, univariate frequencies can be easily retrieved from the protected data set. Note that this procedure does not entail any privacy risk as only some estimates of the frequencies are retrieved, not specific responses that can be traced back to any individual.

RR is based on an implicit privacy guarantee called *plausible deniability* [5]. It equips the individuals with the ability to deny, with variable strength according to the parameterization of P, that they have reported a specific value. In fact, the more similar the probabilities in P, the higher the deniability. In the case where the probabilities within each column of P are identical, it can be proved that *perfect secrecy* in the Shannon sense is reached [15]: observing the anonymized attribute Y gives no information at all on the real value X. Under such configuration, a privacy breach cannot originate from the release of an anonymized data set, as the release does not bring any information that could be used for an attack. However, as exposed in the paper, the price to pay in terms of data utility is high.

A.2 The Permutation Model of SDC

The permutation model of statistical disclosure control conceptually unifies SDC methods by viewing them basically as permutation [4]. Consider an original attribute $X =$

$\{x_1, \ldots, x_n\}$ observed on n individuals and its anonymized version $Y = \{y_1, \ldots, y_n\}$. Assume these attributes can be ranked—even categorical nominal attributes can be, using a semantic distance. For $i = 1$ to n: compute $j = Rank(y_i)$ and let $z_i = x_{(j)}$, where $x_{(j)}$ is the value of X of rank j. Then call attribute $Z = \{z_1, \ldots, z_n\}$ the *reverse-mapped* version of X. For example, if an original value $x_1 \in X$ is anonymized as $y_1 \in Y$, and y_1 is, say, the 3rd smallest value in Y, then take z_1 to be the 3rd smallest value in X. If there are several attributes in the original data set X and anonymized data set Y, the previous reverse-mapping procedure is conducted for each attribute; call Z the data set formed by reverse-mapped attributes.

Note that: *i)* a reverse-mapped attribute Z is a permutation of the corresponding original attribute X; *ii)* the rank order of Z is the same as the rank order of Y. Therefore, any SDC method for microdata—individual records—is functionally equivalent to permutation—transforming data set X into Z—followed by residual noise—transforming Z into the anonymized data set Y. The noise added is residual because by construction the ranks of Z and Y are the same.

A.3 Information Theory

Classically, information theory approaches the notion of information contained in a message as capturing how much the message reduces uncertainty about something [10]. As a result, in this theory information shares the same definition as entropy and choosing which term to use depends on whether it is given or taken away. For example, a high entropy attribute will convey a high initial uncertainty about its actual value. If we then learn the value, we have acquired an amount of information equal to the initial uncertainty, i.e. the entropy we had originally about the value. Thus, information and entropy are two sides of the same coin. In this paper, we propose to apply entropy to a data set in a controlled way. This operation will take away data utility from the user but will in exchange generate protection. As such, data utility and protection also become two sides of the same coin, albeit in that case they are inversely related.

In information theory, a basic way to capture uncertainty is majorization [12]. Assume two vectors $x = (x_1, \ldots, x_N)^T$ and $y = (y_1, \ldots, y_N)^T$ that represent probability distributions, with the elements of each vector pre-ordered in decreasing order. The vector x is said to majorize y, usually noted as $x \succ y$, if and only if the largest element of x is greater than the largest element of y, the largest two elements of x are greater than the largest two elements of y, and so on... [10]. Equivalently, that means that the probability distribution represented by x is more narrowly peaked than y, in turn implying that x conveys less uncertainty than y, thus that x has less entropy than y.

In the privacy literature there is no such well-defined notion of information and no associated concepts such as majorization. What is meant as information for the meaningful exploitation of a data set lies in the eye of the user. For example, one user may be interested in the ability to perform some simple statistical requests such as cross-tabulations and thus will call information the analytical validity of such requests on anonymized data and their close proximity with the same requests performed on the original data set. Another user may be only interested in the ability to perform some econometric analyses, and thus again will qualify an anonymized data as informative given, for example, the validity of some OLS outputs made on it. Of course, and because the needs of users can be quasi-infinitely rich, one is left with a severe problem of diversity for evaluating the information content of an anonymized data set. In the paper, we reasonably assume that the original data set always provides the highest utility and analytical value to the user, and thus that an anonymized data set always entails a loss of utility.

References

1. Chaudhuri, A., Mukerjee, R.: Randomized Response : Theory and Techniques. Marcel Dekker (1988)
2. Clifton, C., Tassa, T.: On syntactic anonymity and differential privacy. Trans. Data Priv. **6**, 147–159 (2013)
3. Cover, T., Thomas, J.: Elements of Information Theory. Wiley (2012)
4. Domingo-Ferrer, J., Muralidhar, K.: New directions in anonymization: permutation paradigm, verifiability by subjects and intruders, transparency to users. Inf. Sci. **337–338**, 11–24 (2016)
5. Domingo-Ferrer, J., Soria-Comas, J.: Connecting randomized response, post-randomization, differential privacy and t-closeness via deniability and permutation (2018). https://arxiv.org/abs/1803.02139
6. Domingo-Ferrer, J., Soria-Comas, J.: Multi-dimensional randomized response. IEEE Transactions on Knowledge and Data Engineering. To appear
7. Dwork, C.: Differential privacy. In: Bugliesi, M., Preneel, B., Sassone, V., Wegener, I. (eds.) ICALP 2006. LNCS, vol. 4052, pp. 1–12. Springer, Heidelberg (2006). https://doi.org/10.1007/11787006_1
8. General Data Protection Regulation. European Union Regulation 2016/679 (2016)
9. Hundepool, A., et al.: Statistical Disclosure Control. Wiley (2012)
10. Jacobs, K.: Quantum Measurement Theory and its Applications. Cambridge University Press (2014)
11. Kooiman, P.L., Willenborg, L., Gouweleeuw, J.: PRAM:A Method for Disclosure Limitation of Microdata. Research Rep. 9705, Statistics Netherlands, Voorburg, NL (1998)
12. Marshall, A.W., Olkin, I., Arnold, B.C.: Inequalities: Theory of Majorization and its Applications. Springer Series in Statistics (2011)
13. Muralidhar, K., Domingo-Ferrer, J., Martinez, S.: ε-differential privacy for microdata releases does not guarantee confidentiality (let alone utility). Lecture Notes in Computer Science, vol. 12276 (Privacy in Statistical Databases - PSD 2020), pp. 21–31 (2020)
14. Samarati, P., Sweeney, L.: Protecting Privacy when Disclosing Information: k-Anonymity and its Enforcement through Generalization and Suppression. SRI International Report (1998)
15. Shannon, C.E.: Communication theory of secrecy systems. Bell Syst. Tech. J. **28**(4), 656–715 (1949)
16. Wang, Y., Wu, X., Hu, D. Using randomized response for differential privacy preserving data collection. In: Proceedings of the EDBT/ICDT 2016 Joint Conference (2016)
17. Wooldridge, J.: Econometric Analysis of Cross Section and Panel Data. MIT Press (2010)
18. Xiao, X., Tao, Y.: Anatomy: simple and effective privacy preservation. In Proceedings of the 32nd International Conferences on Very Large Data Bases-VLDB 2006, VLDB Endowment, pp. 139–150 (2006)

Improvement of Estimate Distribution with Local Differential Privacy

Hikaru Horigome and Hiroaki Kikuchi[(✉)][iD]

Graduate School of Advanced Mathematical Science, Meiji University,
4-21-1 Nakano, Tokyo 164-8525, Japan
{cs212030,kikn}@meiji.ac.jp

Abstract. Personalized high-quality services including route finding and detection of the nearest shops and restaurants are provided based on the current location of the owner of the smart device. However, location trace data are very sensitive data because of privacy concerns. They allow to estimate our home residence or office location to be estimated. Hence, privacy preservation is required for reporting current location traces from smart devices.

This paper studies the privacy preservation of time-series location trace using the local differential privacy (LDP) algorithm Randomized Aggregable Privacy-Preserving Ordinal Response (RAPPOR). Location trace is independently randomized according to given procedures and then is sent to a service provider that aggregates data with noise. To discard noise and estimate true statistics, the maximum likelihood estimation is used in RAPPOR. However, maximum likelihood estimation (MLE) could fail if the data distribution is skewed or the data contain extraordinary-values. To address the problem, we propose the expectation maximization for estimating of true distributions. The proposed algorithm iteratively improves estimated posterior probabilities based on Bayes' theorem until the difference converges for all elements. Our experiment using 6,528 individuals' location traces in Tokyo provided from Nightley Inc. demonstrates that the proposed algorithm performs better than the original MLE used in RAPPOR for every special ward in Tokyo in one day. We found that the accuracy is improved as the privacy budget ϵ decreases and as many populations are provided.

Keywords: Local differential privacy · RAPPOR · Expectation maximization

1 Introduction

Smart devices allow us to have better-personalized service in the era of smart society. For example, commercial services provide route finding and detection of the nearest shops and restaurants based on the current location of the owner of the smart device. As for measuring people's movement in relation to Covid-19, time-series population distributions provided from cellphone service providers play an important role in the evaluation of the restriction of people's movement.

© The Author(s), under exclusive license to Springer Nature Switzerland AG 2022
V. Torra and Y. Narukawa (Eds.): MDAI 2022, LNAI 13408, pp. 68–79, 2022.
https://doi.org/10.1007/978-3-031-13448-7_6

However, location traces are very sensitive data for privacy because the location of the owners' home residence or office can be estimated. The correlation between any given location traces may reveal the personal relationship between them. The location service provider may be compromised by a malicious third party and the platforms may contain a malicious insiders who can steal and disclose the private customer's data. Therefore, the privacy of location trace data must be enhanced to prevent privacy threats.

Differential privacy has been studied so as to guarantee privacy preservation. With the Laplacian mechanism, the statistics are perturbed so that no one can distinguish two neighboring datasets that differ only by one individual. Erlingsson et al. at Google proposed a local differential privacy (LDP) algorithm, Randomized Aggregatable Privacy-Preserving Ordinal Response (RAPPOR) [1]. It is well known that RAPPOR can collect data from a large number of devices without revealing private attributes such as frequencies, categories, and statistics of the devices. RAPPOR is based on randomized response [3] and estimates the true attribute as the most likely value. Maximum Likelihood Estimation (MLE) used in RAPPOR does not always work well. It could fail to estimate true data if the distribution of data is biased or if the data contain extraordinary high/low values. In this paper, we show that unbalanced distribution yields significant error in the estimate presented. Because it estimates the most likely value, just only one illegal value can spoil the overall accuracy. Unfortunately, this could happen for use case of location-based services where the movements of people are not predicted.

In this paper, we propose an iterative approach to improve the estimation accuracy of perturbed data in the LDP algorithm. Our idea is based on Bayes' theorem and the Expectation Maximization (EM) algorithm [5]. It estimates the posterior probability that is most consistent with given perturbed data. Because of iterative processes, the estimate is improved repeatedly. Hence, it is more stable and more robust against the unexpected behavior of hazard records.

We conduct an experiment using SNS-based location traces to demonstrate the feasibility of the proposed algorithm and to clarify accuracy improvement in the real location data. Our data contain 6,528 individuals' location traces in Tokyo provided from Nightley Inc. that are classified into several smaller special wards. We show the comparison between our proposed estimate (EM) and the MLE used in RAPPOR for several privacy budgets ϵ.

Our contribution has two components.

- We propose a new algorithm to estimate the distribution of private data from perturbed data in RAPPOR. Our proposed algorithm improves the accuracy of the estimate based on the iterative process of Bayesian posterior probabilities.
- We show the experimental results using large-scale location trace data in Tokyo with several smaller wards. The result shows that the proposed method performs better than the MLE used in RAPPOR and gives significant improvements.

2   Local Differential Privacy

2.1   Fundamental Definition

Suppose that users periodically submit their location data to a service provider. Differential privacy guarantees that the randomized data do not reveal any privacy disclosure from them. On the other hand, LDP needs no trusted party. The private location data are randomized by users before being submitted to the service provider. LDP is defined as follows.

Definition 1. *A randomized algorithm Q satisfies ϵ-local differential privacy if for all pairs of values v and v' of domain V and for all subset S of range Z ($S \subset Z$), and for $\epsilon \geq 0$,*

$$Pr[Q(v) \in S] \leq e^{\epsilon} Pr[Q(v') \in S]. \tag{1}$$

2.2   RAPPOR [1]

Erlingsson et al. at Google proposed a LDP algorithm, Randomized Aggregatable Privacy-Preserving Ordinal Response (RAPPOR) [1]. It is motivated by an application to track the Chrome browser configuration distribution of users.

Let v_i be the i-th element of v and be flipped according to randomized mechanism Q. In the basic randomized response [3], output z_i is set to be 1 for $v_i = 1$ with probability p, and 0 with probability $q = 1 - p$ as,

$$z_i = \begin{cases} v_i & w/p \ p \\ 1 - v_i & w/p \ q \end{cases}$$

where p and q are probabilities to preserve the original value v_i to be unchanged and changed, respectively.

In RAPPOR, additional uncertainty is added through the use of Bloom filter using d hash functions. With this, input v is so-called "one-hot" encoded as a d-bit vector that contains exactly 1 one and $d - 1$ zeros. Sensitivity Δf, the maximum influence that a single individual can have on the result of a randomized response, is 2 bits. For instance, suppose users 1 and 2 have $v = (0, 1, 0, 0)$ and $v' = (0, 0, 1, 0)$, respectively. A probability that randomized algorithm Q outputs $z = (0, 1, 0, 1)$ for v is

$$Pr[Q(v) = (0, 1, 0, 1) \mid v = (0, 1, 0, 0)] = (1 - q)p(1 - q)q.$$

Similarly, user 2 has the same output z with the probability of $Pr[Q(v') = [0, 1, 0, 1] \mid v'] = (1 - q)q(1 - p)q$. If we set p and q with sensitivity Δf as

$$p = \frac{e^{\frac{\epsilon}{\Delta f}}}{1 + e^{\frac{\epsilon}{\Delta f}}} = \frac{e^{\frac{\epsilon}{2}}}{1 + e^{\frac{\epsilon}{2}}} \text{ and } q = \frac{1}{1 + e^{\frac{\epsilon}{2}}}$$

then, it satisfies ϵ-local differential privacy as follows

$$\frac{Pr[Q(v) = z \mid v]}{Pr[Q(v') = z \mid v']} = \frac{(1 - q)p(1 - q)q}{(1 - q)q(1 - p)q} \leq e^{\epsilon}.$$

Intuitively, no one can distinguish v and v' for users from the randomized output z and hence the local (value) privacy is preserved. The privacy budget ϵ controls the degree of privacy and improves privacy as it is close to 0 (smaller ϵ means stronger privacy).

Generally, n-bit vectors v and v' have a sensitivity of Hamming distance, that is, $\Delta f = \sum_{i=1}^{n} |v_i - v'_i| \leq 2$. Letting r and r' be numbers of inconsistent bits in v and v', respectively. We have $Pr[Q(v) = z \in S|v] = p^{n-r}q^r$ and $Pr[Q(v') = z \in S|v'] = p^{n-r'}q^{r'}$. After all, we confirm that Eq. (1) holds as

$$\frac{Pr[Q(v) = z \mid v]}{Pr[Q(v') = z \mid v']} = \frac{p^{n-r}q^r}{p^{n-r'}q^{r'}} = \left(\frac{p}{q}\right)^{h'-h} = e^{\frac{\epsilon \Delta f}{2}} \leq e^{\epsilon}$$

where $\Delta f = h' - h$.

2.3   Related Works

Idea to preserve privacy of input with randomization has been studied so far. Kikuchi et al. [9] proposed a randomization protocol for voting without a single input being guessed but the aggregated value reveals the estimation accurately. Agrawal and Srikant [11] proposed a privacy-preserving collaboration filtering and an estimation algorithm based on Bayes' theorem, called reconstruction. Polat and Du [12] proposed some collaborative filtering schemes for Pearson correlation-based algorithm. Their idea was based on a hypothesis that the random noise uniformly chosen from range goes to be zero, making the estimation simpler by the scalar product of randomized vectors. Zhang et al. pointed out that an additive perturbation does not preserve privacy as much as had been believed by showing the experiment to derive an amount of the original data in [13,14].

Chen et al. [10] proposed the notion of local differential privacy to provide a privacy guarantee for user. Compared to the conventional differential privacy studies, local differential privacy has been used for many real-world application. For example, Erlingsson et al. introduced RAPPOR [1] to use a Bloom filter to encode input as bit of vector. RAPPOR is a Google Chorome extension to collects Windows process names and some attributes without revealing confidential values. Apple also implements their local differential privacy protocols in the latest iOS and MacOS for discovering major emoji and identifying high memory usage in Safari [2].

Local differential privacy has some limitations. The RAPPOR assumes input as 1-dimensional categorical data. To discard the limitation, several studies have been done so far. Qin et al. [7] propose a heavy hitter estimation over set-valued data. Their idea involves user-server interactions in two rounds. Ono et al. [6] also extend their idea and show some improvement.

Ren et al. proposed a multi-dimensional joint distribution estimation algorithm that satisfies LDP [8]. Their proposed method is also based on the expectation maximization and Lasso regression. They reported the experimental results on real-world datasets and showed that the proposed one outperforms the exiting estimation schemes such as support vector machine and random forest classifications.

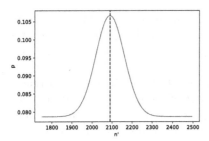

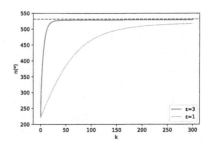

Fig. 1. Probability distribution $Pr(n'|n = 505)$.

Fig. 2. Estimated population n^* with regard to number of iterations k for privacy budgets $\epsilon = 1$ and 3

3   Improvement of Estimate

3.1   Maximum Likelihood Estimate

We consider the problem of estimating the population distribution from the randomization used in RAPPOR in this section.

Let n be the population of city x at a particular time. Suppose that people who live in the city move in their daily life. Consequently, the current population is a dynamic quantity ranging from 0 to the maximum ℓ, such as the total population in the state of that city x. According to the RAPPOR algorithm, Let n' be the randomized population of x according to the RAPPOR algorithm. With probabilities p (true) and q (flipped), the expected value of binomial distribution gives $n' = np + (\ell - n)q$, which leads the maximized likelihood value $L[n]$ as

$$L[n] = \frac{n' - \ell q}{p - q}.$$

Letting h be the number of n individuals who submit 1, we have a probability distribution of n by the addition of binomial distributions as

$$p(n) = \binom{n}{h} p^h q^{n-h} + \binom{\ell - n}{n' - h} p^{\ell - n - n' + h} q^{n' - h}$$

Figure 1 shows the probability distribution of Shinjuku ward's population at 14:00. The randomized population is increased around 21:00.

3.2   Iterative Estimate

MLE used in RAPPOR algorithm works well for most cases but has low estimate accuracy for a biased distribution. Instead, we consider an iterative estimate approach known as the Expectation Maximization (EM) algorithm.

Algorithm 1. EM algorithm for RAPPOR

$\theta_i^{(0)} \leftarrow$ a population of city i.
repeat(E-step)
   $k \leftarrow 1$
   Estimate posterior probability $Pr[V_i = 1|Z]$ in Eq. (3).
   (M-step) Update marginal probability $\theta_i^{(k+1)}$ in Eq. (4).
until $|\theta_i^{(k+1)} - \theta_i^{(k)}| \leq \epsilon'$ **return** $n_i = \ell\theta_i^*$

EM algorithm performs an iterative process for which posterior probabilities are updated through Bayes' theorem. Each iteration estimates the best probabilities θ_i for all cities i that are consistent with the given randomized outputs Z computed in RAPPOR. Hence, it is more robust against unbalanced distribution than the MLE is.

Algorithm 1 shows the proposed EM algorithm for estimating true distribution from randomized data according to RAPPOR. It has two steps; expectation (E-Step) and maximization (M-Step). In the E-Step, Bayes' theorem plays a significant role in estimating, as follows.

Let V_i be a random variable of the population of the i-th city in m cities in the state and Z be that of the randomized one in RAPPOR. Conditional probability given $V_i = 1$ is

$$Pr[Z_i|V_i = 1] = \frac{Pr[Z_i, V_i = 1]}{Pr[Z_i = 1]}. \qquad (2)$$

Bayes' theorem gives the posterior probability of $V_i = 1$ given the randomized value Z as

$$Pr[V_i = 1|Z] = \frac{Pr[Z|V_i = 1]Pr[V_i = 1]}{\sum_{j=1}^{m} Pr[Z|V_j = 1]Pr[V_j = 1]} = \frac{Pr[V_i = 1|Z]\theta_i}{\sum_{j=1}^{m} Pr[Z|V_j = 1]\theta_j}, \qquad (3)$$

where θ_i is the estimated probability of the i-th city.

In the EM algorithm, Bayes' estimate is iterated to improve accuracy. For every iteration, a marginal distribution $\theta_i^{(k)}$ is replaced by the mean of posterior probability as

$$\theta_i^{(k+1)} = \sum_{j \in m} Pr[V_i = 1 \mid V_j = 1]\theta_i^{(k)}. \qquad (4)$$

It continues until the estimate converges for all cities. Let θ_i^* be the converged probability $\theta_i^{(k+1)}$ if $|\theta_i^{(k+1)} - \theta_i^{(k)}|$ is less than a threshold of an iteration that is predetermined for required precision. The final estimate is $n_i^{(*)} = \ell\theta_i^{(*)}$ for city $i \leq \ell$.

Figure 2 shows the improvement of estimated population $n^{(*)}$ with regard to the number of iteration k. Estimated population in RAPPOR with $\epsilon = 1$ and 3 is plotted in Fig. 2, where the dotted line indicates the true population. Obviously, the accuracy is improved as k increases. The result shows that the estimate converged around $k = 200$, even for very strong privacy budget $\epsilon = 1$.

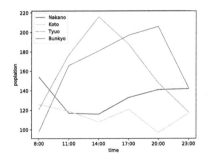

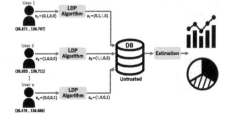

Fig. 3. Time-series population in Tokyo   **Fig. 4.** System flow

4 Experiment

4.1 Objective

The objective of the experiment is to explore the accuracy improvement using open location data and to demonstrate that the proposed algorithm works better than MLE in RAPPOR.

4.2 Data

Our experiment uses the time-series location data published by Nightley Inc. [4]. They are synthetic data based on messages posted in a social networking service. Table 2 shows the specification of the dataset. We use the Nightley dataset that contains location traces for 6,258 individuals for a day. The populations changed as people move from home to office or shops, as shown in Table 1.

The city of Tokyo consists of 23 special wards. For each ward, we identify how many individuals stay for every three hours based on the latitude and longitude provided with the trace (used by Google Map API). The time-series populations for some major wards are shown in Table 3 and Fig. 3. Table 4 gives a change of statistics with respect to a time period. We observe two typical behaviors;

(a) Residential area, where populations are higher in the morning and night, e.g., Nakano and Koto wards
(b) Office area, where many schools, offices, and shops are located and the population in the daytime is higher than in the morning and night, e.g., Tyuo and Bunkyo wards.

Figures 5 and 6 show the heat maps of the population at 8:00 and 14:00. We find the dense area is at the center of Tokyo at 14:00 h, while it is not crowded in the morning (at 8:00). This is typical behavior for people in a metropolitan city, and our target is to estimate this from randomized location traces.

Figure 4 illustrates how location traces are processed in our scheme, where n users move independently and belong to one of 23 special wards. Their current

Table 1. Time-series population Nightley in Tokyo

Time	Population
8:00	2,957
11:00	3,922
14:00	4,640
17:00	4,793
20:00	4,300
23:00	3,283

Table 2. Specification of the Nightley dataset

Surveyed value	Point of Interest (POI), Timestamp (SNS post), The road network
Estimate value	Movement courses, A place of residence, Work location, Stay time, Gender, What they did during their stay (including shopping and leisure)
Area	Tokyo Metropolitan
Target time	July, 2013, October, December
A time unit	As for every five minutes
Geodetic datum	WGS84 (EPSG:4326)
Records	There are approximately 70,000 cases with each csv file
File size	Approximately 100 MB

Table 3. Time-series population in major wards in Tokyo

Ward	8:00	11:00	14:00	17:00	20:00	23:00
Shibuya	262	394	533	532	479	351
Shinjuku	278	414	505	531	454	304
Minato	267	393	509	479	416	284
Chiyoda	186	381	506	496	476	248
Setagaya	295	331	367	403	368	317
Suginami	165	209	227	246	187	188
Tyuo	121	177	216	188	148	118
Bunkyo	98	166	181	197	206	143
Shinagawa	98	147	182	173	147	99
Nakano	154	117	116	133	141	142

Table 4. Statistics of time-series population for 23 wards in Tokyo

Time	8:00	11:00	14:00	17:00	20:00	23:00
Mean	192.4	272.9	334.2	337.8	302.2	219.4
Max	295	414	533	532	479	351
Min	98	117	116	133	141	99

memberships to one of 23 wards are encoded as 23-dimension vector v. They perturb their location in RAPPOR $Q(v)$ before being sent to a service provider. The service provider simply sums all perturbed locations and publishes a distribution of population Z_i for the i-th ward. With either MLE or EM algorithms, we estimate the true distribution of population N_i.

4.3 Method

We apply RAPPOR algorithm to the Nightley data for several privacy budgets ϵ. Our experiment is processed as follows.

1. Each user perturbs his/her current location v in RAPPOR for privacy budgets $\epsilon = 0.5, 1, 1.5, \ldots, 5.0$ to have $Q(v)$.
2. The service provider collects users' location data for every time period and publishes the distribution of populations for 23 wards in Tokyo $Z_1, \ldots, Z_m$.

Fig. 5. Heat map of Tokyo at 8:00

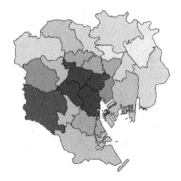

Fig. 6. Heat map of Tokyo at 14:00

3. We estimate populations in MLE and the proposed (EM) algorithms and denote them by N_{MLE} and N_{EM}, respectively.
4. We evaluate the accuracy for two estimates in mean absolute error (MAE), that is, $\sum_{i=1...,m} |N_i - N_{MLE}|$, where N_i is the true population of i-th ward.
5. We repeat the above steps 10 times to estimate mean accuracy for some algorithms.

Note that Step 3, the EM algorithm needs iterative process to esimate until the result is converged. The number of iteration depends on the input data.

4.4   Results

Figure 7 shows the true distribution of populations of the i-th ward, n_i, in Tokyo at 14:00. We perturbed location data in RAPPOR with privacy budget $\epsilon = 0.5$ (very safe) so that no one can be estimated as particular ward, n'_i, as shown in Fig. 8. It shows almost uniform probability distributions and thus the privacy is certainly preserved. The proposed algorithm gives the estimated population $n_i^{(*)}$ as shown in Fig. 9. We observe that the estimated distribution is very close to the true one in Fig. 7.

Figure 10 shows the estimated populations with respect to m wards in Tokyo at 14:00 with privacy budget $\epsilon = 0.5$. The results show that the proposed estimates (labeled as EM, colored in blue) are close to the true population (green) for almost all wards. In contrast, the ML estimates sometimes suffer significant error, e.g., -700 and -900 for the 15th and 20th wards.

For what data does the MLE estimation fails? To answer this question, we show the scatter-plot between true and the estimated populations in Fig. 11. The estimated populations in the EM algorithm are on the line of true population. While, the MLE populations, indicated with red cross, deviate from the true line. The estimated populations are too large when true population is more than 450 and too low when true population is less than 200. In other words, the EM algorithm estimates accurately when the given data are biased.

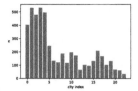

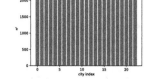

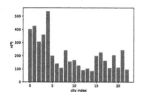

Fig. 7. Distribution of population of i-th ward n_i

Fig. 8. Distribution of populations perturbed in RAPPOR n_i' ($\epsilon = 0.5$)

Fig. 9. Distribution of estimated populations $n_i^{(*)}$

Table 5 shows the mean absolute error of estimations in the proposed algorithm (EM) and the existing one (MLE) for some privacy budgets $\epsilon = 0.5, \ldots, 5.0$. The mean errors of the EM are 60 % of that of the MLE for $\epsilon = 0.5$. The improvement is maximized at the smallest budget.

The accuracy depends on wards and privacy budgets. Thus, we evaluate MAE and depict the MAE results at times 8:00, 11:00, 14:00, 17:00, 20:00 and 23:00 in Figs. 12, 13, 14, 15. This plot shows MAE for both estimate algorithms with respect to privacy budgets $\epsilon = 0.5, 1, 1.5, \ldots, 5.0$. The results show that the proposed algorithm performs better than the MLE used in [1] for every time period. The difference between the two estimates maximizes as the privacy budget decreases (the wider the randomization range, the higher the privacy). We also note that the improvement of accuracy is higher at 8:00 than that at 14:00. This error of MLE is caused because many people are at home in the morning, as shown in Fig. 3 and Fig. 5, and the unbalanced distributions of populations reduce the maximum likelihood. The results show low accuracy for estimating the population of small wards in Fig. 10. This happens for the same reason.

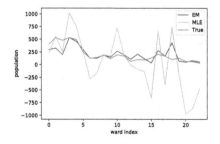

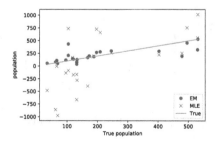

Fig. 10. Estimated populations for m wards in Tokyo at 14:00, $\epsilon = 0.5$ (Color figure online)

Fig. 11. Scatter-plot between true and estimated populations (EM and MLE)

Table 5. Mean absolute error with reagrd to ϵ

ϵ	EM	MLE
0.5	2971.31	4885.28
1.0	1846.69	2256.53
1.5	1404.14	1614.74
2.0	982.69	1072.24
2.5	780.58	849.41
3.0	628.41	710.34
3.5	524.80	601.56
4.0	407.92	503.13
4.5	349.73	434.63
5.0	287.42	363.16

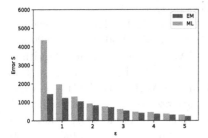

Fig. 12. MLE at 8:00 for privacy budgets ϵ

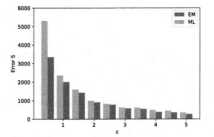

Fig. 13. MLE at 11:00 for privacy budgets ϵ

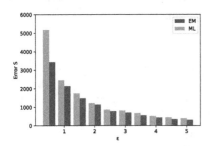

Fig. 14. MLE at 14:00 for privacy budgets ϵ

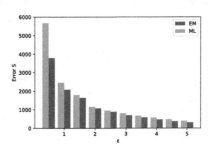

Fig. 15. MLE at 17:00 for privacy budgets ϵ

5   Conclusion

We studied the privacy preservation of time-series location traces using LDP algorithm RAPPOR and proposed the EM for estimating true distributions. The proposed algorithm iteratively improves estimated posterior probabilities based on Bayes' theorem until the difference converged for all elements. Our experiment using 6,528 individuals' location traces in Tokyo provided by Nightley Inc. demonstrates that the proposed algorithm performs better than the original MLE used in RAPPOR for every special ward in Tokyo in one day. The results show that the accuracy improved as the privacy budget ϵ decreased and when many populations were provided. We conclude that the iterative approach works well for data perturbed in the LDP algorithm.

Acknowledgment. Part of this work was supported by JSPS KAKENHI Grant Number JP18H04099 and JST, CREST Grant Number JPMJCR21M1, Japan.

References

1. Erlingsson, Ú., Pihur, V., Korolova, A.: RAPPOR: randomized aggregatable privacy-preserving ordinal response. In: ACM Conference on Computer and Communications Security, pp. 1054–1067 (2014)
2. Learning with Privacy at Scale. https://machinelearning.apple.com/2017/12/06/learning-with-privacy-at-scale.html. Accessed 2019
3. Mochizuki, A., Kikuchi, H.: Privacy-preserving collaborative filtering using randomized response. J. Inf. Process. **21**(4), 617–623 (2012)
4. Nightley Inc.: SNS-based People Flow Data is now available for free download. https://nightley.jp/archives/1954/. Accessed Oct 2019
5. Miyagawa, M.: EM algorithm and marginal applications. Adv. Stat. **16**(1), 1–19 (1987). (in Japanese)
6. Ono, H., Fukuchi, K., Sakuma, J.: Detection of Heavy hitters in restriction of local differential privacy. DEIM Forum 2018 E1-3 (2018). (in Japanese)
7. Qin, Z., Yang, Y., Yu, T.: Heavy hitter estimation over set-valued data with local differential privacy. In: Proceedings of ACM CCS, pp. 192–203 (2016)
8. Ren, X., et al.: LoPub: high-dimensional crowdsourced data publication with local differential privacy. IEEE Trans. Inf. Forensics Secur. **13**(9), 2151–2166 (2018)
9. Kikuchi, H., Akiyama, J., Gobioff, H.: Stochastic voting protocol to protect voters privacy. In: Proceedings of 1999 IEEE Workshop on Internet Applications, pp. 103–111 (1999)
10. Chen, R., Li, H., Qin, A.K., Kasiviswanathan, S.P., Jin, H.: Private spatial data aggregation in the local setting. In: Proceedings of IEEE ICDE, pp. 289–300 (2016)
11. Agrawal, R., Srikant, R.: Privacy-preserving data mining. In: ACM SIGMOD 2000, pp. 439–450 (2000)
12. Polat, H., Du, W.: Privacy-preserving collaborative filtering using randomized perturbation techniques. In: ICDM 2003, pp. 1–15 (2003)
13. Zhang, S., Ford, J., Makedon, F.: Deriving private information from randomly perturbed ratings. In: SIAM-Data Mining Conference (2006)
14. Zhang, S., Ford, J., Makedon, F.: A privacy-preserving collaborative filtering scheme with two-way communication. In: ACM EC 2006, pp. 316–323 (2006)

Geolocated Data Generation and Protection Using Generative Adversarial Networks

Hugo Alatrista-Salas[1] [ID], Peter Montalvo-Garcia[1] [ID],
Miguel Nunez-del-Prado[2,3] [ID], and Julián Salas[4,5(✉)] [ID]

[1] Pontificia Universidad Católica del Perú, Lima, Peru
{halatrista,peter.montalvo}@pucp.edu.pe
[2] Instituto de Investigación de la Universidad Andina del Cusco, Cusco, Peru
[3] Peru Research, Development, and Innovation Center, Lima, Peru
miguel.nunez@peruidi.com
[4] Internet Interdisciplinary Institute (IN3), Universitat Oberta de Catalunya (UOC),
Barcelona, Spain
jsalaspi@uoc.edu
[5] Center for Cybersecurity Research of Catalonia (CYBERCAT), Barcelona, Spain

Abstract. Data mining techniques allow us to discover patterns in large datasets. Nonetheless, data may contain sensitive information. This is especially true when data is georeferenced. Thus, an adversary could learn about individual whereabouts, points of interest, political affiliation, and even sexual habits. At the same time, human mobility is a rich source of information to analyze traffic jams, health care accessibility, food desserts, and even pandemics dynamics. Therefore, to enhance privacy, we study the use of Deep Learning techniques such as Generative Adversarial Network (GAN) and GAN with Differential Privacy (DP-GAN) to generate synthetic data with formal privacy guarantees. Our experiments demonstrate that we can generate synthetic data to maintain individuals' privacy and data quality depending on privacy parameters. Accordingly, based on the privacy settings, we generated data differing a few meters and a few kilometers from the original trajectories. After generating fine-grain mobility trajectories at the GPS level through an adversarial neural networks approach and using GAN to sanitize the original trajectories together with differential privacy, we analyze the privacy provided from the perspective of anonymization literature. We show that such ϵ-differentially private data may still have a risk of re-identification.

Keywords: Differential privacy · Generative Adversarial Networks · Disclosure risk · Information loss · Synthetic trajectories · Privacy

---

H. Alatrista-Salas, P. Montalvo-Garcia and M. Nunez-del-Prado—Contributed equally in the present work.

V. Torra and Y. Narukawa (Eds.): MDAI 2022, LNAI 13408, pp. 80–91, 2022.
https://doi.org/10.1007/978-3-031-13448-7_7

1   Introduction

Geolocated data is a rich source of information. These datasets enable studies about traffic jams, urban planning, population density, health care accessibility, food deserts, and even pandemics dynamics. Nonetheless, location information is a very sensitive piece of information. Location can reveal different aspects of individuals, such as future locations, points of interest, political affiliation, specific diseases, an individual's social network, and even sexual habits. Thus, geolocation has attracted the scientific community's attention [6–9,12] to the point that it is now regulated by the General Data Protection Regulation - GDPR and considered personal data. Accordingly, the challenge is to propose techniques to ensure both individuals' privacy concerns and law compliance to use their location information for studying, for example, the COVID-19 transition dynamic or another phenomenon. In the literature, we find some applications of the synthetic data generation in health [14], transport [20], and to train Machine Learning models [15]. Other works focus more on the privacy mechanism to generate privacy-aware synthetic data [4,22,24]. In the present effort, we analyze the impact of home and work inference over synthetic datasets generated through GAN and DP-GAN, to assess individuals' privacy in terms of information loss and disclosure risk. The rest of the paper is organized as follows. First, Sect. 2 shows the related works, while Sect. 3 depicts the basic concepts. Next, Sect. 4 describes the methodology. In Sect. 5 the experimental protocol and the results are described. Finally, this paper ends with conclusions and future work.

2   Related Works

Several studies were proposed to build synthetic data through Generative Adversarial Networks (GAN). In [15], the authors compare two methods to build spatiotemporal data. The compared methods belong to two different ways: Berlin-MOD, which is an algorithmic method, an RNN, and a GAN based on deep learning. A technique based on the Turing Test was used to determine the realism of the generated data. Methods based on deep learning were built using a batch size of 64, a sequence length of 100, mean absolute error (for RNN), binary cross-entropy (for GAN) as loss functions, and the Adam optimizer. The Data Mobile Challenge and Geolife datasets were used for experimental purposes. Finally, the authors demonstrated that artificial data sets could be distinguished from real in eleven of twelve cases.

Other authors concentrate on human mobility from the existing sets of personal geolocation data. For example, authors in [20] formally define a method to generate and suggest unexplored routes from the existing sets of personal geolocation data using Generative Adversarial Networks. For experiments, data were collected from positioning devices, getting the latitude, longitude, and time information over three years. First, data was pre-treated using a CNN with four layers with each filter size of $2 \times 2 \times 128$, $2 \times 2 \times 64$, $2 \times 2 \times 32$, and $2 \times 2 \times 1$. This pre-processing step was performed to preserve all positioning information in data-generated matrices. Later, CNN with Leaky ReLU was used to transform data into 32×32 matrices. Finally, these 32×32-matrices were used as input for the GAN. As a post-processing step, a CNN-based deconvolution was performed.

In the same spirit, other authors focus on privacy-preservation of density distribution on mobility data against the aggregation attack [22]. Indeed, a discriminator network with four layers was proposed. The first three layers were used to learn the features of the input data, while the last layer was designed to compute the decision value. Also, Relu and Sigmoid were chosen as the activation functions for the first three and four layers, respectively. Later, a GAN-based generator with 4 layers was used to create synthetic data. Also, the Wasserstein distance was used as a loss function. Two open-source datasets were used for experiments: MoMo Mobile App Dataset (MoMo) and San Francisco Cabs Dataset. The proposal's effectiveness evaluation is based on the Utility Loss and the Mean Square Error measures.

In [14], authors couple a GAN and a differential privacy mechanism for generating realistic and private smart health care datasets. To do that, a 4-step process was proposed. First, the dataset containing more than 17M records was gathered from 25 individuals using Fitbit Charge 2 HR smartwatches with the Fitbit App. Participants living in Belgium and Sweden were observed for at least 60 days. Later, a time-series data aggregation step was performed. Then, based on gender and geographical locations, a synthetic data sample was generated through a BGAN. The generator was composed of 2 dense layers with 64 and 32 neurons, coupled to a Leaky ReLU activation and a rate of 0.2. The discriminator uses 2 dense layers with 512 and 256 neurons and the generator's same activation function and rate. Finally, the authors use Information Loss and Accuracy to test their proposal.

In [17], the authors use geo-tagged tweets to train a reliable generator for modeling the real-world distribution telco dataset. First, the authors propose a similarity measure to determine the high-similarity time period of training data, while DBSCAN was used to filter non-hotspots data. Then, a neural network generates a model from the real hotspot distribution through an adversarial process (GAN). The sigmoid cross-entropy in Tensorflow was used to calculate the loss. Also, the RMSprop optimizer was chosen during the training process to find a trade-off between performance and ability of convergence. Finally, the authors found a positive correlation between cellular network traffic and social network to model the intra-cell Tweets traffic distribution by using a neural network.

In [25] a new optimized DP-GAN algorithm for generating synthetic semantic-rich data from three image datasets is proposed. To meet this goal, the authors propose the Advanced DP-GAN, which improves the DP-GAN through different optimization methods. Two main differences exist between our proposal and [25]. First, our proposal generates synthetic data from spatio-temporal data, which is difficult to generate due to the high correlation between temporal and spatial dimensions. Second, authors in [25] use Inception and Jensen-Shannon scores to evaluate their proposal. Both scores capture the utility preserved by the DP-GAN instead of the privacy.

However, as [2] points out, extreme care should be exercised when applying Differential Privacy beyond the setting it was designed for. Otherwise, it may be applied in such a way that contradicts its own core idea: to make the data of any single individual unnoticeable.

Thus, we apply and analyze the privacy protection guarantees of these Differentially Private methods (GANs) considering the literature on anonymization, such as in [19], in which the privacy of a perturbative algorithm for trajectory protection was analyzed by measuring the possibility of reidentification, using the POIs including the Home/Work locations. The justification for such analysis comes from [10] and [23]. In [10], it was shown that workers who revealed their home and work location with noise or on the order of a census block, a census tract, or a county were protected by anonymity sets of sizes 1, 21 and 34,980. In [23], it was shown that the top 2 locations likely correspond to home and work and that the anonymity sets are drastically reduced if an attacker knows such locations.

Our paper thus assesses the privacy protection provided by these differentially private methods for synthetic data generation with a more interpretable measure of the risk of home and work location inference attacks.

3   Background

This section describes the main concepts related to using generative adversarial networks to generate synthetic data.

3.1   GAN and W-GAN

Generative Adversarial Networks (GAN) were fully discussed in [5]. A GAN consist of two components. First, a generator G_{GAN}, which learns the original data distribution P_{data} by mapping a latent distribution P_z. Second, a discriminator D_{GAN} learns to distinguish between samples obtained from P_{data} and those generated by the generator G_{GAN}. Figure 1 depicts the idea behind a GAN.

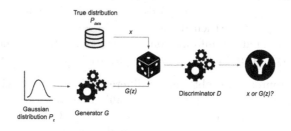

Fig. 1. GAN-based sanitisation process [25]

The goal of a GAN is to train D_{GAN} to maximize the probability that a sample comes from G_{GAN}; analogously, G_{GAN} is trained to minimize the difference of the generated and original data. To formalize it, the $MinMax$ function of G_{GAN} and D_{GAN} over the value function $V(G_{GAN}, D_{GAN})$ is defined in (1).

$$\min_{G_{GAN}} \max_{D} V(D_{GAN}, G_{GAN}) = \mathbb{E}_{x \sim p_{data}(x)}[log D_{GAN}(x)] + \mathbb{E}_{z \sim p_z(z)}[log(1 - D_{GAN}(G_{GAN}(z)))]$$
(1)

Classical Generative Adversarial Networks use Jensen-Shannon divergence. Nevertheless, the measure is not helpful for specific tasks such as synthetic data generation. Thus, the Generative Adversarial Network uses the Wasserstein distance (W-GAN) instead of the Jensen-Shannon divergence to add controlled noise in the gradient. Besides, a W-GAN [1] solves the $minmax$ problem differently, as shown in (2).

$$\min_{G_{GAN}} \max_{w \in W} \mathbb{E}_{x \sim p_{data}}(x)[f_w(x)] - \mathbb{E}_{z \sim p_z(z)}[f_w(G_{GAN}(z))]$$
(2)

where the functions $f_w(x), w \in W$ are all K-Lipschitz continuous values with respect to x for some k. Results of $minmax$ problem solution show better results from a W-GAN concerning a DP-GAN [21]. Nonetheless, this does not solves the privacy issue of generating data that is very similar to the original dataset. Thus, a differential privacy mechanism is applied to solve this problem.

3.2 Differential Privacy

Differential privacy provides formal guarantees of privacy. It is defined as follows [3]: Let $\mathcal{M}$ be an random mechanism, such that: $\mathcal{M} : D \to R$, with D being the domain and R the range. $\mathcal{M}$ is (ϵ, δ) differential private if for any pair of adjacent inputs $d, d' \in D$ and for any subset of outputs $S \subseteq R$ it satisfies (3).

$$\Pr[\mathcal{M}(d) \in S] \leq e^\epsilon \Pr[\mathcal{M}(d') \in S] + \delta$$
(3)

Differential privacy has the following properties that make it very useful for applications such as Deep Learning.

- Composability: if all components of a mechanism are differentially private, the composition is also differentially private.
- Group Privacy: privacy guarantees can be extended for when a group of participants have provided their data.
- Robustness to auxiliary information: privacy guarantees are not affected by any secondary information available to the adversary.

A common approach for obtaining a differentially private mechanism from a real-valued function f is via additive noise calibrated to f's sensitivity S_f, such as the Gaussian noise mechanism, that is used in [21]. Given $f : D \to R$, let S_f be the sensitivity of f, which is the maximum absolute distance: $|f(d) - f(d')|$ for all possible pairs of adjacent input datasets d and d', the Gaussian mechanism is defined in (4).

$$\mathcal{M} \triangleq f(d) + \mathcal{N}(0, S_f^2 \cdot \sigma^2) \tag{4}$$

where $\mathcal{N}$ is the Gaussian distribution, of mean 0 and standard deviation $S_f^2 \cdot \sigma^2$. The function f is (ϵ, δ)-differentially private with $\epsilon < 1$ if $\delta \geq \frac{4}{5} exp(\frac{-(\sigma\epsilon)^2}{2})$.

3.3 DP-GAN

A DP-GAN is a generative adversarial network to which a differential privacy guarantee has been added [13]. Furthermore, several changes were applied to such GANs to improve the differential privacy guarantees. First, an intelligent and adaptive pruning technique is implemented. Also, an intelligent noise distribution is applied, i.e., DP-GANs distribute noise according to each group according to its gradient.

4 Methodology

In the current section, we introduce our methodology to evaluate the performance of GANs and DP-GANs in generating synthetic data. Thus, Fig. 2 depicts the evaluation process. First, the dataset counting original trajectories for different individuals is gathered. This dataset should contain an individual identifier, a timestamp, a latitude, and a longitude. Then, the dataset is pre-processed or cleaned by keeping only weekdays and replacing date and time by the hour of the timestamp. Thus, we capture regular movement points during the weekdays. After the pre-processing stage, we rely on GAN and DP-GAN algorithms to sanitize the dataset by building a synthetic version d' of the original dataset d. The former algorithm inputs the optimizer function, batch size, generator, and discriminator architecture. The latter takes the same inputs of the GAN algorithm with a privacy guarantee parameter epsilon ϵ.

Once the dataset is sanitized, an adversary tries to infer the individuals' home and work locations in the dataset d' by applying a simple heuristic. Thus, individuals' home $H_u' = [Lat, Lon]$ and work $W_u' = [Lat, Lon]$ locations are represented by the centroid of the set of points between midnight to 5AM and 8AM to 6PM, respectively.

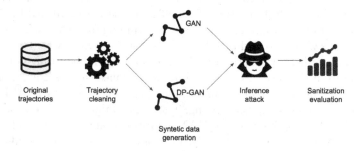

Fig. 2. Sanitization process of geo-referenced data.

Finally, the Information Loss and Disclosure Risk measures were used to evaluate the success of the adversary attack in the synthetized data. Both are described in the following paragraphs.

Information Loss - IL. Inspired by the proposed IL in [18], we defined the information loss as the average distance between the mean of the home H_u and work W_u location inferred from the original dataset and the home H'_u and work W'_u location from the synthetic dataset. Equation 2 formalizes the information loss measure.

$$IL = \frac{1}{|U|} \sum_{u \in U}^{|U|} \frac{dist(H_u, H'_u) + dist(W_u, W'_u)}{2} \qquad (5)$$

where U is the set of users. The information loss expressed in Km allows us to know how much one dataset differs from another. Another essential metric to consider is the disclosure risk.

Disclosure Risk - DR. This metric lets us know the distance between two different models' highest point of interest. According to [11], the DR is defined as the risk that an attacker derives individual information from the original dataset by having access to the synthetic dataset.

$$f(x) = \begin{cases} 1 & \frac{dist(H_u, H'_u) + dist(W_u, W'_u)}{2} < m \\ 0 & \text{otherwise} \end{cases} \qquad (6)$$

where m is a threshold. Accordingly, the DR enables us to quantify the proportion of re-identified home locations within a radius m.

5   Experiment and Results

The present section presents the results obtained from Geolife real data experiments [26]. The experiments were carried out using the methodology previously described. Therefore, the GPS trajectories dataset contains 178 users collected from April 2007 to October 2011. Each GPS trajectory in this dataset is represented by a sequence of points with an identifier, timestamps, latitude, longitude, and altitude. The dataset contains 17 621 trajectories with a total distance of 1 251 654 Km and a total duration of 48 203 h. These were recorded by different GPS devices and phones and have a variety of sampling frequencies. Thus, 91% of the trajectories were recorded in a dense representation, *i.e.*, every 1–5 s or every 5–10 m per record. Importantly, the dataset collected a wide range of outdoor movements from the total users, including life routines such as going home and going to work and some entertainment and sports activities, such as shopping, sightseeing, dining, hiking, and cycling. The original dataset is pre-processed to be the input of the GAN and DP-GAN algorithms, and the result of the processing is a synthetic dataset. Finally, for evaluation, we measure information

Table 1. Parameters of the DP-GAN

Parameter	Value	Parameter	Value
Optimizer	Adam	Generator layers	128, 64,3
	RMSProp		256, 128, 64,3
Batch size	64		512, 256, 128, 64,3
	128		512, 3
	256	Discriminator layers	128, 64, 32, 16, 1
	512		256, 128, 64, 32, 16, 1
ϵ-diff. privacy	1		512, 256, 128, 64, 32, 16, 1
			64, 32, 16, 1

loss and disclosure risk of the home inference in the sanitized dataset using the original dataset as ground truth.

Given the objective of measuring the effectiveness of GAN and DP-GAN against inference attacks, we need to find the most suitable parameters for the generator and discriminator to generate a synthetic dataset. This dataset should be useful while providing enough privacy guarantees. Regarding the optimizer, we consider the *Adam* and *RMSProp* optimization algorithms. Concerning the *batch* size, the considered values ranges from 64 to 512. Concerning generator and discriminator architecture, different configurations were tested as shown in Fig. 1. It is worth noting that the ϵ-differential privacy parameter is constant to find these parameter configurations. Therefore, 128 different configurations were tested.

The two best performances regarding the GAN algorithm are architectures $A17$, $A13$, $R26$, and $R13$. A stands for Adam optimizer, and 17 is the architecture identifier. Regarding the DP-GAN algorithm parametrization, we note that configurations $A17$, $A5$, $R10$, and $R2$ have a less IL value. The comparison of the IL for the different architectures is not shown due to space restrictions.

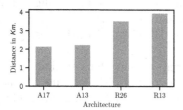

Fig. 3. GAN information loss.

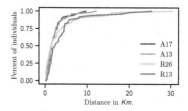

Fig. 4. GAN disclosure risk.

To explore in detail the top 2 best configurations for each optimizer when applying the GAN algorithm, we compare the information loss in Fig. 3 and disclosure risk in Fig. 4. The former shows that the average distance of $A17$ and $A13$ architectures between home and work in the original d and synthetic d' dataset are 2 Km close, while for architectures $R26$ and $R13$, the distances between home and work in the original d and synthetic d' datasets are 3.5 to 3.8 Km away. Consequently, the architecture with less information loss is $A17$. The latter compares the disclosure risk of the different tested architectures. The figure illustrates the error of the adversary's distance in the abscissa axis while inferring the home and work location and the proportion of individuals' home and work the adversary finds with a given error. For instance, the adversary finds 50% of homes successfully when the inference attack threshold is fixed to less than 1.8 Km for $A17$, $A13$, and $R26$. However, for $R13$, the threshold needs to be increased to achieve 50%. Thus, this architecture is more private compared to the other three.

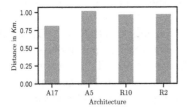

Fig. 5. DP-GAN information loss.

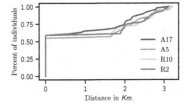

Fig. 6. DP-GAN disclosure risk.

Concerning the DP-GAN algorithm, we compared the best architecture configurations. On the one hand, Fig. 5 portrays that the information loss of the four configurations is less than a kilometer, where $A17$ is the setup with less information loss. On the other hand, Fig. 6 presents the disclosure risk result for the DP-GAN with $\epsilon = 1$. Accordingly, we try to find the architecture configuration that mimics the original dataset's best. Thus, when taking as threshold 1 Km around 60% of the individuals' homes and works are correctly identified.

From previous experiments, we notice that the architecture configuration that best captures human movements in our dataset is $A17$. Hence, we will analyze the impact of the ϵ parameter for the DP-GAN algorithm using the Adam optimizer.

For this experiments, we used different values for epsilon $\epsilon = \{0.001, 0.005, 0.01, 0.1, 1\}$, we report the average for ten different runs for each value of ϵ. Figure 7 evidences the impact of ϵ on the information loss. Thus, the bigger the ϵ value, the less noise in the generator to produce the synthetic dataset, the small information loss. We note that when $\epsilon = 0.001$ (strong privacy) the IL value is more than 15 Km, while when $\epsilon = 1$ the IL decreases to 0.1 Km. Figure 8 illustrates the effect of ϵ over the DR. We remark that when $\epsilon = 1$, the adversary finds the individuals' home and work with less than one Km error. However, when ϵ grows, the privacy guarantee becomes stronger.

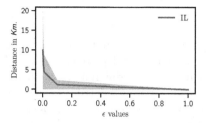

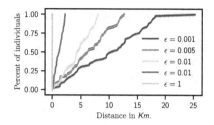

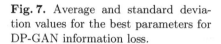

Fig. 7. Average and standard deviation values for the best parameters for DP-GAN information loss.

Fig. 8. Average and standard deviation values for the best parameters for DP-GAN disclosure risk.

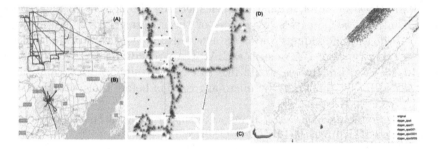

Fig. 9. Synthetic traces through DP-GAN. **(A)** Synthetic traces of a user Bob traveling in a city $\epsilon = 1$. **(B)** Synthetic traces of a user Alice traveling between two a city $\epsilon = 1$. **(C)** Zoom over synthetic traces of a user Charlie original traces and $\epsilon = \{0.1, 1\}$. **(D)** Synthetic traces of a user Charlie for $\epsilon = \{0.001, 0.005, 0.01, 0.1, 1\}$ (Color figure online)

For the sake of comparison, Fig. 9 illustrates the different locations generated for a user using $\epsilon = \{0.001, 0.005, 0.01, 0.1, 1\}$. We note that values close to 1 mimic the original dataset in a more realistic way. On the contrary ϵ small values enhance more individual privacy. We observe that the generation of the geolocated traces is plausible. Figure 9C shows the original points as triangles, and green points are the generated traces with $\epsilon = 1$, while orange points are generated with $\epsilon = 0.1$. Please note that some generated traces could be banded when users travel between cities, as illustrated in Fig. 9D. Besides, the generated geolocated points respect some statistical properties in space and time. For instance, the average distance between generated points is seven meters with $\epsilon = 0.1$ and increases to 22 Km with high epsilon values. Regarding the time dimension in all the synthetic generated data time interval between points every five seconds on average as the original dataset. Nonetheless, if the application using the generated points needs to work with trajectories, the generation should consider only trajectories and not all points in the dataset, as commented in [16].

6   Conclusions and Future Works

We studied the feasibility of generating synthetic geo-located datasets using GANs. This task is far from trivial since human mobility depicts complex and regular mobility patterns, which are helpful in studying different phenomena. However, even for synthetic data, there is a certain risk of inferring knowledge beyond its scope, threatening individuals' privacy. Our experiments demonstrate that we can train deep neural networks to generate synthetic data that maintains individuals' privacy and data quality depending on privacy parameters. Accordingly, based on the privacy settings, we generated data differing a few meters and a few kilometers from the original trajectories. When applying differential privacy, the best parameter for a good privacy/utility trade-off is when $\epsilon = 0.01$. However, after evaluating such methods through the perspective of record linkage, we note that regardless of the ϵ parameter, it is still possible to re-identify individuals' data. As new research avenues, we would like to explore other types of GANs such as LAP-GAN, conditional GAN, InfoGAN, or ALI/BIGAN. Finally, we would like to explore coupling other sanitization methods such as k-anonymity by micro-aggregation before the synthetization.

Acknowledgements. This research was partly supported by the Spanish Government under project RTI2018-095094-B-C22 "CONSENT".

References

1. Arjovsky, M., Chintala, S., Bottou, L.: Wasserstein generative adversarial networks. In: Proceedings of the 34th International Conference on Machine Learning, vol. 70, pp. 214–223, 06–11 August 2017
2. Domingo-Ferrer, J., Sánchez, D., Blanco-Justicia, A.: The limits of differential privacy (and its misuse in data release and machine learning). Commun. ACM **64**(7), 33–35 (2021). https://doi.org/10.1145/3433638
3. Dwork, C., Kenthapadi, K., McSherry, F., Mironov, I., Naor, M.: Our data, ourselves: privacy via distributed noise generation. In: Vaudenay, S. (ed.) EUROCRYPT 2006. LNCS, vol. 4004, pp. 486–503. Springer, Heidelberg (2006). https://doi.org/10.1007/11761679_29
4. Eigenschink, P., Vamosi, S., Vamosi, R., Sun, C., Reutterer, T., Kalcher, K.: Deep generative models for synthetic data. ACM Comput. Surv. (2021)
5. Fan, L.: A survey of differentially private generative adversarial networks. In: The AAAI Workshop on Privacy-Preserving Artificial Intelligence, p. 8 (2020)
6. Gambs, S., Killijian, M.O., Moise, I., del Prado Cortez, M.N.: MapReducing GEPETO or towards conducting a privacy analysis on millions of mobility traces. In: 2013 IEEE International Symposium on Parallel & Distributed Processing, Workshops and Phd Forum, pp. 1937–1946. IEEE (2013)
7. Gambs, S., Killijian, M.O., del Prado Cortez, M.N.: Show me how you move and i will tell you who you are. In: Proceedings of the 3rd ACM SIGSPATIAL International Workshop on Security and Privacy in GIS and LBS, pp. 34–41 (2010)
8. Gambs, S., Killijian, M.O., del Prado Cortez, M.N.: Towards temporal mobility Markov chains. In: 1st International Workshop on Dynamicity Collocated with OPODIS 2011, Toulouse, France, pp. 2-pages (2011)

9. Gambs, S., Killijian, M.O., del Prado Cortez, M.N.: De-anonymization attack on geolocated data. J. Comput. Syst. Sci. **80**(8), 1597–1614 (2014)

10. Golle, P., Partridge, K.: On the anonymity of home/work location pairs. In: Tokuda, H., Beigl, M., Friday, A., Brush, A.J.B., Tobe, Y. (eds.) Pervasive 2009. LNCS, vol. 5538, pp. 390–397. Springer, Heidelberg (2009). https://doi.org/10.1007/978-3-642-01516-8_26

11. Heinle, M.S., Smith, K.C.: A theory of risk disclosure. Rev. Acc. Stud. **22**(4), 1459–1491 (2017). https://doi.org/10.1007/s11142-017-9414-2

12. Heredia-Ductram, D., Nunez-del Prado, M., Alatrista-Salas, H.: Toward a comparison of classical and new privacy mechanism. Entropy **23**(4), 467 (2021)

13. Ho, S., Qu, Y., Gu, B., Gao, L., Li, J., Xiang, Y.: DP-GAN: differentially private consecutive data publishing using generative adversarial nets. J. Netw. Comput. Appl. **185**, 103066 (2021)

14. Imtiaz, S., Arsalan, M., Vlassov, V., Sadre, R.: Synthetic and private smart health care data generation using GANs. In: 2021 International Conference on Computer Communications and Networks (ICCCN), pp. 1–7. IEEE (2021)

15. Kaiser, J., Bavendiek, K., Schupp, S.: Do we need real data? -Testing and training algorithms with artificial geolocation data. In: 50 Jahre Gesellschaft für Informatik, p. 205 (2019)

16. Liu, X., Chen, H., Andris, C.: trajGANs: using generative adversarial networks for geo-privacy protection of trajectory data (vision paper). In: Location Privacy and Security Workshop, pp. 1–7 (2018)

17. Ma, B., Yang, B., Zhang, Z., Zhang, J.: Modelling mobile traffic patterns using a generative adversarial neural networks. In: NOMS 2020–2020 IEEE/IFIP Network Operations and Management Symposium, pp. 1–7. IEEE (2020)

18. Nunez-del Prado, M., Nin, J.: Revisiting online anonymization algorithms to ensure location privacy. J. Ambient Intell. Human. Comput. 1–12 (2019). https://doi.org/10.1007/s12652-019-01371-6

19. Salas, J., Megías, D., Torra, V.: SwapMob: swapping trajectories for mobility anonymization. In: Domingo-Ferrer, J., Montes, F. (eds.) PSD 2018. LNCS, vol. 11126, pp. 331–346. Springer, Cham (2018). https://doi.org/10.1007/978-3-319-99771-1_22

20. Song, H.Y., Baek, M.S., Sung, M.: Generating human mobility route based on generative adversarial network. In: 2019 Federated Conference on Computer Science and Information Systems (FedCSIS), pp. 91–99. IEEE (2019)

21. Xu, C., Ren, J., Zhang, D., Zhang, Y., Qin, Z., Ren, K.: GANobfuscator: mitigating information leakage under GAN via differential privacy. IEEE Trans. Inf. Forensics Secur. **14**(9), 2358–2371 (2019)

22. Yin, D., Yang, Q.: GANs based density distribution privacy-preservation on mobility data. Secur. Commun. Netw. **2018** (2018)

23. Zang, H., Bolot, J.: Anonymization of location data does not work: a large-scale measurement study. In: Proceedings of the 17th Annual International Conference on Mobile Computing and Networking, pp. 145–156 (2011)

24. Zhan, Y., Kyllo, A., Mashhadi, A., Haddadi, H.: Privacy-aware human mobility prediction via adversarial networks. arXiv preprint arXiv:2201.07519 (2022)

25. Zhang, X., Ji, S., Wang, T.: Differentially private releasing via deep generative model (technical report). arXiv preprint arXiv:1801.01594 (2018)

26. Zheng, Y., Fu, H., Xie, X., Ma, W.Y., Li, Q.: Geolife GPS trajectory dataset-user guide. Geolife GPS trajectories **1**, 2011 (2011)

Machine Learning and Data Science

A Strategic Approach Based on AND-OR Recommendation Trees for Updating Obsolete Information

Salma Chaieb[1,4]([✉]) [iD], Ali Ben Mrad[2,4], and Brahim Hnich[3,4]

[1] ISITCom, University of Sousse, 4011 Sousse, Tunisia
salma.chaieb2@yahoo.com
[2] ISAAS, University of Sfax, 1013 Sfax, Tunisia
benmradali2@gmail.com
[3] FSM, University of Monastir, 5000 Monastir, Tunisia
brahim.hnich@fsm.rnu.tn
[4] CES Lab, ENIS, University of Sfax, 3038 Sfax, Tunisia

Abstract. Older adults usually require careful monitoring to detect healthcare problems at an early stage when the problems can be easily treated. Unfortunately, many members of this population are unable or unwilling to detect the existence of critical changes in their own health. One solution for caregivers is to start monitoring elderly patients, directly or via some data collection devices. Information describing a person's health status is constantly evolving and may become obsolete and contradict other acquired information about the same person. So, it is of the utmost importance to monitor and update medical information scattered across healthcare institutions to support in-depth data analysis and achieve personalized healthcare. This study focuses on proposing a decision support system that gives recommendations on how to deal with obsolete personal information. The main objective of our system is to maintain up-to-date and consistent information about elderly patient in order to provide on-demand reliable information regarding the person's current state. The approach outlined for this purpose is based on a polynomial-time algorithm build on top of a causal Bayesian network representing the elderly data. The result is given as a recommendation AND-OR tree with some accuracy level.

Keywords: Causal Bayesian network · Obsolete information · Recommendation tree · Elderly-fall prevention · Real medical study

1 Introduction

The development and implementation of new e-health systems require an immense amount of personal health information that is consistent and up-to-date. Recently, the implementation of tele-medicine solutions has become of great potential among various research communities globally [6,11]. However, with the variety and the unreliability of information acquisition sources, personal information is

© The Author(s), under exclusive license to Springer Nature Switzerland AG 2022
V. Torra and Y. Narukawa (Eds.): MDAI 2022, LNAI 13408, pp. 95–107, 2022.
https://doi.org/10.1007/978-3-031-13448-7_8

often uncertain and incomplete. Furthermore, information describing a person's health status is constantly evolving and may become obsolete and contradict other acquired information about the same person. In the digital healthcare, it is of the utmost importance to monitor medical information scattered across healthcare institutions to support in-depth data analysis and achieve personalized healthcare. The permanent collection of personal information and the constant monitoring of the quality of the information held is a costly and time-consuming process. In addition, not every person can frequently benefit from a full consultation since it requires a lot of time, the presence of specialists, and specific equipment to carry out the examination. A medical information management system for physicians can really help improve this educational work. To be relevant, such a system should require very little time from the physician during a consultation. This article focuses on how to deal with obsolete information in order to always have the right information in real time, in the right form, and of sufficient completeness and quality to meet the current needs.

An Obsolete Information Detection System (OIDS) has been proposed in [1,2] to maintain the consistency of a personal database by detecting obsolete information about an older adult that contradict a newly acquired event on the same person while keeping the latter supposed to be certain in the database. As shown in Fig. 1, the OIDS in [2] is based on the assumption of the existence of a causal Bayesian network (CBN) that encodes the relationships among the features in the database. Obsolete information that contradicts a newly acquired certain event is then detected, in [2], using a polynomial-time algorithm exploiting the CBN. Such obsolete information is then presented, with a certain confidence, in the form of the so-called AND-OR Explanation Tree to describe the possible logical ways the existing information can be in contradiction with the new event.

In this paper, building on the work in [2], we propose an intelligent and autonomous decision support system, Obsolete Information Update System (OIUS), to manage personal information gathered during the patient appointments with their attending physician. The general context of our work is the Elderly-Fall Prevention project, which is part of the ELSAT2020[1] project.

As shown in Fig. 1, our OIUS is composed of two parts, the OIDS defined by [2] and a Recommender System (RS), which is the subject of this paper. Our RS will help practitioners by providing two types of recommendations: (1) recommendations on how to update obsolete information based on the AND-OR Explanation Tree defined by [2] and by answering the following questions: why do we have a contradiction between some information relating to an older adult? What are the possible observations responsible for contradiction? What if we update the values of such observations? and (2) providing in real-time the caregivers with reliable information regarding the person's state with a confidence degree even when some information is missing from the database.

The rest of the paper is structured as follows: In Sect. 2, we describe formal background and notation. In Sect. 3, we give the basics of our recommendation process. In Sect. 4, we present our empirical results. Finally, in Sect. 5, we draw some final conclusions and point out directions for future work.

---

[1] http://www.elsat2020.org/en.

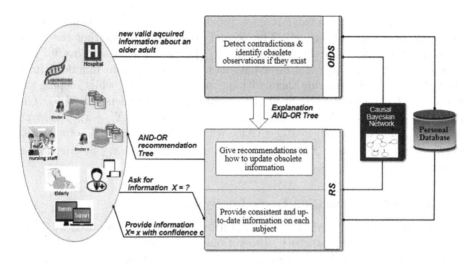

Fig. 1. Obsolete information update system.

2   Formal Background

2.1   Notation

Throughout this paper, the database attributes, i.e. the elderly features, are denoted with uppercase letters such as X_1, X_2, X_3. The domain of an attribute X_i is denoted with $\mathcal{D}(X_i)$. Specific values, also called observations, taken by those attributes are denoted with lowercase letters $x_{1,1}$, $x_{2,1}$, $x_{3,2}$ with $x_{i,j} \in \mathcal{D}(X_i)$, $j \in \{1, ..., |\mathcal{D}(X_i)|\}$. In this paper, we are only concerned with finite domains. At any time, each attribute may be observed or not. New reliable and consistent observations about each elderly are continuously recorded and arriving. We denote by **OBS** the set of pairs representing a variable and its observed value, relating to a single individual of the database $\mathcal{S}$. Let o_{new} denote the newly observed value of a variable O_{new} that is supposed to be certain such that (O_{new}, o_{new}) was not in **OBS** at the previous iteration. Let **OBS'** = **OBS**$\backslash(O_{new}, o_{new})$. We suppose that **OBS'** is consistent before acquiring o_{new}. In this work, we choose to use a CBN [5,7,10] to represent our knowledge.

A CBN is a couple (G, Θ) that consists of a qualitative part, encoding causal relationships among a domain's variables $\mathbf{X} = \{X_1, ..., X_N\}$ in a directed graph G, and a quantitative part, encoding the joint probability distribution Θ, given by the chain rule: $P(\mathbf{X}) = \prod_{i=1}^{n} P(X_i \mid Pa(X_i))$, over these variables, where $Pa(X_i)$ denotes the set of the parents of the node X_i in G.

Each node X_i of the graph represents a random variable and each arc denotes direct *causal influence* between two variables. The most important reasoning in CBNs is to calculate both conditional probabilities and post-interventional probabilities. The first consists in calculating the probability distribution, $P(X_k | X_i = x_{i,j})$, over variables of interest given other observed variables. Efficient statistical inference procedures exist for performing computations over the network [4]. The second consists in calculating the post-interventional probability, $P_M(X_k|do(X_i = x_{i,j}))$, using the *do-calculus* [9]. The *do-calculus* simulates physical interventions by deleting certain functions from the CBN model M, replacing them with a constant $X_i = x_{i,j}$, while keeping the rest of the CBN model unchanged. The resulting model is denoted $M_{x_{i,j}}$. The post-intervention distribution resulting from the action $do(X_i = x_{i,j})$ is given by: $P_M(X_k|do(X_i = x_{i,j})) = P_{M_{x_{i,j}}}(X_k)$, where, following Pearl's notation [8], $do(X_i = x_{i,j})$ means that X_i has been forced to take the value $x_{i,j}$ by an external action.

2.2   Obsolete Information Detection System

An Obsolete Information Detection Algorithm (OIDA) was proposed by [2] to detect all possible contradictory observations, whenever new observations are acquired. As shown in Fig. 1, the input to the method proposed by [2] is a new observation $O_{new} = o_{new}$ about an older adult and the set **OBS'** of previously acquired observations about the same person. The objective is to check if o_{new} is contradictory with **OBS'**, given the representation causal model. In [2], a contradiction between observations occurs when the conditional probability of the new observation given other observations is very close to 0, i.e., **OBS'** is ϵ-Contradictory to o_{new} when $P(O_{new} = o_{new}|\textbf{OBS'}) \leq \epsilon, 0 \leq \epsilon \leq 1$. Indeed, an ϵ-Contradiction occurs when there is a subset $\textbf{S}_{o_{new}}$ of **OBS'** of observations that have become obsolete and contradict o_{new}. In the case where o_{new} contradicts **OBS'**, authors in [2] try to identify among the observations contained in **OBS'** those that have become obsolete because of the arrival of o_{new}. An example of a contradictory scenario is as follows: **OBS** = {(*heartDisease, no*), (*drugsNumber, 0*), (*cardiovascularDrugs, no*)}, the new observation is (*cardiovascularDrugs, yes*). The scenario $\textbf{S}_c$ = {(*cardiovascularDrugs, yes*), (*heartDisease, no*), (*drugs Number, 0*)} is declared ϵ-Contradictory by the definition proposed by [2] since $P(\text{cardiovascularDrugs} = \text{yes} \mid \textbf{OBS'}) \leq \epsilon$. The process of identifying the set of obsolete observations $\textbf{S}_{o_{new}}$ takes place in 3 steps: (1) restrict the ϵ-Contradictory set **OBS'** into $\textbf{S}_{o_{new}}$; (2) decompose the ϵ-Contradictory set to have $\textbf{S}_{o_{new}}$ looking for obsolete observations; and (3) compose the AND-OR Explanation Tree from the set $\textbf{S}_{o_{new}}$. The result from step 1 is the set $\textbf{S}_{o_{new}}$ containing all the observations on the variables of **OBS'** that depend on O_{new} (level 4 of the tree shown in Fig. 2). The result from step 2 is the set $\textbf{S}_{o_{new}}$ subdivided into subsets $\textbf{S}_i$ such that each $\textbf{S}_i$ contains observations on dependent variables and each $\textbf{S}_i$ is ϵ-Contradictory to o_{new}, given the CBN (level 2 of the tree shown in Fig. 2). The restriction and the decomposition phases are based on the concept of *d-separation* [3] in CBNs. Then each set $\textbf{S}_i$ is further divided into two disjoint ϵ-Contradictory subsets $\textbf{S}_i^{AND}$ and $\textbf{S}_i^{OR}$ (level 3 of the tree shown in Fig. 2) such that: $\textbf{S}_i^{AND}$, contains each observation x in $\textbf{S}_i$ that is individually ϵ-Contradictory to o_{new}, given the CBN, i.e., $P(O_{new} = o_{new}|x) \leq \epsilon$; $\textbf{S}_i^{OR}$, contains each observation that is not individually ϵ-Contradictory to o_{new}, given the CBN, and which is likely to be involved in the contradiction. The result from step 3 is an AND-OR Explanation Tree as shown in Fig. 2 constructed as follows: the root node is labeled *AND*. Then, for each subset $\mathbf{S}_i$, an *AND* node whose parent is the root node is created. Next, for each *AND-Set* (resp. *OR-Set*) of $\mathbf{S}_i$, an *AND* (resp. *OR*) node whose parent is the corresponding node of $\mathbf{S}_i$, is added. Finally, a child leaf node for each observation in $\mathbf{S}_i^{AND}$ (resp. $\mathbf{S}_i^{OR}$) is created. Each leaf node is labeled with the obsolete observation. The AND-OR tree represents precisely the set of obsolete observations $\mathbf{S}_{o_{new}}$ and describes the logical relationships among its *AND-Sets* and *OR-Sets* such that all observations of each $\mathbf{S}_i^{AND}$ are obsolete and must all be updated, and at least one observation of each $\mathbf{S}_i^{OR}$ is obsolete. For the observations in $\mathbf{S}_i^{OR}$, authors in [2] state that with the available knowledge at their disposal, they are not able to accurately infer which one(s) should be updated. But they claim that each of these observations may be obsolete. To better understand the full details of the obsolete information detection process, we refer the author to [1,2].

3   Recommender System

The main purpose of our RS is to monitor and assess the risk of falls in older people and subsequently recommend personalized interventions to their caregivers. The RS system offers two main services. One is when there are contradictions and is to recommend which observations should be removed as well as the possible values that can replace them, while the other is to provide the caregivers with information on the current state of their elderly patients even in cases where this information is not available in the database.

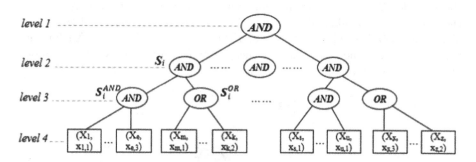

Fig. 2. Hierarchical structure of the AND-OR Explanation Tree.

3.1   Recommendations on How to Update Obsolete Information

In case of a contradiction, and based on the AND-OR Explanation Tree provided by the OIDS, we propose an intervention-based strategy that recommends the possible interventions on how to substitute the obsolete observations using the *do-calculus*. The reason is a very accurate prediction model on its own is not able to guide reasoning about what might happen if we take action, i.e., intervene by changing the values of some variables supposed to be obsolete. In this way, our RS helps us to answer these fundamental questions: which interventions on which variables are the most effective to remove contradiction between observations? What is the effect of each intervention modifying the value of a variable $\in \mathbf{S}_i$ on the probability of having o_{new}, given the other observations? And what would be the likelihood of having such a combination of observations if we had intervened differently? Based on the CBN structure, the *do-calculus* is applied under some constraints. Indeed, operationally, intervening on a variable X_i of the CBN model M leads to wipe out all edges into X_i, i.e., the intervention essentially separates X_i from its direct causes and X_i becomes a root node, all other things remain equal. The resulting model is denoted M_{X_i}. Here two cases arise:

Case 1: if the intervention variable X_i reaches the evidence variables O_{new} in the resulting model M_{X_i}, i.e., X_i still remains dependent of O_{new} in M_{X_i} (case of the variables X_1, X_8, X_2 if X_3 is instantiated, X_4 if X_5 is not instantiated, X_6 if X_7 is instantiated and X_8 is not, in Fig. 3). In this respect, our method is based on studying the *posterior* intervention distributions of (O_{new}, o_{new}) while intervene on a variable $(X_i, x_{i,j})$ of the $\mathbf{S}_i$ by changing its value, given the rest of observation $\mathbf{X} = \mathbf{S}_i \backslash \{(X_i, x_{i,j})\}$, i.e. $P(O_{new} = o_{new} | \mathbf{do}(X_i = x_{i,k}), \mathbf{X})$.

Case 2: if the intervention variable X_i cannot reach the evidence variables O_{new}, i.e. becomes independent of O_{new} in the resulting model M_{X_i} (case of the variables X_3, X_5, X_4 if X_5 is not instantiated, X_6 if X_7 is not instantiated, and X_7 in Fig. 3). Then, intervening on X_i becomes useless and has no contribution to the marginal probability of O_{new}, since $P(O_{new} | \mathbf{do}(X_i = x_{i,k}), \mathbf{X}) = P(O_{new} | \mathbf{X})$. In this case, the *causal inference* does not suit the type of structure that connects the variables X_i to O_{new}. We therefore resort to *statistical inference* by studying the *posterior* probability distribution of O_{new}, given $X_i = x_{i,k}$ and the rest of observations $OR\text{-}Set \backslash \{(X_i, x_{i,j})\}$, i.e. $P(O_{new} = o_{new} | X_i = x_{i,k}, \mathbf{X})$ for each value $x_{i,k}$ of X_i. The reason is that such a prediction may provide information about what we would expect as a logical consequence of the O_{new} cause.

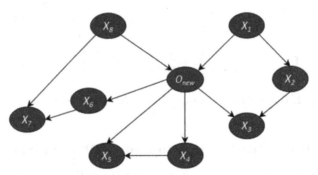

Fig. 3. A part of CBN showing the different intervention cases

As explained in Sect. 2, each set $\mathbf{S}_i$, is composed of two subsets $\mathbf{S}_i^{AND}$ and $\mathbf{S}_i^{OR}$. All the observations contained in $\mathbf{S}_i^{AND}$ must be updated, since they have certainly become obsolete. So for each variable $X_i \in \mathbf{S}_i^{AND}$ our RS recommends all the possible value amongst its modalities that could replace the obsolete one using one of the methods suggested above, as appropriate. We would like to make two remarks here. The first is that when X_i is a binary variable, we recommend directly the complementary observation to replace the obsolete one. The second remark is that when managing observations of the *AND-Sets*, instead of calculating $P(O_{new} = o_{new} | X_i = x_{i,k}, \mathbf{X})$ (resp. $P(O_{new} = o_{new} | \mathbf{do}(X_i = x_{i,k}), \mathbf{X}))$ by varying $x_{i,k}$, we calculate $P(O_{new} = o_{new} | X_i = x_{i,k})$ (resp. $P(O_{new} = o_{new} | \mathbf{do}(X_i = x_{i,k}))$. The reason is that the first probability always remains equal to 0 whatever the value taken by X_i, as long as the other variables of the *AND-Set* $\mathbf{X}$ are not yet updated.

As stated by [2], any observation $X_i = x_{i,j}$ in the *OR-Set* may be obsolete and updating at least one observation of $\mathbf{S}_i^{OR}$ remove contradiction, but we are not able to exactly infer which one(s) should be updated. So in this case and for each variable X_i, we recommend all the possible values that do not contradict O_{new} sorted in descending order of the calculated posterior probability p_x, given the rest of observations. We also order the *OR-Set* such that the nodes with the highest probability are packed from left to right. Then we let the user (i.e. physician) choose which of the variables in the given $\mathbf{S}_i^{OR}$ is most likely to be updated, and which of its recommended values is the most appropriate.

Algorithm 1 shows the main steps of the proposed method. The inputs to our Obsolete Observations Recommendation Algorithm (OORA) are the AND-OR Explanation Tree $\mathcal{T}$ given by the OIDS, the CBN $\mathcal{B}$, and (O_{new}, o_{new}).

As a first step, for each $\mathbf{S}_i \in \mathbf{S}_{o_{new}}$, we inspect its two subsets $\mathbf{S}_i^{OR}$ and $\mathbf{S}_i^{AND}$. For each variable X in the set $\mathbf{S}_i^{OR}$, we extract the mutilated graph $\mathcal{B}_X$ from the CBN $\mathcal{B}$ by calling the function *Mutilation*. This function takes as input the causal graph $\mathcal{B}$ and the variable X, wipes out from $\mathcal{B}$ all edges into X while keeping the rest of $\mathcal{B}$ unchanged, and returns the resulting mutilated graph $\mathcal{B}_X$. Next, we check if the variable X is still reachable from O_{new} in the mutilated graph $\mathcal{B}_X$, given the set **OBS'** of all observed variables by calling the function *d-separated*. In the case where X and O_{new} are independent (resp. independent) given **OBS'** (line 10 (resp. 17)), we try to find out all the values x' of X that can substitute the obsolete one, i.e. whose probability of occurrence with o_{new} and the rest of the observations is beyond the given threshold ϵ. To ensure this we calculate the posterior probability of o_{new} given the new value x' of X and the rest of observations using the initial (resp. mutilated) graph $\mathcal{B}$ (resp. $\mathcal{B}_X$).

Let $\mathbf{S}_i^{OR'} = \{\mathbf{S}_{X_l}, ..., \mathbf{S}_{X_p}\}$, $1 \le l \le N, 1 \le p \le N$. Each subset $\mathbf{S}_X$ of $\mathbf{S}_i^{OR'}$ contains the pair (X, x) representing the obsolete observation followed by $1 \le m \le |D(X) - 1|$ tuples in the form of $(X, x', p_{x'})$ which represent all the possible values x' that can replace x, each is given with the likelihood of its occurrence with the rest of observations. All variables in $\mathbf{S}_i^{OR'}$ are then sorted in descending order of their probabilities. Line 28 traverses all the pairs (X, x) in the subset $\mathbf{S}_i^{AND} \in \mathbf{S}_i$, and for each one, we apply the same treatment used to manage the *OR-Sets*. The result from line 50 of our OORA is the set $\mathbf{S}_{o_{new}} = \{\mathbf{S}_1, ..., \mathbf{S}_k\}$ such that: each $\mathbf{S}_i$ is divided into $\mathbf{S}_i^{AND'}$ and $\mathbf{S}_i^{OR'}$, each part of $\mathbf{S}_i$

Algorithm 1. Obsolete Observations Recommendation Algorithm (OORA)

Input: $\mathcal{T}$, $\mathcal{B}$, (O_{new}, o_{new}), **OBS'**, ϵ: a real number, $0 \leq \epsilon \leq 1$

Output: AND-OR Recommendation Tree

1: let $\mathbf{S}_{o_{new}} = \{\mathbf{S}_1, ..., \mathbf{S}_i, ..., \mathbf{S}_k\}$ the set regrouping all the subsets $\mathbf{S}_i$ of the tree $\mathcal{T}$, such that $\mathbf{S}_i = \{\mathbf{S}_i^{AND}, \mathbf{S}_i^{OR}\}$, $1 \leq k \leq N$

2: **for each** $\mathbf{S}_i \in \mathbf{S}_{o_{new}}$ **do**

3:     $\mathbf{S}_i^{OR'} = \emptyset$

4:     $\mathbf{S}_i^{AND'} = \emptyset$

5:     **for each** $(X, x) \in \mathbf{S}_i^{OR}$ **do**

6:         $\mathbf{S}_X = \emptyset$

7:         let $\mathbf{x}$ the set of all observations $\in \mathbf{S}_i^{OR} \setminus x$

8:         $\mathbf{S}_X = \{(X, x)\}$

9:         $\mathcal{B}_X = Mutilation(\mathcal{B}, X)$

10:        **if** $d\text{-}separated(X, O_{new}, \mathbf{OBS'}, \mathcal{B}_X)$ **then**

11:            **for each** $x' \in D(X) \setminus \{x\}$ **do**

12:                $p_{x'} = P(O_{new} = o_{new} | X = x', \mathbf{x})$

13:                **if** $p_{x'} > \epsilon$ **then**

14:                    $\mathbf{S}_X = \mathbf{S}_X \cup \{(x', p_{x'})\}$

15:                **end if**

16:            **end for**

17:        **else**

18:            **for each** $x' \in D(X) \setminus \{x\}$ **do**

19:                $p_{x'} = P(O_{new} = o_{new} | do(X = x'), \mathbf{x})$

20:                **if** $p_{x'} > \epsilon$ **then**

21:                    $\mathbf{S}_X = \mathbf{S}_X \cup \{(x', p_{x'})\}$

22:                **end if**

23:            **end for**

24:        **end if**

25:        $\mathbf{S}_i^{OR'} = \mathbf{S}_i^{OR'} \cup \mathbf{S}_X$

26:    **end for**

27:    $\mathbf{S}_i^{OR'} = Sort_{p_x}(\mathbf{S}_i^{OR'})$

---

contains elements in the form of $\{\mathbf{S}_{X_l}, ..., \mathbf{S}_{X_p}\}$, $1 \leq l \leq N, 1 \leq p \leq N$, and each $\mathbf{S}_{X_i}$ contains elements in the form of $\{(X_i, x_{i,a}), (x_{i,b}, p_{x_{i,b}}), ..., (x_{i,l}, p_{x_{i,l}})\}$, such that $x_{i,a} \in D(X_i), x_{i,b} \in D(X_i), x_{i,l} \in D(X_i)$. Once we have the new updated set $\mathbf{S}_{o_{new}}$, our OORA update the AND-OR tree $\mathcal{T}$ based on $\mathbf{S}_{o_{new}}$, and returns the AND-OR Recommendation Tree such that for each *OR-Set*, the nodes with the highest probability are packed from left to right, and for each node, the substitute values are sorted in descending order of the calculated posterior probability.

Our OORA runs in $O(N_d \times N_x \times (N_p + N_s))$, where N_d is the size of the set $\mathbf{S}_{o_{new}}$, N_x is the number of pairs (X, x) in $\mathbf{S}_i$, N_p is the number of parents of the variable X, and N_s is the number of states of X.

3.2 Predictions

Now if we don't consider the contradictions, our RS aims to provide the care-givers with reliable information about their elderly patients in real-time even when some information is missing and based on what it already knows about that older adult, denoted by **OBS**. Let (X, x) denotes the requested information x on the variable X that carries the requested information. It consists in inferring the CBN by observing **OBS** and fixing the target variable to X, then returns the predicted information in the form of (X, x, p_x) such that $p_x = P(X = x | \mathbf{OBS})$ represents our belief about $X = x$ taking the observed data into account.

28:    **for** each $(X, x) \in \mathbf{S}_i^{AND}$ **do**
29:      $\mathbf{S}_X = \emptyset$
30:      $\mathbf{S}_X = \{(X, x)\}$
31:      $\mathcal{B}_X = Mutilation(\mathcal{B}, X)$
32:      **if** $d\text{-}separated(X, O_{new}, \mathbf{OBS'}, \mathcal{B}_X)$ **then**
33:        **for** each $x' \in D(X)$ **do**
34:          $p_{x'} = P(o_{new} | X = x')$
35:          **if** $p_{x'} > \epsilon$ **then**
36:            $\mathbf{S}_X = \mathbf{S}_X \cup (x', p_{x'})$
37:          **end if**
38:        **end for**
39:      **else**
40:        **for** each $x' \in D(X)$ **do**
41:          $p_{x'} = PosteriorProba(o_{new} | \mathbf{do}(X = x'))$
42:          **if** $p_{x'} > \epsilon$ **then**
43:            $\mathbf{S}_X = \mathbf{S}_X \cup \{(x', p_{x'})\}$
44:          **end if**
45:        **end for**
46:      **end if**
47:      $\mathbf{S}_i^{AND'} = \mathbf{S}_i^{AND'} \cup \mathbf{S}_X$
48:    **end for**
49:    $\mathbf{S}_i = \{\mathbf{S}_i^{AND'}, \mathbf{S}_i^{OR'}\}$
50:    $Update(\mathbf{S}_{o_{new}}, \mathbf{S}_i)$
51: **end for**
52: $UpdateTree(\mathbf{S}_{o_{new}}, \mathcal{T})$
53: **return** $\mathcal{T}$

---

4   Empirical Results

4.1   Experimental Data

The database *Elderly-Data* available for us includes 1174 patient records, each of which was described by 435 patient-history features gathered in the University Hospital Center of Lille over a 9-year period (2005–2014). We conducted a study of these data in collaboration with hospital experts on fall prevention, which ends by the selection of 41 relevant attributes associated with the elderly features, the main risk factors for fall, and the possible consequences of fall. From this result, in addition to bibliographic research, and the solicitation of domain experts, we built and evaluated a model of the generic knowledge, embedded in a CBN. Once the causal model is validated, we automatically generate a total of 720 scenarios among which 580 are chosen and validated by five experts, three orthopedists, a neurologist, and a general practitioner who did not participate in the construction and CBN validation. It consists of randomly selecting variables from the given CBN, assigning random observations to the selected variables, and arbitrarily choosing a pair (variable, observation) that represents the newly acquired information. Then, for each scenario $\mathbf{S}_i$ a label c_i given by the experts is associated such as: $c_i = 1$ if $\mathbf{S}_i$ is declared contradictory by the experts, $c_i = 0$ otherwise. As a result, we tried to obtain a balanced database $\mathcal{S} = \{(\mathbf{S}_i, c_i)\}$ of 580 scenarios labeled by experts with 290 contradictory scenarios and 290 non-contradictory scenarios. Then, for each of the 290 contradictory scenarios, the experts provided a list of subsets of all possible obsolete observations. The resulting subsets will be compared with the result provided by the OIDS. Furthermore, for each subset of observations, the experts prioritize the obsolete observations and give us the most likely to be updated. These observations will be compared later with those provided by our RS.

The detection of contradictory scenarios is conditioned by a threshold ϵ. In most approximation-based works, the threshold is often hard to set. In this work, we have applied the algorithm proposed by [2], which is based on the receiver operating characteristic curve, on a part of the database $\mathcal{S}$ ($\approx 35\%$ of $\mathcal{S}$) to calculate the ϵ value. The threshold associated with our CBN is set to 10^{-2}.

4.2   Results and Discussion

The validation of our OORA consists of two parts: assess the quality of the AND-OR trees resulting from our OIDS and evaluate the quality of the recommendations provided by our RS.

Step 1 AND-OR Explanation Trees evaluation: we start by applying the OIDS on the rest of the database $\mathcal{S}$ ($\approx 65\%$ of the database) with 380 scenarios divided into 190 contradictory scenarios and 190 non-contradictory scenarios labeled by experts. For each scenario, our OIDS estimates whether it is contradictory or not. For each scenario classified as ϵ-Contradictory, the OIDS generates the associated AND-OR Explanation Tree, which encodes all possible obsolete observations responsible for the contradiction. To facilitate the assessment of the resulted AND-OR trees, we translate them, as well as the results provided by experts, into propositional formulas. Recall that the result of the OIDS is the set $\mathbf{S}_{O_{new}} = \{\mathbf{S}_1, \mathbf{S}_2, ..., \mathbf{S}_k\}$. As explained in Sect. 2, when building the AND-OR tree, we group all the subsets $\mathbf{S}_i$ under a root node labeled AND. This can be presented in the form of: $\mathbf{S}_1 \wedge \mathbf{S}_2 \wedge ... \wedge \mathbf{S}_k$. Then, each subset $\mathbf{S}_i$ is divided in two subsets $\mathbf{S}_i^{AND}$ and $\mathbf{S}_i^{OR}$, such that all observations of the set $\mathbf{S}_i^{AND}$ (resp. $\mathbf{S}_i^{OR}$) are linked with an *AND* (resp. *OR*). The formulas to be compared can therefore take the following form:

$$\underbrace{\underbrace{(a_1 \wedge ... \wedge a_i)}_{\mathbf{s}_1^{AND}} \wedge \underbrace{(b_1 \vee ... \vee b_j))}_{\mathbf{s}_1^{OR}}}_{\mathbf{s}_1} \wedge ... \wedge \underbrace{(\underbrace{(x_1 \wedge ... \wedge x_k)}_{\mathbf{s}_p^{AND}} \wedge \underbrace{(y_1 \vee ... \vee y_l))}_{\mathbf{s}_p^{OR}}}_{\mathbf{s}_p}$$

such that letters correspond to the possible obsolete observations and i, j, k, l, $p \in \{1, ..., N\}$. Subsequently, we compare each formula resulting from our OIDS with that given by the experts. The comparison is made in two levels. At the first level, we check the number of items (the subsets $\mathbf{S}_i$) that appear in each formula. Then, for each proposition $\mathbf{S}_i$, we compare the literals that form each of the clauses $\mathbf{S}_i^{AND}$ and $\mathbf{S}_i^{OR}$, with those provided by the experts.

Step 2 AND-OR Recommendation Trees evaluation: we apply our RS on the AND-OR trees resulting from the OIDS and that conform to those given by the experts. The results are AND-OR Recommendation Trees such that for each *OR-Set* in the tree, the nodes that encodes the most likely obsolete observations are packed from left to right. We compare each $\mathbf{S}_i^{OR}$ in the tree resulting from our RS with the priority order assigned by the experts using a rank correlation that measures the relationship between different rankings of variables in the same set $\mathbf{S}_i^{OR}$. Let $\mathbf{S}_i^{OR} = \{X_1, X_2, ..., X_k\}$. We denote by R and S the assignment of the ordering labels '1', '2', '3', etc. to different variables X_j in $\mathbf{S}_i^{OR}$ assigned respectively by our RS and by the experts. We denote by r_j and s_j the rankings of the variable X_j assigned respectively by our RS and by the experts. Then we compare the two ranks R and S using the Spearman's rank correlation coefficient ρ [12]: $\rho = 1 - \frac{6 \sum d_j^2}{k(k^2-1)}$, where $d_j = r_j - s_j$ is the difference between the two rankings of each variable X_j in $\mathbf{S}_i^{OR}$ and k is the number of variables in $\mathbf{S}_i^{OR}$. The Spearman's rank correlation coefficient can take values from $+1$ to -1. The ρ is high when variables have a similar ranking in both R and S. For each *OR-Set*, we calculate the coefficient ρ and we check if the recommendations given by our RS match those suggested by the experts. We apply the OIDS on the 380 remaining scenarios. The results are summarized in Table 1. Out of the 185 propositional formulas relating to the AND-OR trees provided by the OIDS, 182 are in line with those provided by the experts. Next, we apply our RS on the 182 AND-OR trees resulted from the OIDS that conform to those provided by the experts. We analyze the obtained 182 recommendation trees from which a total of 273 *OR-Sets* are extracted. For each one, we calculate the Spearman's rank correlation coefficient ρ. For the 273 *OR-Sets*, the resulting coefficient ρ ranges from 0.1 to 1 with an average of 0.73 and is satisfactory for 232 *OR-Sets*.

Table 1. 10^{-2} threshold contingency.

		Predicted	
	N = 380	ϵ-contradictory	Not ϵ-contradictory
Actual	Contradictory	**185**	5
	Not contradictory	3	**187**

5   Conclusion

Concluding this paper, emphasis was given in the RS and its simulated results for monitoring and updating personal obsolete information to help preventing falls in older adults. Our RS is based on a 41-node probabilistic causal model representing some elderly features and aims to provide caregivers with recommendations on which observations to update and which values can replace obsolete ones. The main objective is to maintain a consistent and up-to-date personal database in order to always provide the right information regarding the person's current state in real-time, in the right form, and of sufficient completeness and quality. Our approach runs in a polynomial time and returns results in an original way, in the form of an AND-OR Recommendation Tree. It encodes all possible obsolete observations in a priority order and gives for each the values that can replace it. Our approach efficiency is confirmed experimentally since our simulations on a real-life database in the elderly fall prevention context are very encouraging. Of course, our approach has been considered here without an actual testing process and work needs to be done. For the future, a user interface will be proposed in order to perform a set of tests of our OIUS by some physicians, using an iterative and incremental development cycle.

Acknowledgements. This work is supported and co-financed by the Ministry of Higher Education and Scientific Research of Tunisia. The experts who provided the estimates for the used causal Bayesian model and the University Hospital physicians who validated our scenarios are thanked for their participation.

References

1. Chaieb, S., Hnich, B., Mrad, A.B.: Data obsolescence detection in the light of newly acquired valid observations. Appl. Intell. (2022). https://doi.org/10.1007/s10489-022-03212-0
2. Chaieb, S., Mrad, A.B., Hnich, B.: Probabilistic causal model for the detection of obsolete personal information to prevent falls in the elderly. Procedia Comput. Sci. **192**, 1170–1179 (2021)
3. Gogel, W.C., Sturm, R.D.: Directional separation and the size cue to distance. Psychol. Forsch. **35**(1), 57–80 (1971). https://doi.org/10.1007/BF00424475
4. Lauritzen, S.L., Spiegelhalter, D.J.: Local computations with probabilities on graphical structures and their application to expert systems. J. Roy. Stat. Soc.: Ser. B (Methodol.) **50**(2), 157–194 (1988)
5. Luo, G., Zhao, B., Du, S.: Causal inference and Bayesian network structure learning from nominal data. Appl. Intell. **49**(1), 253–264 (2019). https://doi.org/10.1007/s10489-018-1274-3
6. Markert, C., Sasangohar, F., Mortazavi, B.J., Fields, S.: The use of telehealth technology to support health coaching for older adults: literature review. JMIR Hum. Factors **8**(1), e23796 (2021)
7. Pearl, J.: Bayesian Inference. Probabilistic Reasoning in Intelligent Systems: Networks of Plausible Inference, 2nd edn., pp. 29–75. Morgan Kaufmann Publisher, San Francisco (1988)

8. Pearl, J.: Causal diagrams for empirical research. Biometrika **82**(4), 669–688 (1995)
9. Pearl, J.: The do-calculus revisited. In: Proceedings of the Twenty-Eighth Conference on Uncertainty in Artificial Intelligence, UAI 2012, Arlington, Virginia, USA, pp. 3–11. AUAI Press (2012)
10. Pearl, J., Mackenzie, D.: The Book of Why: The New Science of Cause and Effect. Basic Books, New York (2018)
11. Saldivar, R.T., Tew, W.P., Shahrokni, A., Nelson, J.: Goals of care conversations and telemedicine. J. Geriatr. Oncol. **12**(7), 995–999 (2021)
12. Zar, J.H.: Significance testing of the spearman rank correlation coefficient. J. Am. Stat. Assoc. **67**(339), 578–580 (1972)

Identification of Subjects Wearing a Surgical Mask from Their Speech by Means of X-vectors and Fisher Vectors

José Vicente Egas-López[1]([⊠]) and Gábor Gosztolya[1,2]

[1] Institute of Informatics, University of Szeged, Szeged, Hungary
{egasj,ggabor}@inf.u-szeged.hu
[2] ELRN-SZTE Research Group on Artificial Intelligence, Szeged, Hungary

Abstract. This paper addresses the classification of speech recorded from subjects while wearing a surgical mask. Here, we employ two different types of feature extraction methods: the x-vectors embeddings, which is the current state-of-the-art approach for Speaker Recognition; and the Fisher Vector (FV), that is a method originally intended for Image Recognition, but here employed to discriminate utterances. These approaches make use of distinct frame-level representations: MFCC and PLP. Using Support Vector Machines (SVM) as the classifier, we perform a technical comparison between the performances of the FV encodings and the x-vector embeddings for this particular classification task. We find that the Fisher vector encodings provide better representations of the utterances than the x-vectors do for this specific dataset. Moreover, we show that a fusion of our best configurations outperforms all the original baseline scores.

Keywords: Speech recognition · Computational paralinguistics · Fisher vectors · x-vectors · Surgical mask

1 Introduction

The Computational Paralinguistics differs from Automatic Speech Recognition in that the latter seeks to determine the *content* of the speech of an utterance, while the former seeks to understand the *way* that the speech is spoken. There are different types of techniques that attempt to solve this problem in Computational Paralinguistics. Methods such as the i-vector Approach, the Fisher vector, neural networks, among others, are being increasingly used by researchers

This research was supported by the Hungarian Ministry of Innovation and Technology (grants no. NKFIH-1279-2/2020 and TKP2021-NVA-09), by the NRDI Office with grant FK-124413 and within the framework of the Artificial Intelligence National Laboratory Program (MILAB). G. Gosztolya was also funded by the János Bolyai Scholarship of the Hungarian Academy of Sciences and by the Hungarian Ministry of Innovation and Technology New National Excellence Program ÚNKP-21-5-SZTE.

to address paralinguistic issues. This can be seen in studies like diagnosing neurodegenerative diseases using the speech of the patients [1–3]; the discrimination of crying sounds and heartbeats [4]; or the estimation of the sincerity of apologies [5]. These studies aim to distinguish the latent patterns existing within the speech of a subject and not the content of it.

The INTERSPEECH ComParE Challenge, annually organized since 2009 [6], has provided a wide variety of Computational Paralinguistics problems each year. These types of challenges seem to encourage its participants to use or devise state-of-the-art techniques to handle the states and characteristics latent in an audio signal. This year, the challenge offers three tasks; but here we will just focus on one of them, namely, the *Mask* Sub-Challenge.

The 2020's challenge involved speech recordings of German speakers while wearing a surgical mask, and also while not wearing one. The task was to determine whether the utterance corresponds to a speaker whose speech was recorded while wearing the mask or not. The baseline reported by the organizers is an UAR (Unweighted Average Recall) score of 70.8%, which corresponds to a non-fused score. And a 71.8% for the fusion of the best four configurations for the *Mask* Sub-Challenge. Forensics and *'live'* communication between surgeons may benefit from a system that could determine whether a subject is wearing a mask based on their speech [7].

Lots of speaker recognition systems these days are based on i-vectors [8]. The i-vector system utilizes a GMM-UBM (Universal Background Model) to extract a fixed-dimension feature called *i-vector*. This is a robust technique that was and still is the state-of-the-art for many speaker recognition/verification approaches [9,10]. Also, i-vectors have been used in computational paralinguistics and offer promising results when assessing Alzheimer's from speech [11], or at the moment of classifying depressed speech [12]. Nonetheless, there are more meaningful features that seem to provide better representations of frame-level features than the i-vectors do.

Embeddings extracted from a Feed-Forward Deep Neural Network are gradually replacing i-vectors; such embeddings are called *x-vectors*. Regarded as the new state-of-the-art technique for speaker recognition systems [13], x-vectors can capture meta-information such as the gender of the speaker, as well as their speech rate (i.e. long-term speech traits). Researchers are increasingly using such representations in their studies, especially in text-independent approaches (see e.g. [14–17]). Also, *x-vectors* have already been applied to paralinguistics; studies like [18–20] reported high performances at classifying emotions, Alzheimer's, or age and gender of subjects.

As a contribution to the ComParE Challenge, here, we perform the chosen task via two different methodologies. The Fisher Vector (FV) approach [21], which is an encoding method originally developed to represent images as gradients of a global generative GMM of low-level image descriptors; mainly used in image recognition [22]. And we also employ the DNN embeddings approach (i.e. *x-vector system*) where the role of the DNN is to perform a mapping between variable-length utterances and fixed-dimensional embeddings.

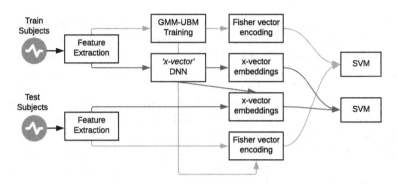

Fig. 1. The generic methodology applied in this study.

The workflow proposed is the following. First, we use two types of frame-level representations, i.e., MFCCs and PLPs extracted from the audio signals. Second, we process the frame-level information obtained utilizing two different techniques: the FV and the x-vector approaches. And third, we classify and evaluate FV and x-vector features individually. Finally, we opt for a late-fusion of the best configurations.

2   Data

The Mask Augsburg Speech Corpus (MASC) comprises recordings of 32 German native speakers. It has a total duration of 10 h 9 min 14 s; segmented into chunks of 1 s. The recordings have a rate of 16 kHz. The total number of utterances is 36554: 10895 for train, 14647 for development, and 11012 for test. The subjects were asked to perform specific types of tasks and recorded their speech while wearing and not wearing a surgical mask. (see more details in [7]).

3   Feature Extraction and Evaluation Methods

As depicted in Fig. 1, the steps carried out in our study are as follows: (1) Feature extraction (MFCCs and PLP); (2a) Train GMM-UBM using utterances from the training set, (2b) Train the DNN for the x-vectors utilizing the training set and its *augmented* version; (3a) Extract Fisher vector features from the datasets employing the GMM-UBM model, (3b) Extract embeddings from the DNN; and, (4a/4b) Independently classify the FV and x-vectors representations using SVM.

3.1   Frame-Level Features

Here, we used the well-known Mel-Frequency Cepstral Coefficients (MFCC) and Perceptual Linear Predictions (PLP) frame-level representations. Both have 13

Table 1. DNN architecture of the x-vector system. It comprises five frame-level layers, a statistics pooling layer, two segment-layers and a final softmax layer as output. N represents the number of training speakers in the softmax layer. The DNN structure here is the same as that shown in Snyder et al. [24].

Layer	Layer context	Tot. context	In, Out
Frame1	[t−2, t+2]	5	120, 512
Frame2	{t−2, t, t+2}	9	1536, 512
Frame3	{t−3, t, t+3}	15	1536, 512
Frame4	{t}	15	512, 512
Frame5	{t}	15	512, 1500
Stats pooling	[0, T}	T	1500T, 3000
Segment6	{0}	T	3000, 512
Segment7	{0}	T	512, 512
Softmax	{0}	T	512, N

dimensions, a frame-length of 25 ms and a sliding window of 3 ms. Moreover, since x-vectors are extracted from a DNN, an additional configuration for the MFCCs called *high-resolution (hires)* was utilized. This allows us to maintain all the cepstra while decorrelating the MFCCs. The MFCC-hires configuration is intended for neural network training. This configuration has the same values as those previously described, except that it extracts 40 cepstral coefficients, the number of mel-bins is 40, and the low and high cut-off frequencies are 20 and −400, respectively (see e.g. in [23]). Also, non-speech frames are removed from all the representations employing VAD.

3.2   X-vectors

The x-vector approach can be thought as of a neural network feature extraction technique that provides fixed-dimensional embeddings corresponding to variable-length utterances. Such a system can be viewed as a feed-forward Deep Neural Network (DNN) that computes such embeddings. Below, we will describe the architecture of the DNN (based on [13]) and the embeddings that are extracted from it.

DNN Structure. Table 1 outlines the architecture of the DNN. The *frame-level* layers have a time-delay architecture, and let us assume that t is the actual time step. At the input, the frames are spliced together; namely, the input to the current layer is the spliced output of the previous layer (i.e. input to layer *frame3* is the spliced output of layer *frame2*, at frames $t-3$ and $t+3$). Next, the *stats pooling* layer gets the T frame-level output from the last frame-level layer (*frame5*), aggregates over the input segment, and computes the mean and standard deviation. The mean and the standard deviation are concatenated and used as input for the next *segment* layers; from any of these layers the *x-vectors* embeddings can be extracted. And finally, the *softmax* output layer (which is discarded after training the DNN) [13, 24, 25].

Instead of predicting frames, the network is trained to predict speakers from variable-length utterances. Namely, it is trained to classify the N speakers present in the train set utilizing a multi-class cross entropy objective function (see Eq. 1). Let K be the number of speakers in N training segments. Then, the probability of the speaker k given T input frames $(x_1^{(n)}, x_2^{(n)}, ..., x_{1:T}^{(n)})$ is given by: $P(spkr_k|x_{1:T}^{(n)})$. If the speaker label for segment n is k, then the quantity of d_{nk} is 1, and 0 otherwise [24].

$$E = -\sum_{n=1}^{N} \sum_{k=1}^{K} d_{nk} \ln P(spkr_k|x_{1:T}^{(n)}). \tag{1}$$

Embeddings. The embeddings produced by the network described above capture information from the speakers over the whole audio-signal. Such embeddings are called *x-vectors* and they can be extracted from any *segment* layer; that is, either *segment6* or *segment7* layers (see Table 1). Normally, embeddings from the *segment6* layer give a better performance than those from *segment7* [13]. In this study, these type of representations can capture meaningful information from each utterance. This embedding may help us to discriminate better the utterances due to the fact that the characteristics are acquired at the utterance level rather than at the frame-level. For this, we used the Kaldi Toolkit [26].

3.3 Fisher Vectors

The Fisher Vector approach is an image representation that pools local image descriptors (e.g. SIFT, describing occurrences of rotation- and scale-invariant primitives [27]). In contrast with the Bag-of-Visual-Words (BoV, [28]) technique, it assigns a local descriptor to elements in a visual dictionary, obtained via a Gaussian Mixture Model for FV. Nevertheless, instead of just storing visual word occurrences, these representations take into account the difference between dictionary elements and pooled local features, and they store their statistics. A nice advantage of the FV representation is that, regardless of the number of local features (i.e. SIFT), it extracts a *fixed-sized* feature representation from each image.

The FV technique has been shown to be quite promising in image representation [21]. Despite the fact that just a handful of studies use FV in speech processing (e.g. for categorizing audio-signals as speech, music and others [29], for speaker verification [30, 31], and for determining the food type from eating sounds [32]), we think that FV can be harnessed to improve classification performance in audio processing.

Fisher Kernel. The Fisher Kernel (FK) seeks to measure the similarity of two objects from a parametric generative model of the data (X) which is defined as the gradient of the log-likelihood of X:

$$G_\lambda^X = \nabla_\lambda \log \upsilon_\lambda(X), \tag{2}$$

where $X = \{x_t, t = 1, \ldots, T\}$ is a sample of T observations $x_t \in \mathcal{X}$, υ represents a probability density function that models the generative process of the elements in $\mathcal{X}$ and $\lambda = [\lambda_1, \ldots, \lambda_M]' \in R^M$ stands for the parameter vector υ_λ [33]. Thus, such a gradient describes the way the parameter υ_λ should be changed in order to best fit the data X. A novel way to measure the similarity between two points X and Y by means of the FK can be expressed as follows [21]:

$$K_{FK}(X,Y) = G_\lambda^{X'} F_\lambda^{-1} G_\lambda^Y. \tag{3}$$

Since F_λ is positive semi-definite, $F_\lambda = F_\lambda^{-1}$. Equation (4) shows how the Cholesky decomposition $F_\lambda^{-1} = L_\lambda' L_\lambda$ can be utilized to rewrite the Eq. (3) in terms of the dot product:

$$K_{FK}(X,Y) = \mathscr{G}_\lambda^{X'} \mathscr{G}_\lambda^Y, \tag{4}$$

where

$$\mathscr{G}_\lambda^X = L_\lambda G_\lambda^X = L_\lambda \nabla_\lambda \log \upsilon_\lambda(X). \tag{5}$$

Such a normalized gradient vector is the so-called *Fisher Vector* of X [33]. Both the FV $\mathscr{G}_\lambda^X$ and the gradient vector G_λ^X have the same dimension.

Fisher Vectors. Let $X = \{X_t, t = 1 \ldots T\}$ be the set of D-dimensional local SIFT descriptors extracted from an image and let the assumption of independent samples hold, then Eq. (5) becomes:

$$\mathscr{G}_\lambda^X = \sum_{t=1}^{T} L_\lambda \nabla_\lambda \log \upsilon_\lambda(X_t). \tag{6}$$

The assumption of independence permits the FV to become a sum of normalized gradients statistics $L_\lambda \nabla_\lambda \log \upsilon_\lambda(x_t)$ calculated for each SIFT descriptor. That is:

$$X_t \to \varphi_{FK}(X_t) = L_\lambda \nabla_\lambda \log \upsilon_\lambda(X_t), \tag{7}$$

which describes an operation that can be thought of as a higher dimensional space embedding of the local descriptors X_t.

The FV extracts low-level local patch descriptors from the audio-signal spectrogram. Then, a GMM with diagonal covariances models the distribution of the extracted features. The log-likelihood gradients of the features modeled by the parameters of such GMM are encoded through the FV [33]. This type of encoding stores the mean and covariance deviation vectors of the components k that form the GMM together with the elements of the local feature descriptors. The utterance is represented by the concatenation of all the mean and the covariance vectors that gives a final vector of length $(2D + 1)N$, for N quantization cells and D dimensional descriptors [33,34]. Here, we use FV features to encode the MFCC features extracted from the audio-signals of the *Mask* dataset.

3.4 Support Vector Machines (SVM)

A linear-SVM classifier was utilized to discriminate the audio-signals. This algorithm was found to be robust even with a large number of dimensions and it was shown to be efficient when used with FV [33,35] due to it being a discriminative classifier that provides a flexible decision boundary. We used the libSVM implementation [36] with a linear kernel. As stated in the paper on this year's challenge [7], since 2009 (and also for this year), Unweighted Average Recall (UAR) has been the chosen metric for evaluating the performance of the classifiers.

4 Experimental Setup

As for the Fisher vectors, the number of K GMM components utilized to compute the FVs ranged from $2, 4, 8,$ to 512. The construction of the FV encoding was performed using a Python-wrapped version of the VLFeat library [37]. Both MFCC and PLP representations were used separately to train the GMM model and extract the FV features. The GMM model was fit utilizing the training set. Fisher vectors were *optimized* employing Power Normalization (PN) and L2-Normalization before training the data; in [33] the authors obtained good performances using this feature pre-processing technique.

The x-vector network was fitted using the training data and its augmented version following the methodology employed in [13]; likewise, we used the same network topology proposed there. Basically, from the original training data, two augmented versions were added, i.e. noise and reverberation. From additive noises and reverberation, two of the following types of augmentation were chosen arbitrarily: babble, music, noise, and reverberation. The first three types correspond to simply adding or fitting a kind of noise to the original utterances, while the fourth one involves a convolution of room impulse responses with the audio, i.e. reverberation (see [13] for more details about the augmentation strategies used). From the artificially generated data, we chose a subset of 40000 utterances to train the DNN, which is roughly four times the number of original training samples. From the *segment6* layer of the DNN, we extracted 512-dimensional neural network embeddings (x-vectors) for the train, development, and test sets, respectively. As Snyder et al. [13], we also found that embeddings from *segment6* gave a better performance than those from *segment7* in our experiments.

Following the techniques suggested in [21], the parameter C of the SVM was set in the range: $10^{-5}, \ldots, 10^{1}$. Since the training and development sets are meant to be combined and used to train the final SVM model, we fused the above-mentioned sets and employed a Stratified k-fold Cross-Validation. We set $k = 10$ to find the best C. The training set has 5353 utterances labeled as *no-mask* and 5542 labeled as *mask*; the development set has 6666 and 7981, as *no-mask* and as *mask*, respectively. Namely, there is a slight class imbalance when combining both sets. As a result, there were 1504 more utterances labeled as *mask* in the combined set. Hence, we set the *class-weight* parameter of the SVM to *balanced*. In this way, the classifier adjusted the weights of the classes automatically.

Table 2. Experiment results. Scores are presented for x-vectors and FVs; both using MFCCs and PLPs. FoB stands for 'fusion of best' (fusion of the ComParE best configurations) [7]. The GMM size corresponds to the K value used for FV; for x-vectors this is not applicable. The dashes (-) in the UAR column indicate that the scores for those configurations are not available due to the limited number of trials for submissions defined by the organizers of the Challenge.

Feature	GMM size	UAR (%)		
		Dev	CV	Test
ComParE baseline	-	-	-	71.81
x-vecs (MFCC)	-	56.86	65.21	-
x-vecs (MFCC-hires)	-	59.87	72.14	-
x-vecs (PLP)	-	58.46	64.80	-
FV (MFCC)	512	57.43	78.18	-
FV (PLP)	256	59.18	71.09	-
FV + FoB	512	-	-	70.30
FV + x-vecs (hires)	512	-	-	70.81
FV + x-vecs (hires) + FoB	512	-	-	74.92

Before classification, all the features were standardized by removing their means and scaling to unit variance.

In addition, we carried out a *late fusion* of our best configurations. Moreover, we also fused our best configurations with those posteriors from *'fusion of best'* of the sub-challenge [7].

5   Results and Discussion

As Table 2 shows, the FV representations produced better performances in the evaluation (i.e. Dev and CV) phase than the x-vectors embeddings did. However, this is mainly true for the CV scores, where FV achieved UAR scores above 70%. Overall, the configuration *FV (MFCC)* attained the best CV score (78.18%). On the other hand, the best configuration for the x-vectors embeddings was that of *high resolution* MFCCs (i.e. MFCC-hires), which gave a 72.14%. In contrast, when we evaluated the features using just the development set, x-vectors presented better scores; nevertheless, the difference compared to those of FV was not significant. Although in this study we did not rely on the development scores to find the best C value for the SVM, we still report the scores obtained when evaluating on this dataset (see Table 2). It should be added that we chose the best C based on the Stratified 10-fold CV experiments.

Furthermore, the FV encodings yielded a significant performance improvement when applying PN and L2-normalization before fitting them (see also [33]). However, here, just the best configurations are reported (the improved FVs). PN reduced the effect of the features that become more sparse as the value of K

increased. Also, L2-normalization helped to alleviate the problem of having different utterances with (relatively) distinct amounts of background information projected into the extracted features. This mainly enhanced the prediction performances. Also, it was found that the higher the number of K, the higher the UAR score. This means that these two are directly proportional to each other. In our study, both MFCC and PLP achieved their best configurations when using a large value for K (512 and 256, respectively). Likewise, MFCC-hires gave a better frame-level feature quality (for the x-vectors) than the standard MFCC configuration. This can be attributed to the DNN training phase, where the neural network exploits in a better way the larger and less correlated frame-level representations.

Table 2 lists the final scores. The fusion of the posteriors of FV_{512} with those of the *fusion of best* (from the challenge) attained a UAR score of 70.3% on the test set. Likewise, the fusion of FV_{512} with x-vectors ($x\text{-}vecs_{hires}$) yielded a score of 70.8%. Finally, the fusion of FV_{512} with $x\text{-}vecs_{hires}$ along with FoB provided a UAR score of 74.9% on the test set.

6   Conclusions

Here, we studied the performance of x-vector and Fisher vector representations as a contribution to the *Mask* Sub-Challenge of the INTERSPEECH 2020 ComParE. These representations were extracted from two different types of frame-level features: MFCC and PLP. As for the FV encodings, we found that MFCCs presented a superior type of frame-level traits of the recordings than the PLP did. Regarding the x-vectors, the configuration of *MFCC-hires* was found to be better than those of the standard MFCC and PLP. Also, we found that PN and L2-Normalization enhanced the quality of the FVs. Although the FV gave better quality features than x-vectors for this particular dataset, x-vectors also captured meaningful phonatory with articulatory information, as their scores are competitive. Moreover, we found that the fusion of our best configurations increased the performance of the final predictions. To conclude, our workflow outperformed the official baseline scores of the *Mask* Sub-Challenge [7]; besides, our feature extraction approach appears to be simpler than those from [7].

References

1. Egas-López, J.V., Orozco-Arroyave, J.R., Gosztolya, G.: Assessing Parkinson's disease from speech using fisher vectors. In: Proceedings of Interspeech (2019)
2. Gosztolya, G., Bagi, A., Szalóki, S., Szendi, I., Hoffmann, I.: Identifying schizophrenia based on temporal parameters in spontaneous speech. In: Proceedings of Interspeech, Hyderabad, India, pp. 3408–3412, September 2018
3. Grósz, T., Busa-Fekete, R., Gosztolya, G., Tóth, L.: Assessing the degree of nativeness and Parkinson's condition using Gaussian processes and deep rectifier neural networks. In: Proceedings of Interspeech, Dresden, Germany, pp. 1339–1343, September 2015

4. Gosztolya, G., Grósz, T., Tóth, L.: General utterance-level feature extraction for classifying crying sounds, atypical & self-assessed affect and heart beats. In: Proceedings of Interspeech, Hyderabad, India, pp. 531–535, September 2018

5. Gosztolya, G., Grósz, T., Szaszák, G., Tóth, L.: Estimating the sincerity of apologies in speech by DNN rank learning and prosodic analysis. In: Proceedings of Interspeech, San Francisco, CA, USA, pp. 2026–2030, September 2016

6. Schuller, B., Batliner, A., Steidl, S., Seppi, D.: Recognising realistic emotions and affect in speech: state of the art and lessons learnt from the first challenge. Speech Commun. 53(9–10), 1062–1087 (2011)

7. Schuller, B.W., et al.: The INTERSPEECH 2020 computational paralinguistics challenge: elderly emotion, breathing & masks. In: Proceedings of Interspeech, Shanghai, China, p. 5, September 2020

8. Dehak, N., Kenny, P.J., Dehak, R., Dumouchel, P., Ouellet, P.: Front-end factor analysis for speaker verification. IEEE Trans. Audio Speech Lang. Process. 19(4), 788–798 (2011)

9. Ibrahim, N.S., Ramli, D.A.: I-vector extraction for speaker recognition based on dimensionality reduction. Procedia Comput. Sci. 126, 1534–1540 (2018)

10. Garcia-Romero, D., Espy-Wilson, C.Y.: Analysis of i-vector length normalization in speaker recognition systems. In: Twelfth Annual Conference of the International Speech Communication Association (2011)

11. Egas López, J.V., Tóth, L., Hoffmann, I., Kálmán, J., Pákáski, M., Gosztolya, G.: Assessing Alzheimer's disease from speech using the i-vector approach. In: Salah, A.A., Karpov, A., Potapova, R. (eds.) SPECOM 2019. LNCS (LNAI), vol. 11658, pp. 289–298. Springer, Cham (2019). https://doi.org/10.1007/978-3-030-26061-3_30

12. Cummins, N., Epps, J., Sethu, V., Krajewski, J.: Variability compensation in small data: oversampled extraction of i-vectors for the classification of depressed speech. In: 2014 IEEE International Conference on Acoustics, Speech and Signal Processing (ICASSP), pp. 970–974 (2014)

13. Snyder, D., Garcia-Romero, D., Sell, G., Povey, D., Khudanpur, S.: X-vectors: robust DNN embeddings for speaker verification. In: Proceedings of ICASSP, pp. 5329–5333 (2018)

14. Silnova, A., Brummer, N., Garcia-Romero, D., Snyder, D., Burget, L.: Fast variational bayes for heavy-tailed PLDA applied to i-vectors and x-vectors. arXiv preprint: arXiv:1803.09153 (2018)

15. Snyder, D., Garcia-Romero, D., Sell, G., McCree, A., Povey, D., Khudanpur, S.: Speaker recognition for multi-speaker conversations using x-vectors. In: Proceedings of ICASSP (2019)

16. Chung, J.S., Nagrani, A., Zisserman, A.: VoxCeleb2: Deep Speaker Recognition. arXiv preprint arXiv:1806.05622 (2018)

17. Novotný, O., Plchot, O., Matejka, P., Mosner, L., Glembek, O.: On the use of x-vectors for robust speaker recognition. In: Proceedings of Odyssey, pp. 168–175 (2018)

18. Zargarbashi, S., Babaali, B.: A multi-modal feature embedding approach to diagnose Alzheimer's disease from spoken language. arXiv preprint arXiv:1910.00330 (2019)

19. Pappagari, R., Wang, T., Villalba, J., Chen, N., Dehak, N.: X-vectors meet emotions: a study on dependencies between emotion and speaker verification. In: Proceedings of ICASSP, pp. 7169–7173 (2020)

20. Raj, D., Snyder, D., Povey, D., Khudanpur, S.: Probing the information encoded in x-vectors. arXiv preprint arXiv:1909.06351 (2019)

21. Jaakkola, T.S., Haussler, D.: Exploiting generative models in discriminative classifiers. In: Proceedings of NIPS, Denver, CO, USA, pp. 487–493 (1998)
22. Song, Y., Zou, J.J., Chang, H., Cai, W.: Adapting Fisher vectors for histopathology image classification. In: Proceedings of ISBI, pp. 600–603. IEEE (2017)
23. Hernandez, F., Nguyen, V., Ghannay, S., Tomashenko, N., Estève, Y.: TED-LIUM 3: twice as much data and corpus repartition for experiments on speaker adaptation. In: Karpov, A., Jokisch, O., Potapova, R. (eds.) SPECOM 2018. LNCS (LNAI), vol. 11096, pp. 198–208. Springer, Cham (2018). https://doi.org/10.1007/978-3-319-99579-3_21
24. Snyder, D., Garcia-Romero, D., Povey, D., Khudanpur, S.: Deep neural network embeddings for text-independent speaker verification. In: Proceedings of Interspeech (2017)
25. Snyder, D., Ghahremani, P., Povey, D., Garcia-Romero, D., Carmiel, Y., Khudanpur, S.: Deep neural network-based speaker embeddings for end-to-end speaker verification. In: Proceedings of SLT, pp. 165–170 (2016)
26. Povey, D., et al.: The Kaldi speech recognition toolkit. In: Proceedings of ASRU (2011)
27. Lowe, D.G.: Distinctive image features from scale-invariant keypoints. Int. J. Comput. Vision **60**(2), 91–110 (2004)
28. Peng, X., Wang, L., Wang, X., Qiao, Y.: Bag of Visual Words and fusion methods for action recognition: comprehensive study and good practice. Comput. Vis. Image Underst. **150**, 109–125 (2016)
29. Moreno, P.J., Rifkin, R.: Using the Fisher kernel method for web audio classification. In: Proceedings of ICASSP, Dallas, TX, USA, pp. 2417–2420 (2010)
30. Tian, Y., He, L., Li, Z.Y., Wu, W.L., Zhang, W.Q., Liu, J.: Speaker verification using Fisher vector. In: Proceedings of ISCSLP, Singapore, Singapore, pp. 419–422 (2014)
31. Zajíc, Z., Hrúz, M.: Fisher vectors in PLDA speaker verification system. In: Proceedings of ICSP, Chengdu, China, pp. 1338–1341 (2016)
32. Kaya, H., Karpov, A.A., Salah, A.A.: Fisher vectors with cascaded normalization for paralinguistic analysis. In: Proceedings of Interspeech, pp. 909–913 (2015)
33. Sánchez, J., Perronnin, F., Mensink, T., Verbeek, J.: Image classification with the fisher vector: theory and practice. Int. J. Comput. Vision **105**, 222–245 (2013)
34. Perronnin, F., Dance, C.: Fisher kernels on visual vocabularies for image categorization. In: Proceedings of CVPR (2007)
35. Smith, D.C., Kornelson, K.A.: A comparison of Fisher vectors and Gaussian supervectors for document versus non-document image classification. In: Applications of Digital Image Processing XXXVI, vol. 8856, p. 88560N. International Society for Optics and Photonics (2013)
36. Chang, C.-C., Lin, C.-J.: LIBSVM: a library for support vector machines. ACM Trans. Intell. Syst. Technol. **2**, 1–27 (2011)
37. Vedaldi, A., Fulkerson, B.: VLFeat: an open and portable library of computer vision algorithms. In: Proceedings of ACM Multimedia, pp. 1469–1472 (2010)

Measuring Fairness in Machine Learning Models via Counterfactual Examples

Rami Haffar[⊠], Ashneet Khandpur Singh, Josep Domingo-Ferrer,
and Najeeb Jebreel

Department of Computer Engineering and Mathematics,
CYBERCAT-Center for Cybersecurity Research of Catalonia,
Universitat Rovira i Virgili, Av. Països Catalans 26, 43007 Tarragona, Catalonia
{rami.haffar,ashneet.singh,josep.domingo,najeeb.jebreel}@urv.cat

Abstract. Machine learning has become a vital resource of the modern society. It is present in everything around us, from a smartwatch to a self-driving car. To train a machine learning model, a heap of data is used. This can be worrisome in the case of that learned models can be discriminatory with respect to protected features such as race or gender. In order to develop fair models and verify the fairness of these models, a plethora of work has emerged in recent years. In this work, we propose a method, based on counterfactual examples, that detects any bias in the machine learning model. Our method works for different data types, including tabular data and images.

Keywords: Machine learning · Fairness · Counterfactual examples · Adversarial examples · GANs

1 Introduction

Artificial intelligence (AI) is undergoing a rapid evolution. Most companies that were evaluating or experimenting with AI not so long ago are now using it. Machine learning (ML) has played a vital role in this advancement. Various industries ranging from information technology, finance, media, gaming, robotics, have already set ML technology in practice.

However, machine learning is still in its early stages and plenty of work needs to be done. In the future, ML will help build self-learning robots and machines that are expected to improve their performance without using any human involvement. In this way, machines will be able to make decisions based on past data to predict the best future action.

Since ML models use high amounts of data, concerns have arisen that learned models may be discriminatory with respect to sensitive features, e.g. race, gender, and socioeconomic status. As a result of these issues, an astounding number of methods for developing fair models and verifying the fairness of existing models have emerged in recent years.

There are two types of fairness definitions that have been considered in the literature [7, 15]:

V. Torra and Y. Narukawa (Eds.): MDAI 2022, LNAI 13408, pp. 119–131, 2022.
https://doi.org/10.1007/978-3-031-13448-7_10

- The vast majority of definitions deal with group fairness, e.g. demographic parity [5], equalized odds [10] or predictive parity [3]. Basically, such definitions pre-identify what attributes or groups should be protected. Group fairness metrics have the advantage that they can be easily computed and they reflect anti-discrimination legislation. These metrics have a solid theoretical foundation as well as practical methods and implementations. Their weakness is that they entail no guarantees for individuals.
- The second type of definitions are about individual fairness. They assume a similarity metric of the individuals for the classification task at hand that is generally hard to find. For instance, unawareness [5] and counterfactual fairness [12]. This type of definitions bind at the individual level.

Any of the metrics mentioned above can be used to calculate disparities in data across groups, but many of them cannot be balanced across subgroups at the same time. As a result, one of the most crucial components of measuring bias in the model is understanding how fairness should be defined for a certain scenario. In this work, we are going to merge the concept of group fairness with that of individual fairness, in the sense that the proposed method protects the individuals of any minority against any bias in the model.

Contribution and Plan of This Paper

The purpose of this paper is to detect any bias in the ML models targeting any individual, regardless of the type of data used in the model. To that end, we leverage counterfactual examples. The key contributions of the paper are: (i) to detect the bias with regard to the ML model behavior and the training data, unlike the previous work [12] that solely focuses on the bias of the training data; (ii) to provide bias detection regardless of the data type (in particular for tabular data and images), thanks to the use of counterfactual examples, which offer developers a straightforward way to measure the fairness of their models.

The rest of this paper is organized as follows. Section 2 introduces the three different fields of ML used in this work and the related work. Section 3 presents the proposed methodologies to measure fairness in ML models. Section 4 reports experimental results. Finally, Sect. 5 gathers conclusions and sketches future research lines.

2   Related Work

This section gives an overview of three distinct fields of machine learning research that are explicitly merged in this paper.

2.1   Fairness

The existing research addressing the topic of fairness in machine learning has focused on how to measure and evaluate fairness (or, equivalently, bias) in models.

The work in [5] introduced the definition of individual fairness, which contrasts with group-based notions of fairness [3,10] that require demographic groups to be treated similarly on average.

Later, [12] introduced a causal, individual-level, definition of fairness, called counterfactual fairness, which states that a decision is fair toward an individual if it coincides with the one that would have been taken in a counterfactual world in which the sensitive attribute was different. More formally, given protected attributes A, remaining attributes Z and output of interest Y, a classifier $\hat{Y}$ is counterfactually fair if, under any context $A = a$ and $Z = z$, we have

$$P(\hat{Y} = \hat{y}_{A=a}|A = a, Z = z) = P(\hat{Y} = \hat{y}_{A=a'}|A = a, Z = z),$$

for any value a' attainable by A.

In relation with group fairness, counterfactual fairness is complementary to the group fairness notion of equality of odds, which demands equality of true positive rates and true negative rates for different values of the sensitive attribute.

2.2 Adversarial Examples

Adversarial examples are inputs to machine learning models that an attacker intentionally constructs to fool the model into returning a false prediction [14]. Adversarial examples are closely related to counterfactual examples: [16] characterize counterfactuals as adversarial examples that perturb inputs in human-interpretable and possibly problematic ways. Thus, whereas adversarial examples try to deceive the model, counterfactual examples try to understand or explain it.

Formally speaking, given a input x, a classifier $\hat{Y}$, a distance metric d (which can be the L_p distance) and a small distance $\epsilon > 0$, an adversarial example is defined as an input $x' \neq x$, such that $d(x', x) < \epsilon$ and $\hat{Y}(x') \neq \hat{Y}(x)$.

In [18], by utilizing adversarial examples for data augmentation, the authors implemented a prototype application to solve the algorithm bias problem. In order to obtain a fair dataset in which the distribution of bias variables is balanced, they apply adversarial attacks to generate examples containing information of bias variables as the enhanced data.

2.3 GANs

Generative Adversarial Networks, or GANs for short, are a type of generative model, that is, a model that can produce new content based on its training data. They were first introduced by [8] and they have a variety of applications. However, their most common use is to generate new images. A GAN consists of two artificial neural networks, a generator G and a discriminator D, that compete against each other. G creates new data instances while D evaluates them for authenticity.

More specifically, G takes as input a random noise vector z and outputs an image $z = G(z)$. D receives as input either a training image x or a synthesized image $G(z)$ from G and outputs a probability distribution $D(\cdot)$ over possible image sources. D is trained to maximize the log-likelihood it assigns to the correct source:

$$L = E_x[\log(D(x))] + E_z[\log(1 - D(G(z)))].$$

The generator G is trained to minimize $E_z[\log(1 - D(G(z)))]$, that is, to minimize the likelihood that its generated images are detected as fake by D.

In [17], the authors develop a GAN for fairness. Their architecture is limited to low-dimensional structured data and only applies to demographic parity. In contrast, our work is geared towards high-dimensional image data and individual fairness.

Another work that measures fairness based on GANs is [1]. The authors propose an adversarial approach, inspired from GANs, in which a sanitizer is learned from data representing the population. In this work, local sanitization is employed to reach algorithmic fairness.

3   Measuring Fairness via Counterfactual Examples

In this section, we introduce our proposed method to measure fairness in ML models. Our approach rests on generating counterfactual examples. To this end, the technique used to generate those counterfactuals may differ depending on the input data type. We next discuss the cases of tabular data and image data.

3.1   Measuring Fairness in Tabular Data

We want to measure the fairness of any ML model, which will ensure that the predictions of the model are not biased against any minority in the data set. To this end, we need to guarantee that the ML model is not making its predictions based on a sensitive attribute. The fairness assurance process should be automated in the sense that it is not enough to change the attribute value and monitor the outcome of the model. At the same time, this process should be model- and data-related, because the bias might be in the training data or in the learned model.

In order to measure the fairness of an ML model f, for a specific data record x, taking into consideration the protected attribute a, we have to satisfy the counterfactual fairness definition mentioned in Sect. 2.1. We propose an automated approach that creates counterfactual examples for each record in the data set. The proposed method uses adversarial examples as a means to create those counterfactual examples. To create an adversarial example, the proposed method targets only the attributes that have the highest effect on the ML model prediction, in an attempt to alter its predicted label with the smallest input changes. In this situation, if the changed attribute is one of the protected attributes, this indicates that the model is not fair to this record.

Algorithm 1 describes the proposed method. Given an ML model f, a maximum allowed value ϵ_{max}, an input record x containing n attributes, the method generates the counterfactual example x_* by changing at most $c \leq n$ attributes from x, where c is the number of protected attributes. First, to set the target classification label y_* we desire for x_*, we compute *probs*, the probability vector that f outputs for x. Then, we set the desired class label y_* to be the index of the second most probable class in *probs*. Choosing this class makes it easier for the proposed method to find the desired x_* with small changes to x. Note that the user can also set y_* to any class label she wants. Then, to select the c attributes which have the highest effect on the model prediction, we compute the gradient of the loss between the model output $f_u(x)$ and the desired output y_* with regard to the attributes of the input record. After that, we take the L_1-norm of the computed gradient ∇_x. Subsequently, we identify the c attributes with the highest L_1-norms as the attributes to be changed when generating x_*. This is done using a weighting vector w which contains 0 s for the unchanged attributes and 1 s for the changed attributes. Using this vector allows us to change only c attributes while creating x_*. Afterwards, we keep repeating the gradient descent step in expression

$$x_* = x - w \cdot \epsilon \cdot \frac{\partial}{\partial x} \mathcal{L}(f(x), y_*),$$

with regard to w until one of two following conditions is satisfied: i) an adversarial example x_* is obtained that fools f into labeling it as y_* or ii) the maximum value ϵ_{max} is reached for ϵ (which means that no x_* close to x could be found). Note that we start with a small $\epsilon = 0.05$ and we increase it by 0.05 at each step. Once we create the adversarial example x_*, we compare it with x to identify the changed attributes. If one or more of the changed attributes belong to a, the set of the protected features, then this indicates bias in the model.

3.2   Measuring Fairness in Image Data

Measuring fairness for image classifiers is more challenging than measuring fairness for tabular data classifiers because the attributes in images are not self-explanatory. To tackle this challenge, we propose a method that generates counterfactual examples for the image data by leveraging the GANs described in Sect. 2.3.

In the proposed method, we use two generators and one discriminator consisting of a trained binary classifier, as shown in Fig. 1. Both generators create images to fool the trained image classifier model. However, each generator can only fool the model into one specific outcome. Generator A creates counterfactual images to be classified by the classifier into class a, whereas generator B's counterfactuals are to be classified into class b. After training both generators, they can be used to create counterfactual examples to detect any bias in the classifier. Any image m from class a that the classifier misclassifies into class b is passed through generator A to generate the counterfactual example m_*. This counterfactual m_* will be classified into class a. By comparing m and m_* we can notice whether they differ in any of the discriminatory attributes (those related

Algorithm 1. Creating the counterfactual example

1: **Input:** Trained model f, record x, maximum allowed ϵ_{max}, maximum number of attributes to be changed c.
2: **Output:** Counterfactual example x_*
3: $probs \leftarrow$ Get_Probabilities($f(x)$)
4: $y_* \leftarrow argmax(probs, 2)$
5: $n \leftarrow$ Number of attributes in x
6: $|\nabla_x| \leftarrow abs(\frac{\partial}{\partial x}\mathcal{L}(f(x), y_*))$
7: $w \leftarrow$ Zero vector of length n
8: $idxs \leftarrow$ Indices of the highest c values in $|\nabla_x|$
9: **for** $idx \in idxs$ **do**
10:     $w[idx] = 1$
11: **end for**
12: $x_* \leftarrow x$
13: $\epsilon \leftarrow 0.05$
14: **while** $f(x_*) \neq y_*$ and $\epsilon \leq \epsilon_{max}$ **do**
15:     $x_* \leftarrow x - w \cdot \epsilon \cdot \frac{\partial}{\partial x}\mathcal{L}(f(x), y_*)$
16:     $\epsilon \leftarrow \epsilon + 0.05$
17: **end while**
18: **if** $f(x_*) = y_*$ **then**
19:     **Return** x_*
20: **else**
21:     **Return** $\emptyset$
22: **end if**

---

to race, such as dark skin or dark hair). Similarly, an image m' from class b misclassified into class a is passed through generator B to create the counterfactual m'_*.

4   Empirical Results

In this section, we evaluate the performance of the proposed approach on two ML tasks: tabular data classification and image classification. For each task, we trained a baseline model with the original data set and a biased model after we did some alterations to the data set. In both data sets, the baseline and biased models had the same architecture. First, we show the performance of the models and then we evaluate the proposed fairness measures.

4.1   Experimental Setup

Data Sets and Provider Models. We evaluated the proposed approach on two data sets:

– **Adult**[1] is a data set from the UCI Machine Learning repository [4]. It is a tabular data set that contains $48,842$ records of census income information

---

[1] https://archive.ics.uci.edu/ml/datasets/adult.

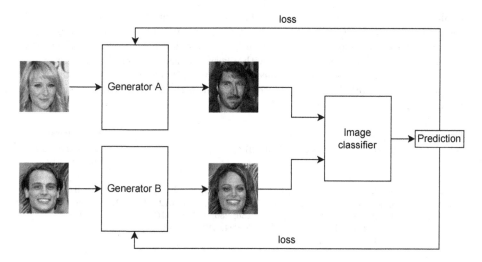

Fig. 1. Training the generator of the counterfactual examples.

with 14 numerical and categorical attributes. From these, we dropped the final weights (*fnlwgt, capital-loss, and capital-gain*), which reveal too much information to the model, and the *education* attribute, which is redundant with *education-num*. We also encoded categorical attributes as numbers. The class label is the attribute *income*, that classifies records into either >50K or ≤50K. We used 80% of the data as training data, and the remaining 20% as validation data.

– **CelebA**[2] is a binary classification data set from Kaggle [13]. It consists of RGB images of male and female faces with a training set of 17,943 female images and 10,057 male images. The validation set contains 2,000 images evenly divided into the two classes. Since the images have large sizes of 1024 × 1024 pixels, we first resized them to 256 × 256 pixels in order to train our models faster.

The architectures of the models used in the experiments are shown in Table 1. We took the same models from [9].

In all experiments, we employed the binary cross-entropy loss function and the Adam optimizer [11].

Training Data for Biased Models. The two original data sets were balanced in terms of sensitive data. To train biased models, we modified both training data sets in order to train the biased model.

– **Adult:** To drive the model to be biased against the attribute *gender*, we selected 45% of the *females* whose *race* was *black* and whose *income* was >50K, and we changed their *income* to ≤50K. Also, we selected 45% of the

---

2 https://www.kaggle.com/dataset/504743cb487a5aed565ce14238c6343b7d650ffd28c0 71f03f2fd9b25819e6c9.

Table 1. Architectures of the models used in the experiments for the Adult and CelebA classification data sets. $C(3, 32, 3, 0, 1)$ denotes a convolutional layer with 3 input channels, 32 output channels, a kernel of size 3×3, a stride of 0, and a padding of 1; $MP(2, 2)$ denotes a max-pooling layer with a kernel of size 2×2 and a stride of 2; and $FC(18432, 2048)$ indicates a fully connected layer with 18,432 inputs and 2,048 output neurons. We used *ReLU* as an activation function in the hidden layers; *lr* stands for learning rate.

Data set	Model architecture	Hyper-parameter
Adult	FC(12, 100), FC(100, 100), FC(100, 2)	lr = 0.001, epochs = 10, batch = 128
CelebA	C(3, 32, 3, 0, 1), C(32, 64, 3, 1, 1), MP(2, 2), C(64, 128, 3, 0, 1), C(128, 256, 3, 1, 1), MP(2, 2), C(256, 512, 3, 0, 1), C(512, 512, 3, 1, 1), MP(2, 2), C(512, 256, 3, 0, 1), C(256, 256, 3, 1, 1), MP(2, 2), FC(16384, 2048), FC(2048, 1024), FC(1024, 512), FC(512, 128), FC(128, 32), FC(32, 2)	lr = 0.001 epochs = 10 batch = 64

> *males* whose *race* was *black* and whose income was ≤50K, and we changed their income to >50k.

- **CelebA:** To train a biased gender classification model, we separated from the female training data the images containing dark skin. In order to do so, we used the unsupervised cluster K-means [2], while keeping track of some cherry-picked images to monitor the outcome of the cluster. The desired class consisted of 1904 images. We changed the class of 60% of those images from female into male.

Evaluation Metrics. We used the following evaluation metrics to measure the performance of the trained surrogate models and the generated explanations:

- *Accuracy*: Number of correct predictions divided by the total number of predictions. We used this metric to measure and compare the performance of the baseline and the biased models.
- *ROC curve* [6]: The Receiver operating characteristic (ROC) is a graph plotting the false positive rate in the abscissae and the true positive rate in the ordinates. It shows the performance of a classification model at all classification thresholds. The AUC (area under the ROC curve) takes values from 0.0 (when the model predictions are 100% wrong), to 1.0 (when the model predictions are 100% correct). AUC is scale invariant, and classification-threshold invariant. In some cases it is a better metric than accuracy.

In this work, we evaluated the fairness of the model based on its performance on the targeted minority, since there are no methods in the literature to compute the individual fairness score.

4.2   Results

Accuracy and ROC-AUC Score. In Table 2, we show the accuracy of the baseline and biased models when evaluated on the full evaluation data set, for both data sets. The baseline model was more accurate than the biased model on both data sets, even though the biased model's accuracy was not much lower than the baseline model's.

Table 2. Accuracy of the baseline and biased model evaluated on the full evaluation data set, for the Adult and the CelebA data sets

Data set	Baseline model	Biased model
Adult	82.80%	79.67%
CelebA	98.52%	86.42%

In Fig. 2, ROC curves are presented for both models on the two data sets. The results are consistent with those of Table 2, where the baseline and the biased models exhibit small performance differences.

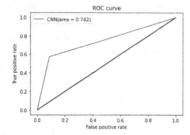

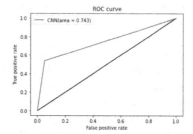

(a) ROC curve of the baseline model on the Adult data set

(b) ROC curve of the biased model on the Adult data set

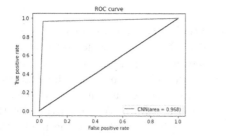

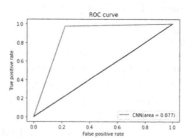

(c) ROC curve of the baseline model on the CelebA data set

(d) ROC curve of the biased model on the CelebA data set

Fig. 2. ROC curve of the baseline and biased models on both data sets

To better understand the performance differences between the baseline and the biased models, we evaluated them on modified data sets, which consist of the samples belonging to the minorities in each data set. On the one side, we derived an evaluation set from Adult by picking all the records with *race* equal to *black*. On the other hand, we derived an evaluation set from CelebA by picking all female images with dark skin. We call those evaluation sets the targeted data sets. Table 3 reports the accuracy of the models when they were evaluated on the targeted sets. For both data sets, the baseline model accuracy was similar to that in Table 2, while the performance of the biased model was very poor: it was around 1% in both data sets. This illustrates that the biased models were precisely biased against the individuals in the targeted data sets.

Table 3. Accuracy of the baseline and biased models evaluated on the targeted data sets derived from Adult and CelebA

Data set	Baseline model	Biased model
Adult	81.90%	0.54%
CelebA	99.60%	1.67%

Fairness of the Trained Models

- **Adult data set:** We generated a counterfactual example for each record in the validation portion of the Adult data set. First, we considered the attribute *gender* as the protected attribute. Then, we used Algorithm 1 with $c = 1$, to restrict the changes to only one attribute when generating the examples. After that, we computed the number of cases where the counterfactual example was created by changing the protected attribute. We found that for the biased model, this happened 1,637 times, while for the baseline model this happened only 12 times. These results indicate that for the baseline model the protected attribute was not essential in the prediction. On the other hand, the protected attribute had a very high impact on the predictions made by the biased model. We present two examples of the counterfactual examples generated by the proposed method in Table 4. Record 1's income was classified as >50K by both models. The first counterfactual example which was created based on the baseline model shows that the original record's prediction can change to ≤50K by reducing the *educational level* from 13 to 9. This recommendation from the proposed method seems logical in the sense that less education yields decreased income. The second counterfactual example which was created based on the biased model recommended changing the *gender* from *male* to *female*, which shows that the model learned a gender bias (income of males is higher than the income of females). On the other hand, Record 2's income was classified as ≤50K by both models. In this case, the counterfactual created by the baseline recommended increasing the *hours-per-week* from 47 to 60, which is also reasonable because more working hours usually means more payout. In contrast, the counterfactual created by the biased model recommended to change the attribute *gender* but this time from *female* to *male*, because the model learned that males earn more.

Table 4. Two examples of records from the Adult data set. Symbol '"' indicates that the value of the attribute did not change during the creation of the counterfactual example.

Features	Age	Workclass	Educational-num	Marital-status	Occupation	Relationship	Race	Gender	Hours-per-week	Native-country	Income
Original record 1	38	State-gov	13	Married	Protective-serv	Husband	Black	Male	52	United-States	>50K
Baseline recommendation	"	"	9	"	"	"	"	"	"	"	$\leq 50K$
Biased model recommendation	"	"	"	"	"	"	"	Female	"	"	$\leq 50K$
Original record 2	43	Local-gov	14	Unmarried	Tech-support	Not-in-family	Black	Female	47	United-States	$\leq 50K$
Baseline recommendation	"	"	"	"	"	"	"	"	60	"	>50K
Biased model recommendation	"	"	"	"	"	"	"	Male	"	"	>50K

- **CelebA data set:** In order to generate the counterfactual examples for the CelebA data set, we selected the female images that were classified into the label male by the biased model and into the label female by the baseline model, because those images were targeted when training the biased model. Even though those images correspond to females, we pass them through the female generator, that is due to the classifier (in this case it is also the discriminator) to classify them as a male. Figure 3 presents five examples of the counterfactual created by the proposed method. In all the images, the proposed method made the skin lighter, and the hair color blond. Those counterfactuals were classified as females by both models. Thus, our method detected that the biased model classified every face image with dark skin and black hair as male.

Fig. 3. Five examples of the counterfactual examples created by the proposed method

5   Conclusion and Future Work

In this paper, we have examined fairness in the scenario of binary classification for two types of input data, tabular and image data. The proposed method is based on generating counterfactual examples to measure fairness in ML models. In the case of tabular data, we used adversarial examples to create the counterfactuals. To achieve this for image data, we used GANs as a generator for the counterfactuals. Our experiments confirm that the proposed method can detect any model bias against protected attributes. As future work, we plan to implement a new measure that characterizes fairness for image classifier models, since there is a limitation in the current literature on this topic. Furthermore, we intend to automate the comparison process between the original data and the counterfactual examples. We also envision generalizing our method to non-binary classification.

Acknowledgements. We acknowledge support from the European Commission (projects H2020-871042 "SoBigData++" and H2020-101006879 "MobiDataLab") and from the Government of Catalonia (ICREA Acadèmia Prize to J. Domingo-Ferrer).

References

1. Aïvodji, U., Bidet, F., Gambs, S., Ngueveu, R.C., Tapp, A.: Local data debiasing for fairness based on generative adversarial training. Algorithms **14**(3), 87 (2021)
2. Ball, G.H., Hall, D.J.: ISODATA: a novel method of data analysis and pattern classification. Stanford Research Institute, Menlo Park, CA (1965)
3. Chouldechova, A.: Fair prediction with disparate impact: a study of bias in recidivism prediction instruments. Big Data **5**(2), 153–163 (2017)
4. Dua, D., Graff, C.: UCI machine learning repository. University of California, School of Information and Computer Science, Irvine, CA (2017). http://archive. ics.uci.edu/ml
5. Dwork, C., Hardt, M., Pitassi, T., Reingold, O., Zemel, R.: Fairness through awareness. In: Proceedings of the 3rd Innovations in Theoretical Computer Science Conference, pp. 214–226. ACM (2012)
6. Fawcett, T.: An introduction to ROC analysis. Pattern Recogn. Lett. **27**(8), 861–874 (2006)
7. Gajane, P., Pechenizkiy, M.: On formalizing fairness in prediction with machine learning. arXiv preprint arXiv:1710.03184 (2018)
8. Goodfellow, I.J., et al.: Generative adversarial networks. In: Advances of Neural Information Processing Systems-NIPS 2014, vol. 27 (2014)
9. Haffar, R., Jebreel, N.M., Domingo-Ferrer, J., Sánchez, D.: Explaining image misclassification in deep learning via adversarial examples. In: Torra, V., Narukawa, Y. (eds.) MDAI 2021. LNCS (LNAI), vol. 12898, pp. 323–334. Springer, Cham (2021). https://doi.org/10.1007/978-3-030-85529-1_26
10. Hardt, M., Price, E., Srebro, N.: Equality of opportunity in supervised learning. In: Advances in Neural Information Processing Systems-NIPS 2016, vol. 29 (2016)
11. Kingma, D.P., Ba, J.: Adam: a method for stochastic optimization. arXiv preprint arXiv:1412.6980 (2014)

12. Kusner, M.J., Loftus, J., Russell, C., Silva, R.: Counterfactual fairness. In: Advances in Neural Information Processing Systems-NIPS 2017, vol. 30 (2017)
13. Liu, Z., Luo, P., Wang, X., Tang, X.: Deep learning face attributes in the wild. In: Proceedings of the IEEE International Conference on Computer Vision, pp. 3730–3738 (2015)
14. Szegedy, C., et al.: Intriguing properties of neural networks. In: International Conference on Learning Representations (2014). arXiv preprint arXiv: 1312.6199
15. Verma, S., Rubin, J.: Fairness definitions explained. In: 2018 IEEE/ACM International Workshop on Software Fairness (FairWare 2018), pp. 1–7. IEEE (2018)
16. Wachter, S., Mittelstadt, B.D., Russell, C.: Counterfactual explanations without opening the black box: automated decisions and the GDPR. CoRR abs/1711.00399 (2017)
17. Xu, D., Yuan, S., Zhang, L., Wu, X.: FairGAN: fairness-aware generative adversarial networks. In: 2018 IEEE International Conference on Big Data (Big Data), pp. 570–575 (2018)
18. Zhang, Y., Sang, J.: Towards accuracy-fairness paradox: adversarial example-based data augmentation for visual debiasing. In: Proceedings of the 28th ACM International Conference on Multimedia, pp. 4346–4354 (2020)

Re-calibrating Machine Learning Models Using Confidence Interval Bounds

Andrea Campagner[1(✉)], Lorenzo Famiglini[1], and Federico Cabitza[1,2]

[1] Dipartimento di Informatica, Sistemistica e Comunicazione,
University of Milano-Bicocca, viale Sarca 336, 20126 Milan, Italy
a.campagner@campus.unimib.it
[2] IRCCS Istituto Ortopedico Galeazzi, Milan, Italy

Abstract. In this article we propose a novel technique for the re-calibration of Machine Learning (ML) models. This technique is based on the computation of confidence intervals for the probability scores provided by any ML model. Compared to existing and commonly used calibration methods, the proposed approach has two important advantages: first, under weak assumptions it provides theoretical guarantees about calibration; second, this method does not require any further data other than the training set used for ML model development. We illustrate the effectiveness of the proposed approach on a benchmark dataset for COVID-19 diagnosis, by comparing the proposed method against commonly used re-calibration techniques.

Keywords: Calibration · Machine Learning · Confidence interval · Trustable AI

1 Introduction

In recent years, the application of Machine Learning (ML) techniques in several practical scenarios has received increasing attention. Despite promising results reported by these methods in terms of accuracy, recent research has highlighted important limitations in terms of other quality dimensions than those related to discrimination, which are of great interest in human decision making, such as robustness, utility and trustworthiness [4,5,19,21].

Among these quality dimensions, *calibration* [21] is a fundamental characteristic of predictive models: intuitively, calibration [2] is information about the extent confidence scores associated with each prediction/classification are good estimates of event occurrence frequencies. Therefore, calibration is an important property of a ML model, especially in critical settings (such as the medical one) [22], in that a calibrated model is "trustworthy" since the confidence scores it produces can be used by human experts to assess the probability that its advice is right [15]. By contrast, a poorly calibrated model can provide misleading predictions [23].

V. Torra and Y. Narukawa (Eds.): MDAI 2022, LNAI 13408, pp. 132–142, 2022.
https://doi.org/10.1007/978-3-031-13448-7_11

Unfortunately, even models with good discrimination power can be poorly calibrated: for example, commonly used non-linear classification models such as deep neural networks [6], support vector machines [30] and tree ensembles [13,18] have extensively been shown to have poor calibration by default.

A possible solution to this problem is to apply a *re-calibration method* [14] as a post-processing step, whose goal is to *correct* the confidence scores provided by a ML model in order to improve its calibration and thus provide probability estimates that are more accurate or as accurate as possible. Several such techniques have been proposed in the literature (e.g., [6,14,17,27,29]); however, the most commonly adopted methods do not provide any sort of statistical guarantee [1,24]: in other words, the adjusted confidence scores are not guaranteed to be more calibrated on any new data. Some techniques have been proposed that provide theoretical guarantees under weak assumptions [9] (e.g., that the sample data instance are i.i.d. or exchangeable); however, also these methods have some drawback: in particular they are generally not sample efficient, in that they need a part of the training set to be reserved and used for re-calibration, what is usually called a *calibration set* [26]. Such data cannot thus be used during the ML model development [12], so as to potentially lead to a conflict between models' accuracy and calibration.

To overcome these limitations, in this article we propose a novel re-calibration method, which is based on the computation of confidence intervals for the confidence scores provided by an ML model. The proposed method provides theoretical guarantees on the post-correction calibration, under weak assumptions; furthermore, this method has low computational complexity and does not need a separate calibration set, so that all available data can be used for model training. In the following sections, we illustrate the derivation of the proposed method (see Sect. 2); we prove its properties, and show its effectiveness in an experimental comparison against different commonly used re-calibration methods (see Sect. 3).

2   Method

Let X be the set of instances and Y the set of classes. In this article we will assume that $Y = \{0, 1\}$, that is, we deal with binary classification tasks. Let $\mathcal{D}$ be a joint probability distribution over $X \times Y$, which is assumed to be the unknown data generating process. We denote with $S = \{(x_i, y_i)\}_{i=1}^n$ the training set, sampled i.i.d from $\mathcal{D}$.

Let h be a scoring classifier, that is $h : X \mapsto [0, 1]$, where $h(x)$ is interpreted as the confidence score associated the positive class (i.e., class 1). Let $k \in \mathbb{N}^+$ be a positive integer greater than 2, then S_k denotes a partition of S into k equal-width bins $S_k^1, \ldots, S_k^k$, obtained by first sorting the elements $\{h(x) : (x, y) \in S\}$ and then splitting the obtained ordered list. In particular we note that if $x_i \in S_k^i, x_j \in S_k^j$ with $i < j$, then $h(x_i) \leq h(x_j)$.

Given a bin S_k^i, we denote with σ_i the average confidence score for the instances in S_k^i, that is $\sigma_i = \frac{1}{|S_k^i|} \sum_{(x,y) \in S_k^i} h(x)$. Similarly, we denote with o_i the observed frequency of the positive class in bin S_k^i, that is $o_i = \frac{|\{(x,y) \in S_k^i : y=1\}|}{|S_k^i|}$.

A scoring classifier h is *strongly calibrated* if $Pr_{x \sim \mathcal{D}_X}(y_x = 1 | h(x) = p) = p$, that is, its confidence scores can be interpreted as probability estimates. Despite being a useful property, strong calibration is not easily achievable by any scoring classifier trained on finite samples [26].

To avoid this limitation, the methodology we propose is based on the computation of confidence intervals around $h(x)$, obtained by inverting a statistic related to the Hosmer-Lemeshow test for calibration [7]. For this purpose, we first introduce the notion of an interval scoring classifier [27] (sometimes also called a multiprobabilistic predictor in the literature), which is a function $s : X \mapsto [0, 1]^2$ s.t. $s(x)_0 \leq s(x)_1$. Intuitively, $s(x)_0$ (resp., $s(x)_1$) is interpreted as a lower (resp., upper) bound on the confidence associated with the positive class $y = 1$. We note that a scoring classifier is a special case of an interval scoring classifier, where $\forall x \in X, s(x)_0 = s(x)_1$.

An interval scoring classifier s is *α-calibrated* if, with probability no smaller than α over the selection of S, $s(x)_0 \leq Pr_{x \sim \mathcal{D}_X}(y_x = 1) \leq s(x)_1$. Given an interval scoring classifier s and instance x, the *interval width* at x is defined as $s(x)_1 - s(x)_0$. Intuitively, the interval width provides an indicator of specificity: the smaller the interval width, the more specific the predictions. Identified a scoring classifier h and $\alpha \in (0, 1)$, our method constructs an interval scoring classifier s^h based on the observed performance of h on the training set. Intuitively, given a new instance x to be classified, we compute the confidence score $h(x)$, then, based on a partitioning S_k of the training set S, we select the bin S_k^i s.t. $h(x) \in S_k^i$ and we compute an interval estimate of $P(y_x = 1)$ based on the observed mis-calibration of h on the corresponding bin. Formally, the above mentioned interval scoring classifier s^h is defined as:

$$s_0^h(x; \alpha) = \max\{0, h(x) - \frac{\sqrt{2\hat{\sigma}_i} \cdot erf^{-1}(\alpha)}{\sqrt{|S_k^i| + 1}}\} \tag{1}$$

$$s_1^h(x; \alpha) = \min\{1, h(x) + \frac{\sqrt{2\hat{\sigma}_i} \cdot erf^{-1}(\alpha)}{\sqrt{|S_k^i| + 1}}\} \tag{2}$$

where $h(x) \in S_k^i$, $\hat{\sigma}_i = \frac{\sigma_i \cdot |S_k^i| + h(x)}{|S_k^i| + 1}$ and erf is the *error function*. That is, s^h is obtained from h by first identifying in which bin S_k^i the confidence score $h(x)$ falls, and then by correcting $h(x)$. The whole procedure to compute s^h is defined in Algorithm 1.

The following theorem provides the main theoretical justification for the proposed method, showing that the obtained interval scoring classifier is calibrated.

Theorem 1. *Assume S, x are sampled i.i.d. from $\mathcal{D}$. Then, for each $\alpha \in [0, 1]$, $s^h(\cdot; \alpha)$ is (asymptotically, that is, as $|S| \to +\infty$) α-calibrated. Furthermore, let $C(\alpha) = \frac{\sqrt{2\hat{\sigma}_i} \cdot erf^{-1}(\alpha)}{\sqrt{|S_k^i| + 1}}$, then the finite sample probability that s^h fails to be α-calibrated is less than $2e^{-2(|S_k^i| + 1)C(\alpha)^2}$.*

Proof. Given a partition S_k of the training set S, denote with $Q = \sum_{i=1}^k \frac{(O_i - \Sigma_i)^2}{\Sigma}$, where $O_i = o_i \cdot |S_k^i|$ and $\Sigma_i = \sigma_i \cdot |S_k^i|$. Q is asymptotically

---

Algorithm 1. The proposed confidence interval-based re-calibration method.

---

procedure INTERVAL_RECALIBRATION(h: ML model, S: training set, k: number of bins, α: confidence level, x : new instance)

    Train h on S

    $H \leftarrow \emptyset$

    for all $(x_i, y_i) \in S$ **do**

        $H.append(h(x_i))$

    end for

    Sort H in increasing order

    Partition H in $H_1, ..., H_k$ equal-sized bins

    Find i s.t. $h(x) \in [\min H_i, \max H_i]$

    $\hat{\sigma}_i \leftarrow \frac{1}{|H_i|} \sum_{j:h_j \in H_i} h_j$

    $s_0^h \leftarrow \max\{0, h(x) - \frac{\sqrt{2\hat{\sigma}_i} \cdot erf^{-1}(\alpha)}{\sqrt{|H_i|+1}}\}$

    $s_1^h \leftarrow \min\{1, h(x) + \frac{\sqrt{2\hat{\sigma}_i} \cdot erf^{-1}(\alpha)}{\sqrt{|H_i|+1}}\}$

    return s_0^h, s_1^h

end procedure

---

distributed as a chi-square with $k - 2$ degrees of freedom, that is $Q \sim \chi_{k-2}^2$ [7]. Consequently, $\frac{(O_i-\Sigma_i)^2}{\Sigma_i}$ is asymptotically distributed as a χ_1^2 and, therefore, $\frac{|O_i-\Sigma_i|}{\sqrt{\Sigma_i}} \sim \chi_1$.

Hence, $|O_i - \Sigma_i| \sim HN(\sqrt{\Sigma_i})$, that is the deviation between the observed frequency and the average confidence score is asymptotically distributed as a half-normal with parameter $\sqrt{\Sigma_i}$. Thus, a confidence interval (with confidence level α) around o_i can be obtained by $h(x) \pm \frac{\sqrt{2\hat{\sigma}_i} \cdot erf^{-1}(\alpha)}{\sqrt{|S_k^i|+1}}$, where $h(x) \in S_k^i$, from which the first part of the result follows. The second part directly follows by applying Hoeffding bound [3] to $|o_i - \sigma_i|$. □

As a consequence of Theorem 1, we note that there is a trade-off, governed by the number of bins k, between the interval width $s_1^h - s_0^h$ and the probability that s^h fails to be (finite sample) α-calibrated. Indeed, as k increases, $\hat{\sigma}_i$ becomes closer to $h(x)$ but the interval width increases (since the denominator in Eqs. (1), (2) becomes smaller) and similarly also the finite sample probability of failure increases (since $C(\alpha)$ decreases), and vice-versa when k decreases. Therefore, in practical applications, the number of bins k, should be carefully set so as to optimize the above mentioned trade-off between coverage and efficiency (i.e., the requirement of having small interval width [25,27]).

Aside from the above mentioned theoretical result, an interesting property of our method (and, more in general, of interval scoring classifiers) is that its calibration can be easily checked by means of a graphical criterion. Indeed, if we plot the reliability curve for s (that is, for each bin S_k^i we plot o_i against $s_0(x), s_1(x)$), then s is calibrated if and only if the bisector lies in-between the lower and upper curves determined by s (we will show an example of this criterion in the Results section). We will further discuss this point in Sect. 4.

Finally, we show that the proposed method is computationally efficient, with sub-linear run-time complexity in the size of the training set:

Theorem 2. *Let S be a training set, $n = |S|$, S_k a k-partition of S, and x a new instance. Then, independently of $\alpha \in (0, 1)$, $s_0^h(x; \alpha), s_1^h(x; \alpha)$ can be computed in time $\Theta(log(k))$ and space $O(k)$. In particular, if k is independent of n, then the proposed method has (run-time) time and space complexity $O(1)$.*

Proof. As shown in Algorithm 1, to compute $s_0^h(x; \alpha), s_1^h(x; \alpha)$, we first need to find S_i^k s.t. $\min_{x' \in S_i^k} h(x') \leq h(x)$ and $h(x) \leq \max_{x' \in S_i^k} h(x')]$, which requires $\Theta(log(k))$ by applying binary search. Then, the desired quantities can be computed in time $O(1)$ and space $O(k)$, if we store the partial averages $\hat{\sigma}_i$, for each bin i. The result follows if the partitioning S_k is computed off-line.

The previous theorem is interesting in that it shows that the proposed method not only is more sample-efficient, but it is also more computationally efficient compared to other re-calibration methods that provide similar guarantees (e.g., Venn predictors [9, 27], whose run-time complexity lies between $O(|C|)$, where C is a separate calibration set, and $O(|S|)$, depending on whether we consider inductive or transductive implementations [11]).

2.1   Experimental Analysis

In order to assess the effectiveness of the proposed method, we performed an experiment in which we compared our method against different calibration techniques proposed in the literature. All methods were evaluated on a publicly available dataset for the task of COVID-19 diagnosis from routine blood exams, collected in Northern Italy during the first and second waves of the pandemic [4]. In particular, the training set encompassed a collection of 1736 samples (one for each patient) collected between February and May 2020 at the IRCCS Ospedale San Raffaele (OSR) and IRCCS Istituto Ortopedico Galeazzi, in Milan, Italy. On the other hand, the test set encompassed a collection of 224 samples collected in November 2020 at IRCCS OSR. Thus, the training and test sets pertained to two different waves of the pandemics: we decided to use two separate datasets, with data from different pandemics waves, in order to assess the robustness of considered re-calibration methods with respect to possible violations of the i.i.d. assumption [28]. Both datasets encompassed 21 features, including the complete blood count (CBC), age, biological sex, and presence of suspect symptoms. The full list of features, as well as descriptive statistics for both the continuous and discrete features, for the train and test sets, is reported in Table 1.

In regard to model development, as scoring classifier we adopted a SVM-based pipeline model (encompassing a k-nearest neighbors-based imputation step for missing data imputation, and a feature standardization step) which was shown to obtain state-of-the-art performance on the considered task [4]. As baseline, we considered the model trained on the full training set. We then considered four re-calibration methods to be compared:

Table 1. The list of the 21 parameters, along with the target, used by the validated Machine Learning models. For each continuous parameter we report the mean and the extremes of the 95% confidence intervals, as well as the missing rate in the training set (in parenthesis). For the discrete features, as well as for the target, we report the distribution of values, as well as the missing rate for the training set (in parenthesis). No value was missing in the test set.

Parameter	Unit of measure	Train (Missing)	Test
Age	Years	60.93 ± 0.92 (3.11)	60.53 ± 0.2
Hematocrit (HCT)	%	39.21 ± 0.26 (3.63)	39.67 ± 0.1
Hemoglobin (HGB)	g/dL	13.14 ± 0.10 (3.63)	12.86 ± 0.0
Mean Corpuscular Hemoglobin (MCH)	pg/Cell	29.21 ± 0.13 (3.63)	29.51 ± 0.0
Mean Corpuscular Hemoglobin Concentration (MCHC)	g Hb/dL	33.45 ± 0.06 (3.63)	33.00 ± 0.0
Mean Corpuscular Volume (MCV)	fL	87.29 ± 0.3 (3.63)	89.41 ± 0.1
Red Blood Cells (RBC)	$10^{1}2/L$	4.52 ± 0.0 (3.63)	4.46 ± 0.0
White Blood Cells (WBC)	$10^9/L$	8.72 ± 0.2 (3.63)	9.53 ± 0.1
Platelets (PLT1)	$10^9/L$	235.66 ± 4.4 (3.63)	218.00 ± 0.7
Neutrophils (NE)	%	72.35 ± 0.6 (20.85)	72.48 ± 0.1
Lymphocytes (LY)	%	18.58 ± 0.5 (20.85)	17.96 ± 0.2
Monocytes (MO)	%	7.83 ± 0.2 (20.85)	8.13 ± 0.0
Eosinophils (EO)	%	0.88 ± 0.1 (20.85)	0.60 ± 0.0
Basophils (BA)	%	0.34 ± 0.0 (20.85)	0.32 ± 0.0
Neutrophils (NET)	$10^9/L$	6.45 ± 0.2 (20.85)	6.76 ± 0.0
Lymphocytes (LYT)	$10^9/L$	1.37 ± 0.0 (20.85)	1.82 ± 0.1
Monocytes (MOT)	$10^9/L$	0.62 ± 0.0 (20.85)	0.64 ± 0.0
Eosinophils (EOT)	$10^9/L$	0.07 ± 0.0 (20.85)	0.05 ± 0.0
Basophils (BAT)	$10^9/L$	0.02 ± 0.0 (20.85)	0.02 ± 0.0
COVID-19 specific symptoms at triage (Suspect)	Yes/No	68%/32% (0)	82%/18%
Gender	M/F	57%/43% (0)	63%/37%
COVID-19 Positivity (Target)	Positive/Negative	53%/47%	53%/47%

- Sigmoid regression (SR) (or, Platt scaling) [17], obtained by 5-fold cross-validation (CV) on the training set;
- Isotonic regression (IR) [14], obtained by 5-fold CV on the training set;
- Venn prediction (VP) [9,11], based on a 80/20 split of the training set into training proper and calibration set. The underlying classifier was trained on the training proper, while the calibration set was used to compute the interval estimates for instances in the test set;
- Our proposed method, with $\alpha = 0.90$ (that is, we considered 90% confidence intervals). The underlying classifier was trained on the full training set, which was then subsequently used also for the computation of the confidence intervals for instances in the test set.

As previously mentioned, after training, all models were compared in terms of performance on the separate test set. Model comparison was performed in terms of the Brier score $\frac{1}{n}\sum_{i=1}^{n}(h(x_i) - y_i)^2$ and graphical analysis based on reliability diagrams. In particular, for the interval predictors (i.e. Venn prediction and the proposed method), we considered a generalization of the Brier score, defined as $\frac{1}{n}\sum_{i=1}^{n} \mathbb{1}_{y_i \notin [s_0^h, s_1^h]} * \min\{(s_0^h(x_i)-y_i)^2, (s_1^h(x_i)-y_i)^2\}$: that is, for each instance x_i, the mis-calibration w.r.t. the correct label y_i is computed as the distance from the value in $[s_0^h, s_1^h]$ closest to y_i. For Venn prediction and for our proposed method, we also considered the average interval width (that is, $\frac{1}{n}\sum_{i=1}^{n} s_1(x_i) - s_0(x_i)$).

3   Results

The reliability diagrams and Brier scores for the evaluated models are reported in Figs. 1 and 2. The proposed method reported an average interval width of .15, while the Venn prediction method reported an average interval width of .02.

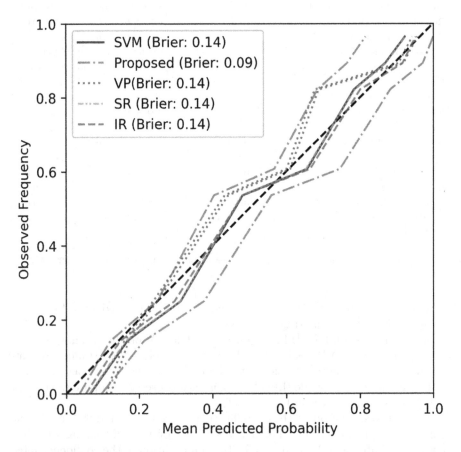

Fig. 1. Results of the experimental analysis, represented as a reliability diagram. The dashed line denotes perfect calibration. For interval-based methods (that is, the proposed method and Venn prediction), calibration curves are obtained from the confidence intervals, and are hence represented by a lower and a upper bound: the more the bisector line lies within these bounds, the better.

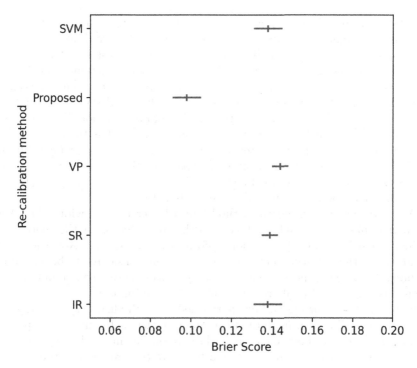

Fig. 2. Results of the experimental analysis, in terms of Brier scores and corresponding 99% confidence intervals: the lower the Brier score, the better.

The number of instances for which the bisector of the reliability diagram was not within the interval produced by our method was 21 (9.4%), which was lower than the value of α (10%).

4   Discussion

As shown in Figs. 1 and 2, the proposed method resulted in a larger reduction in the Brier score compared to the other considered re-calibration methods. In particular, we note that both isotonic and sigmoid regression did not provide any improvement in terms of the Brier score. Similarly in terms of calibration curves, it is easy to observe that sigmoid regression did not provide any calibration improvement w.r.t. to the baseline model (indeed, the curves for the baseline SVM model and the sigmoid regression coincide), while isotonic regression provided only a small improvement. Interestingly, also the Venn prediction method did not provide any improvement compared to the baseline SVM model. Venn prediction is known to provide weakly calibrated interval classifiers under the i.i.d. assumption [27] (and even under the weaker assumption of exchangeability [26]): therefore, the observed violation of calibration could be to attributed to the fact that the training data and the test data came from two different waves of the COVID-19 pandemics, which were associated with different characteristics of the impacted population [4] and thus violates the i.i.d. assumption. By contrast, the proposed confidence interval methods reported a consistent improvement in calibration and robustness to the mentioned violation of its assumptions (indeed, we note that, the i.i.d. assumption is also an hypothesis in Theorem 1), as shown by the fact that the bisector line was almost entirely included within the interval bounds. In particular, we note that the fraction of instances for which the bisector line was not included within the interval bound was less than $1 - \alpha = 0.1$, thus showing that the proposed technique was (empirically) α-weakly calibrated on the test set. We believe this results to be particularly interest as it shows that, in this experiment, the proposed technique is more robust to small violations of the i.i.d. assumption as compared to Venn prediction.

We note that the proposed method had a larger interval width than Venn Prediction: in general, smaller interval widths are preferable as they correspond to higher efficiency and hence more informative predictions. Nonetheless, we recall that in the literature, efficiency is not usually considered to be a desirable property *per se* [25]: indeed, efficiency only makes sense when comparing two method that are equally calibrated, as, ultimately, calibration is the desired property. In this sense, our method out-performed Venn Prediction since it reported much better calibration, in spite of the lower efficiency. In any case, a possible explanation for the above mentioned observation lies in the low power of the Hosmer-Lemeshow test, which was used to derive the proposed method.

The above analysis highlights how, differently from standard re-calibration methods, the calibration of our method can be easily evaluated by means of a simple graphical criterion. Indeed, the interval predictions are calibrated *if and only if* the bisector line is contained within the computed interval bounds, except possibly for a fraction of size approximately equal to α of the test set. This verification provides a simple and interpretable criterion for the assessment of calibration, as compared to existing alternative criteria based on scoring functions lacking clear standard or consensus-based thresholds to interpret the corresponding scores.

5   Conclusion

The importance of calibration cannot be overestimated for its role in allowing agile model updates in front of concept drifts [8], in making models more accurate on uncertain, borderline instances, and in making models more trustworthy, due to their capability to estimate accuracy at instance level. In this article we proposed a novel technique for ML model re-calibration, based on the computation of confidence interval estimates of the unknown event frequency.

Through a theoretical analysis and an illustrative experiment, we showed that the proposed technique provides some advantages compared to existing re-calibration methods, both in statistical and computational terms, as well as in terms of ease of interpretation. Despite these advantages, we note that the proposed method may provide wider confidence intervals than other similar techniques (such as Venn prediciton). This can possibly be due to the low power of the Hosmer-Lemeshow test [10] that we used to derive our approach. We believe that further research should be aimed at studying techniques to reduce the interval width and improve efficiency , for example by adopting more powerful tests [20]. Similarly, it would be interesting to design algorithms that automatically determine the optimal number of bins k, possibly also by allowing for unevensized bins [16]. Furthermore, further research should be devoted at extending the proposed method to the general, multi-class case. Finally, despite the promising result we reported in this contribution, further and more extensive experimental validation of the proposed technique should be conducted.

References

1. Angelopoulos, A., Bates, S., Malik, J., Jordan, MI.: Uncertainty sets for image classifiers using conformal prediction. arXiv preprint arXiv:2009.14193 (2020)
2. Bella, A., Ferri, C., Hernández-Orallo, J., Ramírez-Quintana, M.J.: Calibration of machine learning models. In: Handbook of Research on Machine Learning Applications and Trends: Algorithms, Methods, and Techniques, pp. 128–146. IGI Global (2010)
3. Boucheron, S., Lugosi, G., Massart, P.: A Nonasymptotic Theory of Independence. Concentration Inequalities. Oxford University Press, Oxford (2013)
4. Cabitza, F., et al.: The importance of being external. methodological insights for the external validation of machine learning models in medicine. Comput. Methods Program. Biomed. **208**, 106288 (2021)
5. Campagner, A., Conte, E., Cabitza, F.: Weighted Utility: a utility metric based on the case-wise raters' perceptions. In: Holzinger, A., Kieseberg, P., Tjoa, A.M., Weippl, E. (eds.) CD-MAKE 2021. LNCS, vol. 12844, pp. 203–210. Springer, Cham (2021). https://doi.org/10.1007/978-3-030-84060-0_13
6. Guo, C., Pleiss, G., Sun, G., Weinberger, K.Q.: On calibration of modern neural networks. In: International Conference on Machine Learning, pp. 1321–1330. PMLR (2017)
7. Hosmer Jr., D.W., Lemeshow, S., Sturdivant, R.X.: Applied Logistic Regression, vol. 398. John Wiley & Sons (2013)
8. Huggard, H., Sing Koh, Y., Dobbie, G., Zhang, E.: Detecting concept drift in medical triage. In: Proceedings of the 43rd International ACM SIGIR Conference on Research and Development in Information Retrieval, pp. 1733–1736 (2020)
9. Johansson, U., Löfström, T., Boström, H.: Well-calibrated and sharp interpretable multi-class models. In: Torra, V., Narukawa, Y. (eds.) MDAI 2021. LNCS (LNAI), vol. 12898, pp. 193–204. Springer, Cham (2021). https://doi.org/10.1007/978-3-030-85529-1_16
10. Lai, X., Liu, L.: A simple test procedure in standardizing the power of Hosmer-Lemeshow test in large data sets. J. Stat. Comput. Simul. **88**(13), 2463–2472 (2018)
11. Lambrou, A., Nouretdinov, I., Papadopoulos, H.: Inductive venn prediction. Ann. Math. Artif. Intell. **74**(1), 181–201 (2015)
12. Luo, R., et al.: Sample-efficient safety assurances using conformal prediction. arXiv preprint arXiv:2109.14082 (2021)
13. Niculescu-Mizil, A., Caruana, R.: Obtaining calibrated probabilities from boosting. In: UAI, vol. 5, pp. 413–20 (2005)

14. Niculescu-Mizil, A., Caruana, R.: Predicting good probabilities with supervised learning. In: Proceedings of the 22nd International Conference on Machine Learning, pp. 625–632 (2005)
15. Nixon, J., Dusenberry, M.W., Zhang, L., Jerfel, G., Tran, D.: Measuring Calibration In Deep Learning. In:CVPR Workshops, vol. 2 (2019)
16. Nobel, A.: Histogram regression estimation using data-dependent partitions. Ann. Statist. **24**(3), 1084–1105 (1996)
17. Platt, J., et al.: Probabilistic outputs for support vector machines and comparisons to regularized likelihood methods. Adv. Large Margin Classif. **10**(3), 61–74 (1999)
18. Stickland, A.C., Murray, T.: Diverse ensembles improve calibration. arXiv preprint arXiv:2007.04206 (2020)
19. Toreini, E., et al.: The relationship between trust in AI and trustworthy machine learning technologies. In Proceedings of the 2020 conference on fairness, accountability, and transparency, pp. 272–283 (2020)
20. Vaicenavicius, J., et al.: Evaluating model calibration in classification. In: The 22nd International Conference on Artificial Intelligence and Statistics, pp. 3459–3467. PMLR (2019)
21. Van Calster, G., et al.: Calibration: the achilles heel of predictive analytics. BMC Med. **17**(1), 1–7 (2019)
22. From Utopia to Empirical Data: Van Calster, B., eral.: A calibration hierarchy for risk models was defined. J. Clin. Epidemiol. **74**, 167–176 (2016)
23. Van Calster, B., Vickers, A.J.: Calibration of risk prediction models: impact on decision-analytic performance. Med. Decision making **35**(2):162–169 (2015)
24. Vovk, V.: Venn predictors and isotonic regression. CoRR abs/1211.0025 (2012)
25. Vovk, V., Fedorova, V., Nouretdinov, I., Gammerman, A.: Criteria of efficiency for conformal prediction. In: Gammerman, A., Luo, Z., Vega, J., Vovk, V. (eds.) COPA 2016. LNCS (LNAI), vol. 9653, pp. 23–39. Springer, Cham (2016). https://doi.org/10.1007/978-3-319-33395-3_2
26. Vovk, V., Gammerman, A., Shafer, G.: Algorithmic Learning in a Random World. Springer, New York (2005). https://doi.org/10.1007/b106715
27. Vovk, V., Petej, I.: Venn-Abers predictors. arXiv preprint arXiv:1211.0025 (2012)
28. Wald, Y., Feder, Greenfeld, D., Shalit, U.: On calibration and out-of-domain generalization. Adv. Neural Inf. Process. Syst. **34** (2021)
29. Wenger, J., Kjellström, H., Triebel, R.: Non-parametric calibration for classification. In: International Conference on Artificial Intelligence and Statistics, pp. 178–190. PMLR (2020)
30. Zadrozny, B., Elkan, C.: Transforming classifier scores into accurate multiclass probability estimates. In: Proceedings of the eighth ACM SIGKDD International Conference on Knowledge Discovery and Data Mining, pp. 694–699 (2002)

An Analysis of Byzantine-Tolerant Aggregation Mechanisms on Model Poisoning in Federated Learning

Mary Roszel$^{(\boxtimes)}$, Robert Norvill, and Radu State

University of Luxembourg, 29 Avenue John F. Kennedy, 1855 Luxembourg,
Luxembourg
{mary.roszel,robert.norvill,radu.state}@uni.lu

Abstract. Federated learning is a distributed setting where multiple participants jointly train a machine learning model without exchanging data. Recent work has found that federated learning is vulnerable to backdoor model poisoning attacks, where an attacker leverages the unique environment to submit malicious model updates. To address these malicious participants, several Byzantine-Tolerant aggregation methods have been applied to the federated learning setting, including Krum, Multi-Krum, RFA, and Norm-Difference Clipping. In this work, we analyze the effectiveness and limits of each aggregation method and provide a thorough analysis of their success in various fixed-frequency attack settings. Further, we analyze the fairness of such aggregation methods on the success of the model on its intended tasks. Our results indicate that only one defense can successfully mitigate attacks in all attack scenarios, but a significant fairness issue is observed, highlighting the issues with preventing malicious attacks in a federated setting.

1 Introduction

Federated Learning is an emerging distributed machine learning (ML) setting where multiple clients can collaboratively train an ML model without sharing private data [16]. Typically orchestrated by a central server, federated learning follows a multi-round, multi-agent-based strategy. In each round, the server distributes a current global ML model to a random subset of participants, who then separately leverage private data to locally update the model. The updated models are sent back to the server, which aggregates the updates into a new global model. Due to its strength in allowing many participants to collaborate, federated learning has gained popularity, with applications in mobile devices [13], speech and image recognition [15], finance [14], and medicine [11].

The crux of federated learning lies in the fact that no single entity owns or verifies the training data that participants utilize to train model updates. However, many scholars have shown that federated learning is still vulnerable to adversarial attacks [1,2,4,7,8,21]. As federated learning allows an attacker to have access to the modeling process, attackers can leverage model poisoning

V. Torra and Y. Narukawa (Eds.): MDAI 2022, LNAI 13408, pp. 143–155, 2022.
https://doi.org/10.1007/978-3-031-13448-7_12

in a federated environment to significantly impact the performance of a global model. One way this can be done is through the insertion of backdoors during the learning process, where the goal is to corrupt the global model to lead to a misclassification of a *specific* task, rather than affecting the performance of the entire model. Model poisoning greatly outperforms traditional data poisoning and is of great concern among federated learning researchers [8].

Along with this increase in concern about model poisoning has been an increase in research on methods to defend and harden federated learning systems against adversarial attacks through alternative aggregation mechanisms. However, many of these mechanisms can be circumvented by sophisticated attacks [1,6,7,20,21], and as such creating robust federated learning against model poisoning attacks is an open problem. While the majority of works focus on how attackers can circumvent specific defenses, there are no current works that address the performance of such defenses on model poisoning in general.

In this work, we aim to provide an analysis of the behavior of byzantine aggregation mechanisms against model poisoning in a federated learning setting. In particular, we analyze the performance of popular defenses such as Krum, Multi-Krum [3], Norm-Difference Clipping [20], and RFA [18], and conduct model poisoning within federated learning environments under various adversarial settings. These defenses are chosen due to their applicability and strength in defending federated learning systems.

2   Background

2.1   Federated Learning

Federated Learning is a machine learning (ML) setting where the training of a model is distributed across multiple clients to create a collaborative or global model [16]. Generally orchestrated by a central server S, federated learning follows a multi-round, multi-agent based strategy. The system consists of K participants, each with access to private data. In each round t, the server distributes a global model w^t to a random subset of participants' k, who then separately leverage private data to locally train updated models l^{t+1}. Each participant separately and concurrently sends the difference between the current global model and their updated model back to the server, which updates the global model through aggregation $w^{t+1} = w_t + \frac{\eta}{K} \sum_{i=1}^{k} (l_i^{t+1} - w^t)$ where η is the server learning rate. Local data is never shared with server S, nor with other participants.

2.2   Byzantine-Tolerant Aggregation

Federated learning relies on aggregation rules to combine local model parameters into global model parameters. The most basic aggregation rules work through averaging local model parameters but rely on the assumption that all participants are honest. An attacker can take advantage of simple aggregation rules to compromise worker devices [3,22], or model updates [1,2,6], compromising the global model for all participants. Recent work has focused on the development of Byzantine-Tolerant aggregation rules, where the goal is to ensure convergence in the presence of Byzantine participants [3,4,20,22]. However, many of these byzantine-robust methods assume that the attacker intends to prevent *convergence* of the model, which is not the case in a backdoor attack scenario.

Krum and Multi-Krum. Krum and Multi-Krum are alternative byzantine aggregation methods that intend to tolerate Byzantine participants in a distributed setting by selecting fewer models for aggregation, attempting to exclude malicious participants [3]. In Krum, only one of the participants' local models is chosen to be used as the global model. It is designed to tolerate c compromised participants out of n. For each round, the pairwise distances between all local models submitted are computed. Then, the server sums up the $n - c - 2$ closest distances, and the model with the lowest sum is chosen as the global model for the next round. Multi-Krum is a variation of Krum where instead of one model being chosen, the top $m = n - c$ models are chosen to be averaged into a new global model.

Norm-Difference Clipping. This method relies on the theory that malicious models are likely to produce large norms and that a simple clipping defense could thwart attackers [20]. Norm-difference clipping works by examining the norm-difference of local models submitted to the server, as compared to the current global model, and clipping model updates that have a norm difference larger than threshold M.

RFA. The RFA aggregation mechanism uses a modified method to compute a weighted geometric median using the *smoothed Weiszfeld's algorithm* [18].

2.3   Related Work

Many recent works have discovered methods to insert backdoors in Federated Learning using *model poisoning*. In federated learning, this is conducted with the aim of causing the global model to misclassify a set of chosen inputs while maintaining high accuracy in the original classification tasks. The first of such works demonstrated that model poisoning was effective in a federated learning system, utilizing a novel method to allow the attacker to send back *any* model they want to be aggregated into the global model, known as *model replacement* [1]. Similarly, Bhagoji et al. proposed a modification that leveraged boosting to increase the learning rate of the backdoor inputs [2]. Further, Wang et al. proposed a method of inserting edge-case backdoors, further demonstrating that the federated learning settings are vulnerable to both model poisoning and model replacement attacks [21].

3   Threat Model

We assume that the attacker has control over the local training process and system of one random participant, including training data, hyperparameters, and training process. We assume that attackers are singular entities and are not working toward a common goal with other participants. We assume that all other participants are behaving honestly and correctly. In all experiments, we limit the scenario to having no more than one attacker per round. The attacker does not have access to the training data of other participants, nor does it know their identities. The attacker does not have control of the server and does not control the defense mechanism utilized to aggregate local models into a new global model each round.

3.1 Backdoor Attacks

For consistency with previous work in the domain, our threat model is inspired by existing literature [1, 20, 21]. We consider backdoor attacks, where an attacker aims to manipulate the performance of a model on a particular subtask (hereby called the 'attack task') while maintaining high accuracy on the model's intended tasks (hereby called the 'main tasks'). The main goal of the attacker is to manipulate the federated learning system to produce a global model that performs with high accuracy on the model's intended tasks as well as an attacker-chosen subtask. For example, a given model's intended task may be to correctly classify pictures of animals or numbers. In these scenarios, the attack task may be to classify pictures of cats as birds, or the number '6' as the number '2', without impacting the model's performance on its original tasks. By maintaining high accuracy on the model's main tasks, it is more likely that the attack task will go unnoticed.

3.2 Model Replacement

We consider attacks *with* and *without* model replacement. In scenarios *without* model replacement, the attacker trains the current global model with their data to achieve high accuracy in both the main tasks and the chosen attack task. The poisoned model is submitted to the server and aggregated into the global model, according to the associated aggregation method.

Alternatively, in model replacement scenarios, the attacker aims to replace the global model with any model of their choice. Model replacement occurs in conjunction with the backdoor attack. Generally, this can be achieved through a weight re-scaling method, where the attacker re-scales the weights of the global model to resubmit as an adversarial model along with their goals. In this paper, we scale the weights using the constrain-and-scale technique developed by Bagdasaryan et al. [1] This approach typically requires that the attacker has knowledge about the current global model and the federated environment, and requires model convergence.

4 Experiments

4.1 Experimental Setup

Our simulated federated learning environment is modeled after [16]. The setup consists of K clients, each with access to data. This data is not shared with the server S. For each federated learning round t, the server randomly selects a subset of clients k and provides the current global model to each. Participants' conduct local model training separately and compute a model update. Each participant sends back updated model weights to the server for aggregation.

Table 1. Parameters for experimental set up including datasets and model type used.

Experiment	Scenario 1 CIFAR-10	Scenario 2 EMNIST
Model	VGG-9	LeNet
Data points	50,000	341, 873
Classes	10	10
Clients K	3,383	200
Clients per round k	10	10
Epochs E	2	5
Learning rate	0.2	0.1

We conduct experiments on the effectiveness and limits of Byzantine-tolerant aggregation mechanisms on preventing attacks by adversaries in a federated environment. We consider four different aggregation mechanisms (Krum, Multi-Krum, RFA, and Norm-Difference Clipping), compared to a setting where no defense and the standard aggregation method is used, Federated Averaging [12].

We explore the impact of the frequency of adversarial attacks, particularly measuring fixed-attack frequencies of one attack per round (i.e. an attack every round), one attack every 5 rounds, and one attack every 10 rounds. We consider situations where only one random client is the attacker. As a baseline, we provide a comparison to a setting with no adversaries. In these settings, hereby called a 'no attack' scenario, we still provide an analysis on the behavior of the attack task. This serves to ensure that the attack task does not naturally increase in accuracy through normal model training. For comparison purposes, our experiments utilize the same data and experimental setups utilized by previous work in the domain [1,20,21], and the values of all hyperparameters can be found in Table 1. For all experiments, the subset of clients k is set to 10 (i.e. 10 clients participate per round), and the number of federated rounds t is set to 500. All experiments are implemented in PyTorch [17]. We run experiments on a server with two NVidia Tesla K80 GPUs and 132 GB of RAM.

4.2 Datasets and Learning Models

As the goal of our paper is limited to analyzing the defense characteristics of aggregation mechanisms and not to introducing novel datasets or poisoning attacks, we consider poisoned datasets used previously in the literature [2,20,21].

Experiment Scenario 1 focuses on image classification using the CIFAR-10 dataset [9]. We replicate the experimental setup in [21], where photos of Southwest Airline planes are collected and poisoned to be labeled 'truck'. In total, there are 784 and 196 examples in the training and test sets. We utilize the VGG-9 model [19], beginning with a model with 77.53% accuracy. The model is initialized with a learning rate of 0.2 for two epochs.

Experiment Scenario 2 focuses on digit classification. In this experiment, we utilize the EMNIST [5] and ARDIS [10] datasets. We prepare the data and the model in the same way as [21]. For the non-malicious participants, there are 660 images used for training. For malicious participants, 66 images of the number '7' are labeled '1' and mixed with 100 randomly sampled images from the EMNIST dataset. For evaluation, 1000 images from the ARDIS dataset are used. We utilize the LeNet-5 architecture for image classification as in the PyTorch MNIST example[1]. The model is initialized with a model with 88% accuracy, with a learning rate of 0.1 for five epochs.

4.3   Experimental Fairness

In general, Byzantine-tolerant aggregation methods focus primarily upon ensuring the convergence of the model in the presence of adversaries. However, this does not directly imply that the aggregation method will be fair. Indeed, some aggregation methods have been found to negatively impact the main performance of the model [3, 21].

We consider the algorithm 'fair' if the success of the main task is left unhindered while the defense is deployed, and 'unfair' if the defense has a significant negative impact on the success of the algorithms main tasks, regardless of whether or not the defense was successful at mitigating a potential attack. Further, a 'fair' model should accurately classify all tasks consistently, without misclassifying one or more tasks (i.e. if the algorithm classifies 1 task incorrectly consistently, it is not a fair algorithm).

To measure the impact of this fairness concern, we utilize the **Accuracy Parity** (AP) ratio as formulated in [21]. This ratio measures the fairness of the model on each task. As formulated, we calculate AP ratio as $APratio = \frac{p_{min}}{p_{max}}$. A classifier satisfies AP if $p_i = p_j$ for all pairs i, j where p_i is the accuracy of class i. This metric would equal 1 if perfect parity exists (i.e. all classes are measured correctly), and 0 only if one or more class is completely misclassified.

5   Experimental Results

The results of Experiment Scenario 1 and 2 are displayed in Fig. 1 and 2. The accuracy rates of the attack task can be found in Tables 2 and 3.

In all cases, the main model is unaffected by the backdoor poisoning method, and an increase in the accuracy of the backdoor task is noted. This indicates that the poisoning method was successful in poisoning only a specific subtask and maintaining high accuracy on the model's intended tasks. For both datasets, there is no accuracy growth observed for the attack task in the 'no attack' scenario, indicating that the rise of the attack task is in fact due to the backdoor

---

[1] https://github.com/pytorch/examples/tree/master/mnist.

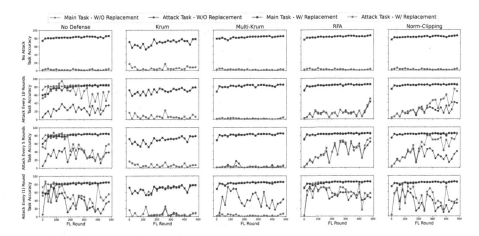

Fig. 1. Experiment Scenario 1: accuracy of model performance on the main and attack tasks under the four attack settings and five defense scenarios.

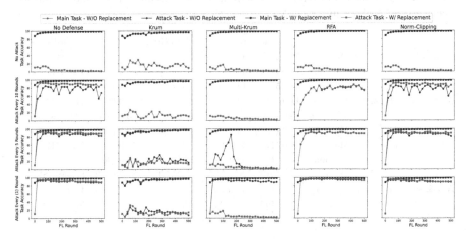

Fig. 2. Experiment Scenario 2: accuracy of model performance on the main and attack tasks under the four attack settings and five defense scenarios.

attack. Further, as expected, the frequency of the attack highly impacts its success, with more frequent attacks resulting in higher attack task accuracy. In regards to model replacement, in all cases, there is a clear delimitation between the effectiveness of defenses with and without model replacement. The effectiveness of mitigation of model replacement by each defense method is detailed in the following sections.

5.1 Aggregation Mechanisms and Defenses

No Defense. For comparison purposes, we first observe scenarios where the standard aggregation method is used (Federated Averaging). This is considered

Table 2. Experiment Scenario 1: without model replacement (with model replacement). Attack task accuracy percentages for all scenarios.

		No defense	Krum	Multi-Krum	RFA	Norm-Difference
No attack	Minimum	0.0 (0)	0.0 (0)	0.0 (0)	0.0 (0)	0.0 (0)
	Maximum	11.1 (11.1)	43.9 (43.9)	15.6 (15.6)	10.6 (10.6)	10.0 (10)
	Mean	2.2 (2.2)	6.4 (6.4)	2.1 (2.1)	2.1 (2.1)	2.0 (2)
Attack every 10 rounds	Minimum	0.0 (2.2)	0.0 (0)	0.0 (0)	0.0 (0)	0.0 (0)
	Maximum	44.4 (94.4)	45.6 (45.6)	17.8 (11.7)	42.2 (49.4)	43.9 (73.9)
	Mean	11.4 (33.3)	6.2 (6.2)	1.8 (1.6)	8.2 (8.5)	10.0 (13.4)
Attack every 5 rounds	Minimum	0.0 (1.1)	0.0 (0)	0.0 (0)	0.0 (0)	0.0 (0)
	Maximum	58.9 (92.8)	55.0 (55)	39.4 (12.8)	70.6 (75.6)	61.1 (83.3)
	Mean	20.7 (39.7)	6.0 (6)	3.0 (2.2)	23.7 (25.7)	18.7 (28.2)
Attack every (1) round	Minimum	1.1 (2.2)	0.0 (0)	0.0 (0)	2.8 (1.1)	1.7 (1.1)
	Maximum	74.4 (93.3)	53.9 (53.9)	75.0 (14.4)	77.8 (85)	71.7 (86.7)
	Mean	34.8 (53.6)	6.8 (5.6)	41.4 (2.1)	52.2 (57)	35.0 (47.9)

Table 3. Experiment Scenario 2: without model replacement (with model replacement). Attack task accuracy percentages for all scenarios.

		No defense	Krum	Multi-Krum	RFA	Norm-Difference
No attack	Minimum	2.0 (2)	3.0 (3)	1.0 (1)	2.0 (2)	2.0 (2)
	Maximum	17.0 (17)	42.0 (42)	23.0 (23)	20.0 (20)	17.0 (17)
	Mean	5.1 (5.1)	14.8 (14.8)	5.4 (5.4)	6.4 (6.4)	5.1 (5.1)
Attack every 10 rounds	Minimum	11.0 (11)	2.0 (2)	2.0 (2)	11.0 (11)	11.0 (11)
	Maximum	93.0 (100)	40.0 (40)	23.0 (23)	93.0 (93)	93.0 (99)
	Mean	81.9 (90.8)	12.8 (12.8)	5.4 (5.4)	79.0 (79.5)	81.6 (89.2)
Attack every 5 rounds	Minimum	11.0 (11)	3.0 (3)	2.0 (2)	11.0 (11)	11.0 (11)
	Maximum	95.0 (100)	54.0 (50)	96.0 (18)	95.0 (96)	95.0 (99)
	Mean	87.5 (91.8)	20.6 (15.7)	20.3 (5.4)	87.9 (88.2)	87.6 (90.8)
Attack every (1) round	Minimum	11.0 (11)	4.0 (4)	9.0 (2)	11.0 (11)	11.0 (11)
	Maximum	97.0 (100)	55.0 (62)	97.0 (19)	98.0 (98)	97.0 (99)
	Mean	90.8 (92.6)	16.6 (13.8)	91.3 (5.6)	94.9 (95.6)	90.9 (92.3)

a scenario where there is no defense for an adversarial attack, as this aggregation method simply averages the contributions of all participants, including the malicious participant.

In both cases, where there is no defense, and no attack, the attack task maintains low accuracy while the main task maintains a stable, high accuracy rate. This is expected behavior and indicates that the model is not poisoned at the start and that it improves over time through iterations. However, in each case where an attack is observed (every 10 rounds, 5 rounds, and each round), an increase in the success of the attack task is observed, with model replacement typically resulting in higher success rates. An increase in the success of the attack task is observed in both scenarios, with more frequent attacks typically resulting in higher attack task accuracy rates.

Overall, these results indicate that 1) the attack task is successful in both cases, and 2) the experimental setup is robust enough to measure the success of the defenses on a basic model poisoning scenario. Where there is no attack, the consistent observation of low attack task accuracy indicates that our setup is robust enough to measure the impact of an attack on both main and attack task accuracy. Further, this provides a benchmark of comparison for the effectiveness of the byzantine defenses on decreasing attack success.

Krum. Overall, the Krum defense is successful in defending against the attack task in every case. Even in the most aggressive case, it protects against the attack task, maintaining a low accuracy (below 40% in all cases), with less than 20% accuracy observed after 500 rounds. This is observed in both cases with and without model replacement. However, the Krum method negatively impacts the performance of the model even where there is no attack. A notable decrease in the performance of the main tasks is observed in all cases. This is likely due to the protocol choosing only one local model to use as the global model, decreasing the information gained in each round. This issue will be discussed further in Sect. 5.2.

Multi-Krum. As an extension to Krum, Multi-Krum produces similar results. In all cases, Multi-Krum successfully defends against model replacement scenarios, where the attack task accuracy is kept below 20% throughout all 500 rounds. In scenarios without model replacement, Multi-Krum fails in three cases.

In the first scenario, Multi-Krum can defend against attacks successfully up to an attack every round. When an attack is observed every round without model replacement, the accuracy of the attack task oscillates throughout the 500 rounds, with a minimum accuracy of 0% and maximum accuracy of 75%. The defense is overall not effective, as a steady increase is observed in the attack task accuracy to 47.2% at 500 rounds, with a mean accuracy across all rounds of 41.36%. A similar trend is observed in scenario 2 in regards to protecting from attacks with low frequency and failing to defend where an attack is conducted each round. However, with a frequency of five attacks per round, the accuracy of the attack task rapidly increases to nearly 40% by round 200, where it appears Multi-Krum detected and eliminated the attack within the provided 500 rounds.

RFA. RFA is not successful in completely mitigating attacks in any case but does indicate some effectiveness in protecting against model replacement attacks. In all experiments without model replacement, RFA does not succeed in decreasing the effectiveness of the attack, often actually increasing the overall accuracy of the attack task. It appears that this defense is particularly weak to aggressive (frequent) attacks, where the success of the attack task increases even more aggressively than observed in the no-defense scenario.

However, RFA does show moderate success in the case of model replacement. At first glance, the success of RFA appears consistent between replacement and non-replacement scenarios, as we observe nearly equal attack task accuracy levels in all sets of experiments. However, as model replacement is generally deemed as more aggressive, this equality indicates that RFA is more robust against replacement attacks. Indeed, RFA greatly decreases the success of the attack in model replacement scenarios that without a defense were observed to excel immediately. For example, in scenario 1 the mean attack success decreased from 33.3% and 39.7% with no defense to 8.5% and 25.6% with RFA, for attacks every 10 and 5 rounds respectively. From these experiments, it appears that RFA does not aid in scenarios without replacement in decreasing attack task accuracy, often increasing it in more aggressive scenarios. Further, while RFA is not as successful as Krum and Multi-Krum, there is no impact of the method on the overall success of the main tasks.

Norm-Difference Clipping. The norm-difference clipping defense produces similar results as RFA. The most notable difference between the two is that norm-difference clipping does not exhibit the same behavior of increasing the effectiveness of the attack in any case.

Considering scenarios without model replacement, in all cases utilizing the norm-difference clipping defense, we observe attack task accuracy rates that are nearly identical to those observed in the no defense scenario (Tables 2 and 3). However, this defense was successful in decreasing the success of attacks aided with model replacement, with varying degrees of success.

5.2   Defense Fairness

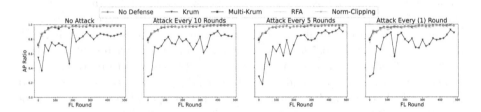

Fig. 3. AP ratio under each aggregation mechanism in Scenario 2.

Our scenarios focus on backdoor attacks, where the goal of the attacker is to increase the accuracy of a poisoned sub-task while maintaining high accuracy on the models' main tasks. In all cases, this assumption is confirmed. However, there are some fairness concerns in respect to defenses impacting the accuracy of the main tasks, even when there is no attack. Utilizing AP Ratio, we can observe the fairness of the algorithm in correctly classifying the intended input (Fig. 3). Here, we only show the results of Scenario 2, however, these results are similar to those observed in Scenario 1.

In all cases, the AP ratios of no defense, Multi-Krum, RFA, and Norm-Difference Clipping are observed as higher than the AP ratios observed under Krum. This indicates a problem with the fairness of Krum. This can also be readily observed in the accuracy values of the main tasks. In the case of the first scenario, a significant decrease in the accuracy of the main tasks is observed. While the model should have an accuracy over 80%, the main tasks are observed to have accuracy below 70%, with an average accuracy of 69% in all cases. This effect is less pronounced but still present in the second scenario, where the main model accuracy drops to 93% on average. While the Krum defense is the most effective at mitigating attacks, it is the only defense that produces this behavior.

In an environment where the accuracy of the model is already low, such as scenario 1, this decrease in the success of the model on its intended tasks could have significant detrimental impacts on the model performance and cause it to be completely ineffective for legitimate use. Although it is a variation of Krum, Multi-Krum does not exhibit this flaw. This is likely because choosing more than one model allows for richness in the global model throughout rounds. Users should consider this fairness concern while utilizing Krum in regards to their specific use case.

6   Discussion and Conclusion

It has been well established here, and in the literature, that model poisoning is a significant concern in a federated learning environment. An attacker can manipulate the global model to produce high accuracy on hidden tasks while maintaining appropriate behavior on main tasks, potentially exposing federated participants to manipulated models that produce an undesired result.

However, defending against these attacks is a difficult task. We have demonstrated that current byzantine defenses, such as Krum, Multi-Krum, RFA, and Norm-Difference Clipping, have inconsistent effectiveness in defending against backdoor attacks. The results of our experiments indicate that Krum is the most effective at mitigating attacks, followed by Multi-Krum, RFA, and Norm-Difference Clipping. All defenses perform better than a no-defense scenario, indicating success in protecting against backdoor attacks.

However, while Krum has the most success mitigating against malicious attackers in a backdoor attack scenario, it has a negative impact on the main model, calling into question the fairness of such a defense. Multi-Krum does not share this same fairness concern, indicating that it may be a better defense for all cases except those with the most aggressive attacks, where Multi-Krum may not damage the main model but could fail to prevent attacks.

This work has highlighted that the current aggregation methods cannot adequately prevent model poisoning attacks without affecting the main performance of the model. This indicates that further work is needed to harden federated learning against attacks, especially where the joint model is used in sensitive areas, such as health care. Alternative aggregation methods may provide more thorough protection without hindering the success of the model.

References

1. Bagdasaryan, E., Veit, A., Hua, Y., Estrin, D., Shmatikov, V.: How to backdoor federated learning. In: International Conference on Artificial Intelligence and Statistics, pp. 2938–2948. PMLR (2020)
2. Bhagoji, A.N., Chakraborty, S., Mittal, P., Calo, S.: Analyzing federated learning through an adversarial lens. In: International Conference on Machine Learning, pp. 634–643. PMLR (2019)
3. Blanchard, P., El Mhamdi, E.M., Guerraoui, R., Stainer, J.: Machine learning with adversaries: Byzantine tolerant gradient descent. In: Proceedings of the 31st International Conference on Neural Information Processing Systems (2017)
4. Chen, Y., Su, L., Xu, J.: Distributed statistical machine learning in adversarial settings: Byzantine gradient descent. Proc. ACM Measur. Anal. Comput. Syst. $1(2)$, 1–25 (2017)
5. Cohen, G., Afshar, S., Tapson, J., Van Schaik, A.: EMNIST: extending MNIST to handwritten letters. In: 2017 International Joint Conference on Neural Networks (IJCNN), pp. 2921–2926. IEEE (2017)
6. Fang, M., Cao, X., Jia, J., Gong, N.: Local model poisoning attacks to Byzantine-Robust federated learning. In: 29th USENIX Security Symposium (USENIX Security 2020), pp. 1605–1622 (2020)
7. Fung, C., Yoon, C.J., Beschastnikh, I.: Mitigating sybils in federated learning poisoning. arXiv preprint arXiv:1808.04866 (2018)
8. Kairouz, P., et al.: Advances and open problems in federated learning. arXiv preprint arXiv:1912.04977 (2019)
9. Krizhevsky, A., Hinton, G., et al.: Learning multiple layers of features from tiny images (2009)
10. Kusetogullari, H., Yavariabdi, A., Cheddad, A., Grahn, H., Johan, H.: ARDIS: a Swedish historical handwritten digit dataset. Neural Comput. Appl. **32**(21), 16505–16518 (2020). https://doi.org/10.1007/s00521-019-04163-3
11. Li, L., Fan, Y., Tse, M., Lin, K.Y.: A review of applications in federated learning. Comput. Ind. Eng. **149**, 106854 (2020)
12. Li, X., Huang, K., Yang, W., Wang, S., Zhang, Z.: On the convergence of FedAvg on Non-IID data. arXiv preprint arXiv:1907.02189 (2019)
13. Lim, W.Y.B., et al.: Federated learning in mobile edge networks: a comprehensive survey. IEEE Commun. Surv. Tutor. **22**(3), 2031–2063 (2020)
14. Long, G., Tan, Y., Jiang, J., Zhang, C.: Federated learning for open banking. In: Yang, Q., Fan, L., Yu, H. (eds.) Federated Learning. LNCS (LNAI), vol. 12500, pp. 240–254. Springer, Cham (2020). https://doi.org/10.1007/978-3-030-63076-8_17
15. Luo, J., et al.: Real-world image datasets for federated learning. arXiv preprint arXiv:1910.11089 (2019)
16. McMahan, B., Moore, E., Ramage, D., Hampson, S., Aguera y Arcas, B.: Communication-efficient learning of deep networks from decentralized data. In: Artificial Intelligence and Statistics, pp. 1273–1282. PMLR (2017)
17. Paszke, A., et al.: PyTorch: an imperative style, high-performance deep learning library. In: Advances in Neural Information Processing Systems, vol. 32, pp. 8026–8037 (2019)
18. Pillutla, K., Kakade, S.M., Harchaoui, Z.: Robust aggregation for federated learning. arXiv preprint arXiv:1912.13445 (2019)
19. Simonyan, K., Zisserman, A.: Very deep convolutional networks for large-scale image recognition. arXiv preprint arXiv:1409.1556 (2014)

20. Sun, Z., Kairouz, P., Suresh, A.T., McMahan, H.B.: Can you really backdoor federated learning? arXiv preprint arXiv:1911.07963 (2019)
21. Wang, H., et al.: Attack of the tails: yes, you really can backdoor federated learning. arXiv preprint arXiv:2007.05084 (2020)
22. Yin, D., Chen, Y., Kannan, R., Bartlett, P.: Byzantine-robust distributed learning: towards optimal statistical rates. In: International Conference on Machine Learning, pp. 5650–5659. PMLR (2018)

Effective Early Stopping of Point Cloud Neural Networks

Thanasis Zoumpekas[1]([✉]) [iD], Maria Salamó[1,2] [iD], and Anna Puig[1,3] [iD]

[1] WAI Research Group, Department of Mathematics and Computer Science,
University of Barcelona, Barcelona, Spain
{thanasis.zoumpekas,maria.salamo,annapuig}@ub.edu
[2] UBICS Institute, University of Barcelona, Barcelona, Spain
[3] IMUB Institute, University of Barcelona, Barcelona, Spain

Abstract. Early stopping techniques can be utilized to decrease the time cost, however currently the ultimate goal of early stopping techniques is closely related to the accuracy upgrade or the ability of the neural network to generalize better on unseen data without being large or complex in structure and not directly with its efficiency. Time efficiency is a critical factor in neural networks, especially when dealing with the segmentation of 3D point cloud data, not only because a neural network itself is computationally expensive, but also because point clouds are large and noisy data, making learning processes even more costly. In this paper, we propose a new early stopping technique based on fundamental mathematics aiming to upgrade the trade-off between the learning efficiency and accuracy of neural networks dealing with 3D point clouds. Our results show that by employing our early stopping technique in four distinct and highly utilized neural networks in segmenting 3D point clouds, the training time efficiency of the models is greatly improved, with efficiency gain values reaching up to 94%, while the models achieving in just a few epochs approximately similar segmentation accuracy metric values like the ones that are obtained in the training of the neural networks in 200 epochs. Also, our proposal outperforms four conventional early stopping approaches in segmentation accuracy, implying a promising innovative early stopping technique in point cloud segmentation.

Keywords: Deep learning · Point clouds · Segmentation · Efficiency · Early stopping

1 Introduction

Since the popularity and the demand in 3D point cloud data analysis is constantly increasing, the rigorous evaluation of intelligent techniques dealing with such data is becoming a need. In particular, the appearance of 3D sensors, such as LIDAR and RGB-D cameras, among others, has favoured the creation of 3D-representations of areas (e.g., map) or objects (e.g., car). The set of data points

© The Author(s), under exclusive license to Springer Nature Switzerland AG 2022
V. Torra and Y. Narukawa (Eds.): MDAI 2022, LNAI 13408, pp. 156–167, 2022.
https://doi.org/10.1007/978-3-031-13448-7_13

in the x, y and z coordinated 3D space appearing in these 3D-representations is called point cloud and represents a 3D shape or object. Their speciality is derived by their noisy and irregular nature and because of this, analysis tasks, such as segmentation, that are common to deal efficiently and effectively in the 2D data domain, portray additional challenges in terms of efficiency and robustness in 3D.

Neural Networks (NN) are the most suitable machine learning algorithms to segment point cloud data due to their ability to handle and take advantage of the huge amount of points (i.e. millions in most cases) that a 3D point cloud dataset contains [2]. Different NN architectures have been proposed recently to segment inner structures of point cloud [11,12,14]. However, recent studies show that training and evaluating these models are a greatly time-consuming task and, in some cases, the number of epochs and time spend is not proportional to the accuracy achieved [18,19]. Indeed, in this process, it is important not just to solely upgrade the accuracy-related metrics of the learning, such as accuracy, precision, recall or F1-score, but also to achieve a balance between efficiency and accuracy [19].

In this paper, we concentrate on 3D point cloud part segmentation analysis and on the upgrade of the trade-off between segmentation accuracy and efficiency of the learning process of NN models. By employing fundamental mathematical methodologies, we propose an algorithmic way that defines an early stopping criterion on the learning process of the models which aims to finish the learning process at an early point but maintaining an accurate enough model for making predictions on the test data. Our results show that by employing our early stopping technique to four of the most well-known neural networks in point cloud segmentation, the trade-off between training time efficiency and segmentation accuracy of the models is greatly improved. The models achieve in just a few epochs comparable segmentation accuracy metric values to the ones obtained in the training of the NN. Besides, the comparison with four conventional early stopping techniques in terms of obtained accuracy and loss analysis indicates that our proposal is a promising novel technique of early stopping in the NN models dealing with point cloud segmentation.

2 Related Work

The study of the ways to enhance the learning process of NN models to achieve higher accuracy and efficiency are major open issues. In the point cloud segmentation field, there are numerous studies dealing with advancements in the architectures or the learning parameters of the developed models to achieve higher segmentation accuracy [2,6,8,17]. However, research must go beyond pure accuracy-metrics and another open issue of utmost importance is the efficiency of such deep learning models dealing with 3D point clouds, although it is still in its early steps of research. Recent studies highlight that the efficiency of 3D point cloud segmentation models is a serious concern for the community [5,17,19]. However, the majority of new and advanced deep learning models emphasize on the improvement of segmentation accuracy, providing almost no information on the models' efficiency [7,9,12,13].

On the other hand, certain techniques of early stopping of the neural networks are utilized to handle either specific learning issues or time efficiency in the training phase. Caruana et al. [3] showed that when huge neural networks have learnt models that are similar to those learned by smaller ones, early stopping can be employed to stop their training process without significant loss in generalization performance.

Specifically, early stopping aims to stop the optimization of the training process of a neural network at an early stage in order to, firstly, mitigate the performance issues caused by overfitting, such as loss of generalization of the network, and secondly to improve the training time cost, i.e. time efficiency [10]. While there are many strategies for dealing with overfitting issues, such as regularization, network-reduction strategy, or data expansion, the early stopping techniques are the most used ones [16]. Data science researchers mostly utilize early stopping techniques based on a threshold monitoring a loss function's values [1,10]. For instance, the stopping of training when the error on the validation data is higher than the one recorded in the previous epoch or epochs. Although, the aforementioned technique is theoretically correct, there is always more than one local minimum in real validation error curves and, thus several stopping criteria utilize windows (or fixed intervals of epochs) capturing the evolution of validation error are employed in order to deal with this [10]. Recently, Bai et al. [1] proposed a progressive early stopping technique, in which they split a neural network into multiple parts and train them individually. Rather than employing traditional early stopping techniques, which require training the entire neural network at once, they train and optimize parts of a neural network by using early stopping criteria in those parts.

In summary, the majority of the related works propose early stopping techniques aiming to deal with learning issues of the models, such as overfitting, in order to lead to higher accuracy values in unseen data (test data), i.e. improve the model's generalization performance. They either rely on the whole network learning process (traditional early stopping) or in specific areas and segments of the NN (progressive early stopping). However, at the time of writing this paper, there are no studies dealing with early stopping of the models with a goal to provide a more efficient, in terms of time, learning process but also a highly accurate model. Thus, in an attempt to fill this gap we propose an effective early stopping aiming to get a model in a state that is highly accurate but also having spent a low amount of time in its training (efficient in run-time). For this, our approach focuses on the segmentation accuracy-related performance metrics instead of the loss function values (see Sect. 3). We categorize our study in the traditional early stopping techniques, mainly because we do not split the architecture of the utilized neural networks into smaller parts.

3   Early Stopping of Point Cloud Neural Networks

This section presents, first, our early stopping criteria, and then, the algorithmic way to select the early stopping of the learning process of the models.

3.1   Early Stopping Criteria

We propose an automatic and online way of stopping the learning process of a point cloud part segmentation task based on the analysis of a stop-window containing the values of a monitored performance metric. Please, note that the monitored performance metric can be any segmentation accuracy-related metric. However, we have selected the $ImIoU$, i.e. the mean value of IoU across all point cloud Instances, explained in [9], because it provides a general segmentation accuracy evaluation across all the available point cloud instances. For completeness, $ImIoU = \frac{\sum_{k=1}^{n} IoU_k}{n}$, where n denotes the number of instances and the subscript k in the sum takes values in range $[1, n]$.

Initially, performance metric values x are obtained by testing the NN in the whole test set after each training epoch. Indeed, in every epoch we train, validate and test the NN. The testing time after each epoch consists of an almost negligible cost compared to the training-validation phases, because it is a forward pass of the data to the model and, as Zhang et al. [17] showed, it is on the scale of milliseconds or even seconds.

Assuming that the performance metric values are samples that can be approximated by a continuous smooth and differentiable (monotonic) function $f(x)$ that converges to a maximum upper bound value, we can calculate the first and second derivative values of $f(x)$, being $f'(x)$ and $f''(x)$ respectively. We approximate the first and second derivatives of $f(x)$ using the formulation appearing in Eqs. 1 and 2 respectively.

$$f'(x) = \frac{f(x+h) - f(x)}{h} \quad , \tag{1}$$

$$f''(x) = \frac{f'(x+h) - f'(x)}{h} \quad , \tag{2}$$

where h is the distance between the data points. The data points are evenly spaced, because we have one performance metric value at every epoch ($h = 1$).

First, we define a **window**, w_{ij}, to be the set of sampled values of $f(x)$ in the interval (x_i, x_j), with $x_i < x_j$, and considering that $f(x_i)$, $f(x_j)$ are local maximum and minimum respectively. Please, note that x_i refers to the i-th and x_j refers to the j-th epoch. Moreover we define $size(w_{ij}) = j - i$, as the length of the interval domain, and $range(w_{ij}) = \{f(x_i) - f(x_{i+1}), ..., f(x_{j-1}) - f(x_j)\}$ the interval range vector. The $range(w_{ij})$ is defined as a vector containing all the differences between each pair of consecutive performance metric values inside the window.

The underlying function of an accuracy-related metric oscillates between local minimum and maximum values. Note that we aim to define intervals to detect when the function oscillates less and converges to a certain value. To do this we could use: (i) Fixed-size intervals (i.e. windows of fixed-size) but they are not adaptive, i.e. taking into account the oscillations of the function, (ii) Adaptive intervals, where we detect the oscillations between local minimum and maximum values to observe the amplitude of the window. Indeed, it could be between a local maximum and a local minimum. In our case, we opted for the latter. The rationale behind our decision is that by starting the stop window at a local maximum, the model reached a peak in its accuracy, thus it seems like a spot to initiate an analysis. Then, we stop at the local minimum after the local maximum, because the model reached a trough spot or alternatively a negative peak, implying that no higher accuracy can be obtained within this interval.

Fundamentally, the **local minimum** of a function can be found where the first derivative of the function is equal to zero, i.e. $f'(x) = 0$, and the second derivative in this exact spot is greater than zero, i.e. $f''(x) > 0$. The approximation of **local maximum** is likewise the same ($f'(x) = 0$) but in this case the second derivative of the function in that spot should be less than zero ($f''(x) < 0$).

Therefore, we define the **stop-window** as the window, w_{ij}, that fulfils certain conditions. In our case, we utilize the following conditions:

1. $size(w_{ij}) \geq N$, with N taking values within $[2, maxEpochs - 1]$, and
2. $\forall k \in range(w_{ij}) : |k| < D$, with D taking values in the range of $(0, 2]$.

The $size(w_{ij})$ is defined as the minimum distance in epochs between the local maximum and local minimum point. For instance, if $N = 4$, then the distance between the local maximum and local minimum should be at least 4 epochs. For clarification, the second condition implies that all the elements of the vector $range(w_{ij})$ should be less than a certain D, taking into consideration that the accuracy-related metric is measured in $[0,100]$. The first condition (i) guarantees a certain size of the window's interval to avoid noisy samples in terms of consecutive local maximums and minimums, while the second condition (ii) ensures the absence of big oscillations in the sampled values inside the window. Please note that, in our proposal we consider a maximum value of $D = 2$ to avoid extreme oscillations of values. However, the selection of N and D values is open for future experimentation.

3.2   The Selection of the Stop-Window

Following the above-mentioned mathematical foundations, we explain our proposal in Algorithm 1. The algorithm is capable of selecting a stop-window of learning during the learning process, i.e. online, where the model is accurate enough.

First, in lines 1–9 of the algorithm we initialize the variables that we will use. Specifically, min_{point} and max_{point} denote the local minimum and local maximum respectively. Also, the variable $epoch$ denotes the current epoch learning process, while $Swindow$ and $stopping$ denote the initialization of the stop-window and the stopping state shows the Boolean condition according to which we will stop the training. The *stopEpoch* variable denotes the selected epoch to stop the training process of the model. The variables D and N denote the maximum range of the window and minimum size of the window respectively. While a NN model is training after each epoch, we evaluate its performance on the test data using the *ImIoU* metric and the value is returned to $f(epoch)$ variable. By calculating the $f'(epoch)$ and $f''(epoch)$, we check if the conditions to form local minimum (code lines 13–14) and local maximum (code lines 15–16) apply. In line 17, we check for the appearance of a local maximum prior to a local minimum of the performance metric and we define a window. Finally, in lines 19–22, we check the conditions to declare a window (w) as a stop-window (*Swindow*) and then we set the window to be qualified as a stop-window. Then, we keep the epoch where the model achieved its maximum *ImIoU* value inside the *Swindow*, i.e. *stopEpoch*, otherwise we continue the training process of the NN. The function returns both the *Swindow* and *stopEpoch*.

Algorithm 1: Method of locating the Stop-window

```
1  min_point = 0;
2  max_point = 0;
3  maxEpochs = 200 // can be changed to any value
4  epoch = 0;
5  Swindow = [];
6  stopEpoch = 0 ;
7  stopping = False;
8  D = 2 // D can be changed to any value in (0,2]
9  N = 4 // N can be changed to any value in [2, max epoch - 1]
10 while (!stopping) and (epoch ≤ maxEpochs) do
11     model@epoch = training() // returns model @ current epoch
12     f(epoch) = testing(model@epoch) // performance metric evaluation
13     if f'(epoch) == 0 and f''(epoch) > 0 then
14     |   min_point = epoch // local minimum at this epoch
15     if f'(epoch) == 0 and f''(epoch) < 0 then
16     |   max_point = epoch // local maximum at this epoch
17     if max_point ¡ min_point then
18     |   w = [max_point, min_point] // w denotes a window
19     |   if (size(w) ≥ N)) and (∀k ∈ range(w) : |k| < D)) then
20     |   |   Swindow = w;
21     |   |   stopEpoch = epoch where max(f(epoch)) ∈[Swindow];
22     |   |   stopping = True;
23     |   epoch++;
24 return Swindow, stopEpoch;
```

Note that, we stop the training once the first *Swindow* is encountered. Besides, we return the *stopEpoch*, i.e. the epoch of *Swindow* in which the model achieved the best accuracy-related metric. Thus, the final model corresponds to the model trained until *stopEpoch*. It is worth-mentioning that the policy rules to select a stop-window (lines 19–22) of the code can be reformulated.

4   Evaluation

This section describes our evaluation process and findings. Initially, we provide our evaluation protocol and then we show the utilized data and models.

4.1 Evaluation Protocol

We have established a standard evaluation protocol. For the training, validating, and testing of the NN models, the split proposed by Chang et al. [4] is used. Specifically, it comprises of 12137 point clouds for training, 1870 point clouds for validation, and 2874 point clouds for testing. Regarding the parameterization of the utilized NN, we set the batch size to be 16 and the optimizer to be Adam. We also use exponential learning rate decay and batch normalization on every epoch. Finally, following each epoch's training phase, all of the NN were validated and tested.

In the parameters of our early stopping algorithm we have set $D = 2$, $N = 4$, $maxEpochs = 200$ and the monitored segmentation accuracy-related performance metric is $ImIoU$, as defined in [9].

4.2 Data and Models

To evaluate our learning stopping strategy, we use the *ShapeNet* [4,15] part segmentation data, which is one of the most utilized datasets in the field. It comprises of 16881 3D point clouds categorised in 16 distinct classes of objects.

In addition, for the analysis of data we use four accurate deep learning models in the field of 3D point cloud segmentation: (i) **PointNet** [11], (ii) **PointNet++** [12], (iii) **KPConv** [13] and (iv) **RSConv** [9]. We utilize this selection of models because it consists of models with differences in their architecture and it encapsulates distinct approaches of part-segmentation, such as multi-layer perceptrons and convolutions.

4.3 Analysis of Our Proposal

Table 1 displays the proposed stop-windows accompanied with statistical measurements monitoring the $ImIoU$ metric for each model. The proposed stop-window in each model is denoted as **Swindow**. We display the average $ImIoU$ value of the stop-window, **SwAvg**, the standard deviation of it, **SwStd** and the maximum $ImIoU$ value, **SwMax**. We further show the maximum value of $ImIoU$ achieved in the whole learning process of 200 epochs, **Max**, the ratio of **SwMax** with the **Max**, $\textbf{SwMaxRatio} = \frac{SwMax}{Max}$, i.e. 0 means highly different and 1 means no difference, and the ratio of **SwAvg** versus the **Max**, $\textbf{SwAvgRatio} = \frac{SwAvg}{Max}$.

We can observe that the models stopped in the proposed stop-windows achieve approximately the same $ImIoU$ values as the best achieved in whole learning process of 200 epochs. For instance, it can be seen that the learning of KPConv model can be stopped at any epoch inside the window of $Swindow = [10, 14]$, which has a maximum value of $SwMax = 82.80$ with a deviation of only $SwStd = 0.24$. The difference between the window's average ($SwAvg = 82.42$) and max ($SwMax = 82.80$) from the general max recorded in 200 epochs ($Max = 84.22$) are $SwMaxRatio = 0.9831$ and $SwAvgRatio = 0.9786$ respectively, indicating that the stopping of training can be done early while having

Table 1. Summary of the process of detecting stop-windows monitoring $ImIoU$.

	PointNet	PointNet++	KPConv	RSConv
Swindow (epochs)	[38, 41]	[22, 26]	[10, 14]	[12, 21]
SwAvg ($ImIoU$)	81.67	83.48	82.42	84.42
SwStd ($ImIoU$)	0.10	0.14	0.24	0.24
SwMax ($ImIoU$)	81.76	83.63	82.80	84.82
Max ($ImIoU$)	84.24	84.93	84.22	85.47
SwMaxRatio ($ImIoU$)	0.9706	0.9847	0.9831	0.9924
SwAvgRatio ($ImIoU$)	0.9695	0.9829	0.9786	0.9877

a highly accurate model (almost identical to the best $ImIoU$ obtained in 200 epochs). According to a recent performance benchmark shown in [19], KPConv needs a great amount of time to complete the learning process on ShapeNet dataset and specifically more time than its competitors.

> **Observation 1.** *The process of learning becomes way less time consuming, while the test accuracy in all the analyzed models is approximately similar to the maximum accuracy achieved in 200 epochs. Thus, by employing our stopping algorithm the process can become much more time efficient, while the models still achieve high accuracy.*

4.4   Comparison to Conventional Early Stopping Techniques

We also compare our proposal with four common early stopping techniques, which deal with the overfitting issues of the models. The cross entropy segmentation loss in being monitored in the following conventional early stopping strategies: (i) **EarlyS1:** It stops the training process of the NN when the validation loss in the current epoch is higher than in the previous one; (ii) **EarlyS2:** It stops the training process when the validation loss in the current epoch is higher than the previous one by a 5%; (iii) **EarlyS3:** A more advanced early stopping technique that considers a patience parameter. Patience refers to the number of epochs with no improvement in the monitored loss. For example a *patience* $= 5$ indicates that the training will be stopped after 5 consecutive epochs of no improvement in the validation loss. In our case, we set *patience* $= 2$; (iv) **EarlyS4:** It stops the training of the NN with *patience* $= 3$.

Table 2 shows a comparison of our proposed technique (**Our Technique**), which is the epoch that corresponds to the maximum $ImIoU \in$ Swindow, versus the four above-mentioned techniques. We denote $IMaxRatio$ the division of the obtained $ImIoU$ in each strategy (stopEpoch, EarlyS1, EarlyS2, EarlyS3, EarlyS4) with the general max of $ImIoU$ of each model obtained in 200 epochs, and shows the difference of each metric versus the maximum obtained by the model in 200 epochs, i.e. 0 means highly different and 1 means no difference. Also, we denote $EffGain = (1 - \frac{Ep}{200}) * 100$, where Ep is the epoch that we stopped

Table 2. Comparison of our proposed technique versus four conventional early stopping techniques. We use dark grey and light grey cell colors to denote the best and the second best score per metric of each row respectively.

Model	Metric	Our Technique	EarlyS1	EarlyS2	EarlyS3	EarlyS4
PointNet	$ImIoU$	81.76	75.07	79.54	78.6	77.26
	$IMaxRatio$	0.9706	0.8911	0.9406	0.9330	0.9171
	$EffGain$	Ep 39: 80.5(%)	Ep 3: 98.5(%)	Ep 18: 91(%)	Ep 14: 93(%)	Ep 15: 92.5(%)
PointNet++	$ImIoU$	83.63	78.66	76.71	80.94	83.45
	$IMaxRatio$	0.9847	0.9261	0.9032	0.9530	0.9826
	$EffGain$	Ep 26: 87(%)	Ep 3: 98.5(%)	Ep 7: 96.5(%)	Ep 11: 94.5(%)	Ep 63: 86.5(%)
KPConv	$ImIoU$	82.80	78.33	81.04	82.13	83.15
	$IMaxRatio$	0.9831	0.9301	0.9622	0.9752	0.9873
	$EffGain$	Ep 12: 94(%)	Ep 3: 98.5(%)	Ep 7: 96.5(%)	Ep 11: 94.5(%)	Ep 63: 68.5(%)
RSConv	$ImIoU$	84.82	81.84	84.42	81.87	84.82
	$IMaxRatio$	0.9924	0.9575	0.9877	0.9579	0.9924
	$EffGain$	Ep 20: 90(%)	Ep 5: 97.5(%)	Ep 21: 89.5(%)	Ep 6: 97(%)	Ep 20: 90(%)

the training according to each early stopping technique. $EffGain$ shows the efficiency gain of each model in each one of the early stopping strategies.

Observing the Table 2, we can note that in our proposed stop epoch (**SwMax**) the models achieved higher $ImIoU$ values than the models obtained from the other early stopping strategies. Regarding, the $IMaxRatio$ metric, which is the division of $ImIoU$ obtained according to each strategy with the general max of $ImIoU$ obtained in 200 epochs, our strategy (**SwMax**) comes first in almost all the models, with the exception of KPConv ($IMaxRatio = 0.9831$) in which it comes second. For example, in RSConv and PointNet++ we achieve values equal to $IMaxRatio = 0.9924$ and 0.9847 respectively, indicating almost similar $ImIoU$ values with the maximum obtained in 200 epochs. Although in the $EffGain$ metric, our strategy comes last compared to its competitors, the obtained values of $EffGain$ are pretty close to the others, with the exception the PointNet ($EffGain = 80.5\%$).

> **Observation 2.** *As the ultimate goal is to have a highly accurate model but also efficient in training time, in comparison to other techniques, our approach can be considered as the winner in selecting this model and an effective early stopping technique to be utilized in a point cloud segmentation task.*

Figure 1 shows a comparison of all the utilized early stopping strategies versus our proposal. In PointNet, we observe that our proposed stopping comes after the other early stopping techniques while achieving higher $ImIoU$ values. In the loss plot, we can see that our proposed stop-window takes place where the model starts to overfit, achieving lower loss values than its competitors. In PointNet++, we observe that our proposal behaves similar with the early stopping 4 strategy and they also detect better the spot where the overfitting of the model starts. Approximately the same behaviour appears in KPConv and RSConv models, with our proposed stop-windows competing well against their competitors.

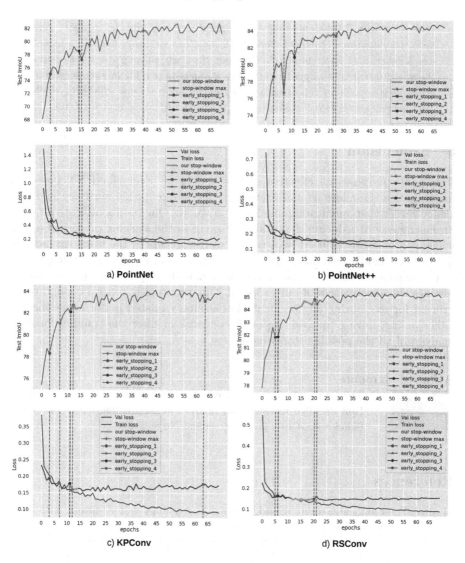

Fig. 1. Application of the conventional early stopping techniques versus our stop-window technique in four neural networks.

Observation 3. *It seems that our proposal not only provides a higher segmentation accuracy (ImIoU) model than the other strategies but also a model which generalizes better in unseen data, i.e. the cross entropy loss is lower and the model learning is stopped right before it starts to overfit. In summary, our proposal is capable of returning a model highly accurate and efficient, which also competes well with the other strategies in identifying overfitting issues.*

5   Conclusion

This paper proposes an effective early stopping of point cloud NN based on mathematical foundations and focuses on the segmentation accuracy and efficiency rather than monitoring loss function values. Our results indicate a rather promising way of reducing the total time spent in the learning process of a NN, which can be easily utilized by a variety of researchers in the field. An individual can get highly accurate point cloud segmentation results in a time-efficient way. The comparison with several conventional early stopping techniques further justifies the effectiveness of our proposal. Our proposal is general enough to be utilized for monitoring any segmentation accuracy-related performance metric, either online, during the training of the network or after the training for data analysis of all the possible stop-windows.

Acknowledgments

Marie Skłodowska-Curie
Actions

This project has received funding from European Union's Horizon 2020 research and innovation programme under the Marie Skłodowska-Curie grant agreement No 860843.

References

1. Bai, Y., et al.: Understanding and Improving early stopping for learning with noisy labels, June 2021 https://arxiv.org/abs/2106.15853v1
2. Bello, S.A., Yu, S., Wang, C., Adam, J.M., Li, J.: Review: deep learning on 3D point clouds. Remote Sens. **12**(11), 1729 (2020). https://doi.org/10.3390/rs12111729
3. Caruana, R., Lawrence, S., Giles, L.: Overfitting in neural nets: backpropagation, conjugate gradient, and early stopping. In: NIPS'00: Proceedings of the 13th International Conference on Neural Information Processing Systems (2000). https://dl.acm.org/doi/10.5555/3008751.3008807
4. Chang, A.X., et al.: ShapeNet: an information-rich 3D model repository. arXiv (12 2015), http://arxiv.org/abs/1512.03012
5. Garcia-Garcia, A., Orts-Escolano, S., Oprea, S., Villena-Martinez, V., Martinez-Gonzalez, P., Garcia-Rodriguez, J.: A survey on deep learning techniques for image and video semantic segmentation. Appl. Soft Comput. **70**, 41–65 (2018). https://doi.org/10.1016/j.asoc.2018.05.018
6. Guo, Y., Wang, H., Hu, Q., Liu, H., Liu, L., Bennamoun, M.: Deep learning for 3D point clouds: a survey. IEEE Trans. Pattern Anal. Mach. Intell. **43**(12), 4338–4364 (2021). https://doi.org/10.1109/TPAMI.2020.3005434

7. Hegde, S., Gangisetty, S.: PIG-Net: inception based deep learning architecture for 3D point cloud segmentation. Comput. Graph. (Pergamon) **95**, 13–22 (2021). https://doi.org/10.1016/j.cag.2021.01.004

8. Liu, W., Sun, J., Li, W., Hu, T., Wang, P.: Deep learning on point clouds and its application: a survey (2019). https://doi.org/10.3390/s19194188

9. Liu, Y., Fan, B., Xiang, S., Pan, C.: Relation-shape convolutional neural network for point cloud analysis (2019). https://doi.org/10.1109/CVPR.2019.00910

10. Prechelt, L.: Early stopping — but when? In: Montavon, G., Orr, G.B., Müller, K.-R. (eds.) Neural Networks: Tricks of the Trade. LNCS, vol. 7700, pp. 53–67. Springer, Heidelberg (2012). https://doi.org/10.1007/978-3-642-35289-8_5

11. Qi, C.R., Su, H., Mo, K., Guibas, L.J.: PointNet: deep learning on point sets for 3D classification and segmentation (2017). https://doi.org/10.1109/CVPR.2017.16

12. Qi, C.R., et al.: PointNet++: deep hierarchical feature learning on point sets in a metric space (2017). https://doi.org/10.5555/3295222

13. Thomas, H., Qi, C.R., Deschaud, J.E., Marcotegui, B., Goulette, F., Guibas, L.: KPConv: flexible and deformable convolution for point clouds, April 2019. https://doi.org/10.1109/ICCV.2019.00651

14. Yan, X., Zheng, C., Li, Z., Wang, S., Cui, S.: PointASNL: robust point clouds processing using nonlocal neural networks with adaptive sampling (2020). https://doi.org/10.1109/cvpr42600.2020.00563

15. Yi, L., et al.: A scalable active framework for region annotation in 3D shape collections. ACM Trans. Graph. **35**(6) (2016). https://doi.org/10.1145/2980179.2980238

16. Ying, X.: An overview of overfitting and its solutions. J. Phys. Conf. Ser. **1168**(2), 022022 (2019). https://doi.org/10.1088/1742-6596/1168/2/022022

17. Zhang, J., Zhao, X., Chen, Z., Lu, Z.: A review of deep learning-based semantic segmentation for point cloud. IEEE Access **7**, 179118–179133 (2019). https://doi.org/10.1109/ACCESS.2019.2958671

18. Zoumpekas, T., Molina, G., Puig, A., Salamó, M.: CLOSED: a Dashboard for 3d point cloud segmentation analysis using deep learning. In: Proceedings of the 17th International Joint Conference on Computer Vision, Imaging and Computer Graphics Theory and Applications, pp. 403–410 (2022). https://doi.org/10.5220/0010826000003124

19. Zoumpekas, T., Molina, G., Salamó, M., Puig, A.: Benchmarking deep learning models on point cloud segmentation. In: Artificial Intelligence Research and Development, vol. 339, pp. 335–344, October 2021. https://doi.org/10.3233/FAIA210152

Representation and Interpretability of IE Integral Neural Networks

Aoi Honda[1]([⊠]), Yudai Kamata[1], and Simon James[2]

[1] Kyushu Institute of Technology, 680-2 Kawazu, Iizuka, Fukuoka 820-8502, Japan
aoi@ai.kyutech.ac.jp
[2] School of Information Technology, Deakin University, Geelong, Australia
sjames@deakin.edu.au

Abstract. While there has been a lot of research attention given to neural networks and other black-box machine learning methods, recent works on aggregation functions and fuzzy sets have highlighted the appeal of incorporating fuzzy integrals into network implementations in order to achieve interpretability. We present an application of the recently proposed inclusion-exclusion integral neural network to the Boston House-Price dataset to illustrate its potential and examine the settings leading to better performance.

Keywords: Nonlinear integral · Neural network · Explainable AI · Interpretable machine learning

1 Introduction

The machine learning and artificial intelligence research areas have enjoyed a number of well-publicized successes in recent years, with hardware developments now being able to implement established theory and models [8,20]. While the increased attention has allowed these fields to flourish, there has also been increased scrutiny and skepticism [4] with interpretability of what is going on inside the 'black-box' being important not only for understanding the successes but also for anomalous behavior and failures [18,19].

In general, there is a trade-off between interpretability and inferential performance. In some cases, simpler but more transparent models such as multiple regression analysis are employed to locally interpret inferences made by the more complex machine learning techniques. However, there is still a desire for 'white-box' analysis methods, which are interpretable but also have high predictive performance.

The concept of explainable artificial intelligence has now gained popularity [2,20], with goals to which theory in fuzzy sets and aggregation have a lot to offer. In particular, the alignment between fuzzy measure or capacity-based aggregation functions and neural networks has become a topic of interest [13,17]. The inclusion-exclusion integral [15,16], which generalizes the Choquet integral [22], can be implemented as a neural network with a structure reflecting the interactions between inputs modeled by the defining fuzzy measure. The details of this

V. Torra and Y. Narukawa (Eds.): MDAI 2022, LNAI 13408, pp. 168–180, 2022.
https://doi.org/10.1007/978-3-031-13448-7_14

model have been developed in [12], with performance comparable to deep learning methods. The key promise of the fuzzy measure based methods is our ability to analyse model behavior according to the fuzzy measure values obtained. The rich theory on fuzzy integrals [3,9] and their associated behavioral indices developed over the last few decades puts a number of easily implemented tools at our fingertips.

This contribution will focus on an application of the inclusion-exclusion (IE) integral neural network developed in [12]. The article will be set out as follows. In Sect. 2, we present the background for the inclusion-exclusion integral based neural network model, while Sect. 3 focuses on its implementation. In Sect. 4, we present two sets of experiments, which examine the effect of different network implementations and choices for the interaction operator. In Sect. 5, we provide discussion around these results before making some final remarks.

2 Preliminaries

Here we present the definitions and background required for implementing and analysing the proposed inclusion-exclusion integral neural network. Many of the results and further detail can also be found in [12].

We assume the set of explanatory variables in our model correspond with a finite J-point set, $X = \{1, \ldots, j, \ldots, J\}$, with $\mathcal{P}(X)$ denoting the power set. Inputs are further assumed to lie in the unit interval, i.e., such that $f = (x_1, x_2, \ldots, x_J) \in [0, 1]^J$ with x_i either representing the arguments themselves or the values after suitable data transformations. The notation, $|A|$ will be used to denote the cardinality of a subset $A \subseteq X$.

The IE integral allows weights to be assigned to each subset of the input set, which are represented by way of a monotone measure $\mu : \mathcal{P}(X) \to [0, +\infty]$, with $A \subseteq B \to \mu(A) \leq \mu(B)$ for all $A, B \subseteq X$. Such measures generalize additive measures and so are sometimes referred to simply as non-additive measures or *fuzzy* measures if $\mu(X) = 1$.

The inclusion-exclusion integral of f, as introduced in [15,16], is given as:

$$\int^{IE} f \, d\mu := \sum_{A \in \mathcal{P}(X)} \left(\sum_{B \supseteq A} (-1)^{|B \setminus A|} \bigotimes_{i \in B} x_i \right) \mu(A),$$

where $\otimes$ is an extended symmetric operator defined for any number of arguments, referred to as the *interaction operator*. The following definition uses the Möbius transform to simplify the expression.

Definition 1. (Inclusion-exclusion integral [16]**).** *Let μ be a monotone measure on $(X, \mathcal{P}(X))$ and $\otimes$ be an interaction operator on $[0, 1]^{|A|}$ for $|A| = 1, \ldots, J$. Then, the inclusion-exclusion integral of $f = (x_1, \ldots, x_j, \ldots, x_J)$ with respect to μ and $\otimes$ is*

$$\int^{IE} f \, d\mu := \sum_{A \in \mathcal{P}(X)} \left(\bigotimes_{i \in A} x_i \right) m^{\mu}(A),$$

where m^μ is the Möbius transform of μ,

$$m^\mu(A) := \sum_{B \subseteq A} (-1)^{|A \setminus B|} \mu(B).$$

The weight information contained within the fuzzy measure values can be used to interpret the importance of individual inputs and coalitions of inputs and their relative impact on the overall output. However, the interaction operator $\otimes$ will also influence the function behavior, usually by affecting the degree to which the output tends toward higher or lower inputs (the 'orness' or 'andness' of the function [14]). Using the logical product (or minimum function) for the interaction operator will result in the IE integral being equivalent to the Choquet integral, and while previous studies have usually focused on the use of t-norms, other choices, including averaging and disjunctive functions are also possible.

When the IE-integral is used as a regression model, we can denote the objective or target variable by y with the explanatory variables given by $x_1, \ldots, x_J$. We then have,

$$\hat{y} = \sum_{A \in \mathcal{P}(X)} \beta_A \left(\bigotimes_{i \in A} x_i \right),$$

with a correspondence between the coefficients β_A and $m^\mu(A)$. For example, in the case of $X = \{1, 2, 3\}$, we have

$$\hat{y} = \beta_\emptyset + \beta_{\{1\}} x_1 + \beta_{\{2\}} x_2 + \beta_{\{3\}} x_3 + \beta_{\{1,2\}} x_1 \otimes x_2$$
$$+ \beta_{\{1,3\}} x_1 \otimes x_3 + \beta_{\{2,3\}} x_2 \otimes x_3 + \beta\{1,2,3\} x_1 \otimes x_2 \otimes x_3. \tag{1}$$

Comparing with the simplest linear regression model,

$$\hat{y} = \beta_0 + \beta_1 x_1 + \beta_2 x_2 + \beta_3 x_3. \tag{2}$$

we can see the similarity of the two, with the first four terms identical. The IE-integral model can hence be seen as a form of linear regression with interaction terms, generalizing not only the standard Choquet integral model, but also the interaction effects sometimes incorporated in statistical regression models [7].

The key advantage in use of the IE-integral model is not so much in its flexibility, but moreso in the interpretability that we gain from calculations like the Shapley indices [6,9], which can be used to interpret the average importance of variables and their coalitions.

3   Inclusion-Exclusion Integral Network

This section describes how to implement the IE-integral model in a neural network. As noted above, the IE-integral model generalizes the classical linear regression model, which stands as a well-established 'white-box' data analysis method. While various methods have been proposed to solve the black-box problem of neural networks, here we contend that the IE-integral network offers the potential for interperting the mechanisms at play within the network. This is achieved by configuring the network according to the structure of the IE-integral, from which it is then possible to interpret the relationship between the explanatory variables and predictions directly from the structure of the network and the values of the parameters after training.

3.1   Network Implementation

Figure 1 illustrates the IE-integral model with a network when the input dimension is 3. Transformation of variables or preprocessing is achieved within the network at the first layer, which we refer to as the *preprocessing layer*. The second half of the network is the IE-integral layer. Learning and implementation of the IE-integral network can be implemented using common neural network libraries. For our experiments in the following section, TensorFlow [1] and Keras [5] were used. Figure 2 shows the implementation of the network in Fig. 1, which was constructed using the Keras Functional API.

Compared to a more general network, there are unconnected units and unweighted edges in the IE-integral model. For unconnected units, the value of the weight parameter for edges between units is set to 0, and the value of the weight parameter is set to 0 for unweighted edges, so that these weights are fixed without being learned. A four or more input network can be designed and implemented in the same way, however as n increases, the number of units in the IE-integral layer in Fig. 1 and the number of *multiply* parts in Fig. 2 increase exponentially.

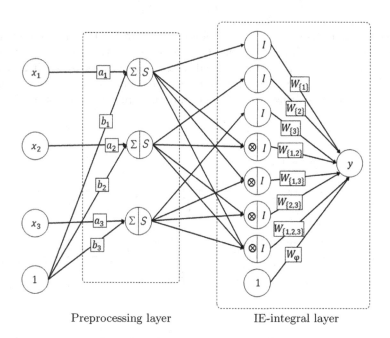

Fig. 1. 3-input Möbius type IE-integral network

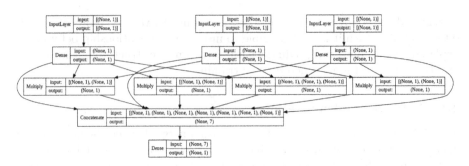

Fig. 2. Implementation of IE-integral network (n = 3) using the Keras Functional API

3.2   Additive Representation of the Interaction Operator

Where the interaction operation $\otimes$ lends itself to an additive representation, incorporating this into the network structure is naturally achieved since it aligns with existing approaches to neural networks. In particular, Archimedean t-norms can be represented by means of a continuous generating function t.

Theorem 1. (Schweizer et al. [21]). *Let T be a t-norm on $[0, 1]$. If T is continuous and strictly monotone, then there exists a strictly monotone decreasing continuous function t with $\lim_{a \to 0+} t(a) = +\infty, t(1) = 0$ such that*

$$T(a,b) = t^{-1}(t(a) + t(b)), \ 0 \leqq a, b \leqq 1. \tag{3}$$

The function t is referred to as an additive generating function. For example, in the case of the algebraic product, the generating function is $t(a) = -\log a$. By Theorem 1, the t-norm can be modeled within the network by setting $t(a)$ and the inverse $t^{-1}(a)$ as activation functions, with t being applied to each argument and $t^{-1}(a)$ to the resulting sum. A programmatic implementation of this is shown in Fig. 3.

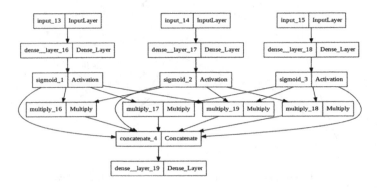

Fig. 3. Implementation of the IE-integral network with additive generation function

As was observed in the previous section, the Choquet integral can be recovered when the minimum (or logical product) is used as the interaction operator in the IE-integral. The minimum and maximum can only be represented using the additive representation as limiting cases, however they can be implemented in the network using the rectified linear unit functions (ReLU), which are often employed in neural network models. We observe the following relationship between these functions and the minimum and maximum.

Proposition 1. *For any $a, b \in \mathbb{R}$, it holds that $a \wedge b = -ReLU(a-b) + a$, $\quad a \vee b = ReLU(a-b) + a$, where $ReLU(a) := a \vee 0$.*

We hence have several choices for the interaction operator, all of which can be represented easily within standard neural network implementations.

3.3   Other Network Models

Various types of models based on mathematical concepts have been proposed for neural networks. A network model similar to the IE neural network model proposed here is the sum and product model [10]. Both are intuitive graph models and have the similarity of being composed of a network with sum and product as internal nodes. They have excellent performance as classifiers, achieving high classification accuracy on the CIFAR-10 image dataset classification problem. The sum-product model is a graphical representation of a Bayesian network, where the nodes of the product represent probabilistic causal relationships. In contrast, the IE model emphasizes interpretability, where the nodes of the product represent interactions between features.

4   Application to Regression and Classification Datasets

We aim to demonstrate the potential for data analysis by applying an IE-integral network to a real dataset and interpreting the resulting parameters. For this we use the Boston House-Price dataset, which is aimed at regression problems [11].

4.1   Dataset: Boston House-Price Data

This well-known dataset has 506 observations with information pertaining to 13 explanatory variables. The objective is to predict the median home price in each region. For the purposes of our experiments, sets of 3 to 6 variables will be selected from those summarized in Table 1. The values of LSTAT, TAX and NOX, which are negatively correlated with the objective variable, are inverted.

4.2   Experiment 1 – Comparison of Two Equivalent Networks

While the additive representation of the interaction operator results in a mathematically equivalent function, whether one calculation is used over another can

Table 1. Boston House-Price data

			Min	Max	Average	cor. with y
y		Median owner-occupied home price	5	50	22.53	1.00
x_1	LSTAT	Lower status of the population	1.73	37.97	12.65	0.74
x_2	RM	Average of rooms per dwelling	3.561	8.78	6.28	0.70
x_3	PTRATIO	Pupil-teacher ratio	12.6	22	18.46	0.51
x_4	INDUS	Prop. of non-retail business acres	0.46	27.74	11.14	0.48
x_5	TAX	Full-value property-tax rate	187	711	408.24	0.47
x_6	NOX	Nitric oxides concentration	0.385	0.871	0.55	0.43

affect the learning performance. In order to investigate the differences, we implemented the IE-integral network model using both the standard product (IEI) and its additive representation in the network using generators (Additive).

We set the same initial values for the corresponding parameters of the two networks. These are not chosen randomly in general, but rather selected to provide the optimal starting conditions, e.g. values that balance the output of the sigmoid function over the value range of the data in the input layer and values that maximize the entropy of the fuzzy measure in the IE-integral layer (the additive and symmetric fuzzy measure). The fitting performance was examined using all 506 instances of the dataset. Mean squared error was used as the loss function and Adam as the optimization method for training. Analysis of the error for models with 3, 4, 5 and 6 inputs showed that, while the error varied slightly, the overall trend of mean squared error as the number of epochs increased was essentially the same. This was also true for the coefficients of determination between the predicted and observed values.

Table 2. Learning speed (sec)

	3-input		4-input		5-input		6-input	
Epoch	IEI	Additive	IEI	Additive	IEI	Additive	IEI	Additive
100	4.6	5.1	5.2	4.6	6.8	4.9	10.8	6.3
500	17.8	18.9	17.7	17.1	21.3	17.5	32.1	20.7
1000	32.8	34.2	33.0	33.1	38.7	32.6	52.3	40.1
1500	48.6	50.3	48.6	47.5	55.3	48.4	79.6	58.0
2000	69.0	70.2	74.7	62.7	72.8	64.0	112.1	75.6
3000	100.0	99.7	95.3	93.1	108.4	94.8	157.4	114.5
4000	130.4	134.2	126.4	124.5	143.5	125.6	208.3	152.1
5000	161.1	166.2	156.3	154.4	179.6	157.5	258.5	187.7

Differences did emerge however, between the two networks in terms of learning speed. As shown in Table 2, the differences in learning speed between the two networks grew larger as the input dimension was increased. We might expect this difference to be more pronounced when the input dimension is much larger.

At the surface, the network with the standard product representation of the interaction operator may be easier to interpret due to the conceptual alignment between the network structure and the IE-integral's mathematical representation. However, the learned parameters corresponding with the fuzzy measure used to interpret the network's behavior are still easily extracted from the additive generator representation. The latter would therefore seem to provide a clear advantage when it comes to implementation and calculation speed.

4.3   Experiment 2 – Comparison of Interaction Operators

Another key consideration for implementing this model is the choice of interaction operator. We hence conducted some additional experiments to compare the performance of networks with different interaction operations. The five interaction operations used were the algebraic product (AP), logical product (min) and sum (max), Łukasiewicz's product and sum (LP and LS). These operators are defined on $[0, K]$ for any number of arguments as follows.

$$\bigotimes_{i \in A}^{AP} x_i := \frac{1}{K^{|A|-1}} \prod_{i \in A} x_i, \quad \bigotimes_{i \in A}^{\min} x_i := \bigwedge_{i \in A} x_i, \quad \bigotimes_{i \in A}^{\max} x_i := \bigvee_{i \in A} x_i,$$

$$\bigotimes_{i \in A}^{LP} x_i := \left(\sum_{i \in A} x_i - (|A| - 1)K \right) \vee 0 \quad and \quad \bigotimes_{i \in A}^{LS} x_i := \left(\sum_{i \in A} x_i \right) \wedge K.$$

These five operators were primarily chosen due to being representative of those typically investigated in research, varying as they do in strength of conjunction and disjunction. We further note that use of the algebraic product results in an operator consistent with linear regression models incorporating interaction terms, and use of the logical product results in the IE-network being equivalent to the Choquet integral.

Since the output of the preprocessing layer passes through a sigmoid activation function in the networks used, the input values of the IE-integral layer will be in the $[0, 1]$ range and hence we can set $K = 1$.

In addition to comparing the different IE-networks defined with respect to each of the interaction operators, four neural network models were also tested for

Table 3. Simple neural network models for comparison

	Hidden layers	Units of hidden layer(s)	Act. func. of preprocessing	Act. func. of integral
NN1	1 Layer	4 units	Sigmoid	Identity
NN2	1 Layer	4 units	ReLU	Identity
NN3	2 Layers	4,16 units	Sigmoid	Identity
NN4	2 Layers	4,16 units	ReLU	Identity

comparison, the key details of which are summarized in Table 3. Simple structures were assumed for all four network models with their layers fully connected.
The optimization method and loss functions were the same as for Experiment 1.

The mean squared error (MSE) results from training of the five IE-integral
network models and the four neural network models are shown in Table 4 and
Fig; 4. The order of fitting performance after 2000 epochs with both MSE and
coefficient of determination R^2 is summarized in Table 5. We note that while the
IE-integral models were not the top-performing in this respect, it is clear that a
similar level of accuracy as neural networks of comparable depth was achieved.

Table 4. Learning progress with epoch increase for each network (MSE)

Epoch	AP	Min	Max	LP	LS	NN1	NN2	NN3	NN4
0	0.9867	0.9639	0.9762	0.9960	0.9451	0.2693	0.3835	3.3320	0.1700
100	0.0249	0.0227	0.0258	0.0217	0.0210	0.0232	0.0125	0.0344	0.0096
500	0.0120	0.0122	0.0120	0.0092	0.0110	0.0135	0.0084	0.0139	0.0077
1000	0.0110	0.0113	0.0113	0.0089	0.0093	0.0127	0.0080	0.0121	0.0079
1500	0.0107	0.0111	0.0111	0.0088	0.0087	0.0121	0.0080	0.0112	0.0069
2000	0.0105	0.0109	0.0110	0.0088	0.0086	0.0112	0.0080	0.0101	0.0070

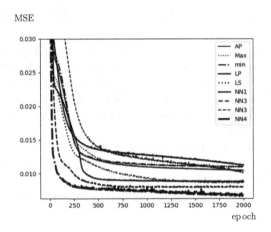

Fig. 4. Visual representation of learning progress results shown in Table 4

Table 6 shows the weights after training. Due to the randomness of the order
of the training data, slight differences may occur from experiment to experiment,
however the initial values of the weights and the hyperparameters of the network
are the same each time, so the learning for weight values are also similar. One
interesting observation from these results was that, in the case of Łukasiewicz's
products, the weights obtained for $w_{1,3}$ and $w_{1,2,3}$ were zero, which makes the

Table 5. Mean squared error and determination coefficient of each network model after 2000 epochs of training

Rank	Model	MSE	R^2
1	NN4	0.0070	0.8401
2	NN2	0.0080	0.8095
3	LS	0.0086	0.7942
4	LP	0.0088	0.7896
5	NN3	0.0101	0.7592
6	AP	0.0105	0.7498
7	Max	0.0110	0.7377
8	Min	0.110	0.7368
9	NN1	0.112	0.7314

resulting model quite easy to interpret. It is an advantage of the Łukasiewicz's product that we can obtain zero weights without adding a regularization term. The model is equivalent to

$$\hat{y} = 1.1312x_1' + 0.2077x_2' + 0.4602x_3' + 1.9158(x_1' \otimes x_2') + 1.3602(x_2' \otimes x_3') - 0.1059,$$

where each x_j' is the output of the preprocessing layer. It provides a straight-forward explanation of the inference that positive synergy is modeled between x_1 and x_3, and between x_2 and x_3. Table 7 shows the Shapley values when the t-norm is a logical product, logical sum, and Łukasiewicz product. The weights in Table 6 have some discrepancies, but the Shapley values are similar among the three t-norms. For the other operators, the Shapley values were not calculated because the fuzzy measures did not satisfy the monotonicity condition. In fact, in the case of the algebraic product model, we have $\mu(\{x_1, x_3\}) = 0.6682 + 0.2827 - 0.4497 = 0.5012 < 0.6682 = \mu(\{x_1\})$. From the Shapley values, it can be seen that LSTAT, RM, and PTRATIO affect the objective variable in that order. Also, from the weights, a strong positive inter-

Table 6. Weight of IE-integral part after learning

	AP	Min	Max	LP	LS
$w_{\{1\}}$	0.6682	1.3434	1.3678	1.1312	1.4736
$w_{\{2\}}$	0.8248	1.1005	1.1954	0.2077	1.5031
$w_{\{3\}}$	0.2827	0.5764	0.9699	0.4602	0.8816
$w_{\{1,2\}}$	1.3886	0.1005	0.3621	1.9158	−0.7996
$w_{\{1,3\}}$	−0.4497	0.3688	−0.2215	0	0.2052
$w_{\{2,3\}}$	0.5492	0.1005	−0.0298	1.3602	−0.6982
$w_{\{1,2,3\}}$	2.2653	0.1005	−0.2215	0	−0.0995

action is at work for RM and PTRATIO, indicating that large values of both of these have a strong positive impact on the objective variable. In other words, the average price of a house is synergistically higher when the two conditions of a large average number of rooms and a low percentage of lower status are combined.

Table 7. Shapley values for each attribute in the case of Min, Max, LP

		Min	Max	LP
x_1	LSTAT	0.4362	0.4244	0.4150
x_2	RM	0.3347	0.3932	0.3650
x_3	PTRATIO	0.2291	0.1823	0.2201

5   Discussion

We have conducted two sets of experiments to examine settings that may lead to improved performance of IE-integral neural networks. Many kinds of IE-integral network were shown to have an equivalent network representation as a regular neural network using additive generators, which was shown to provide similar results with less learning time required. In the second set of experiments, we investigated the difference in performance depending on the interaction operator (or t-norm) used in the IE-integral. We also compared the performance with that of general neural networks. The proposed model was shown to have performance close to that of a neural network, however we stress that networks constructed in this way retain their interpretability. In particular, use of the Łukasiewicz product led to high performance. We can observe that the ramp or ReLU function performed better than the sigmoid function as the activation function for the neural networks tested, and so there may be some underlying feature of the data that responds better to these linear calculations. Although the number of inputs in this experiment is small and further research is needed, our experiments have emphasized the potential for fuzzy integral based network models for data analysis.

While researchers studying aggregation functions and fuzzy integrals have often benchmarked these techniques against state-of-the-art machine learning methods for prediction and analysis tasks, approaches that blend or merge techniques from both sides have been less explored. With the current focus on explainability, interpretability, and integrity in data analysis, there is a growing opportunity for the theory of fuzzy integrals to work towards solving a number of real-world problems. The results provided here, both in terms of the transparent network structure and learning performance, should provide some optimism not only for the IE-integral neural network but also for similar ideas arising from aggregation and fuzzy integral theory.

Acknowledgement. S. James were supported by the Australian Research Council Discovery Project DP210100227.

References

1. Abadi, M., et al.: Tensorflow: a system for large-scale machine learning. In: 12th USENIX Symposium on Operating Systems Design and Implementation (OSDI 2016), pp. 265–283 (2016)
2. Arrieta, A.B., et al.: Explainable artificial intelligence (XAI): concepts, taxonomies, opportunities and challenges toward responsible AI. Inf. Fusion **58**, 82–115 (2020)
3. Beliakov, G., James, S., Wu, J.-Z.: Learning fuzzy measures. In: Discrete Fuzzy Measures. SFSC, vol. 382, pp. 205–239. Springer, Cham (2020). https://doi.org/10.1007/978-3-030-15305-2_8
4. Castelvecchi, D.: The black box of AI. Nature **538**, 20–23 (2016)
5. Chollet, F., et al. Keras. GitHub (2015). https://github.com/fchollet/keras
6. Choquet, G.: A value for n-person games. Ann. Inst. Fourier **5**, 131–295 (1953)
7. Cutaways, V., Stock, T.: Interaction. Auto. Tech. Review. **5**(3), 4–11 (2016). https://doi.org/10.1365/s40112-016-1097-8
8. Dwivedi, Y.K., et al.: Artificial intelligence (AI): multidisciplinary perspectives on emerging challenges, opportunities, and agenda for research, practice and policy. Int. J. Inf. Manag. **57**(101994), 1–47 (2021)
9. Grabisch, M.: Set Functions. Games and Capacities in Decision Making. Springer, Berlin, New York (2016)
10. Domingos, P., Poon, H.: Sum-product networks: a new deep architecture. In: Proceedings of the 12th Conference on Uncertainty in Artificial Intelligence (UAI), pp. 337–346 (2012)
11. Harrison, D., Rubinfeld, D.L.: Hedonic prices and the demand for clean air. J. Environ. Economics and Management **5**, 81–102 (1993)
12. Honda, A., Itabashi, M., James, S.: A neural network based on the inclusion-exclusion integral and its application to data analysis. preprint (2021)
13. Honda, A., James, S.: Parameter learning and applications of the inclusion-exclusion integral for data fusion and analysis. Inf. Fusion **56**, 28–38 (2020)
14. Honda, A., James, S., Rajasegarar, S.: Orness and Cardinality Indices for Averaging Inclusion-Exclusion Integrals. In: Torra, V., Narukawa, Y., Honda, A., Inoue, S. (eds.) MDAI 2017. LNCS (LNAI), vol. 10571, pp. 51–62. Springer, Cham (2017). https://doi.org/10.1007/978-3-319-67422-3_6
15. Honda, A., Okamoto, J.: Inclusion-exclusion integral and its application to subjective video quality estimation. In: Hüllermeier, E., Kruse, R., Hoffmann, F. (eds.) IPMU 2010. CCIS, vol. 80, pp. 480–489. Springer, Heidelberg (2010). https://doi.org/10.1007/978-3-642-14055-6_50
16. Honda, A., Okazaki, Y.: Theory of inclusion-exclusion integral. Inf. Sci. **376**, 136–147 (2017)
17. Islam, M.A., Anderson, D.T., Pinar, A.J., Havens, T.C., Scott, G., Keller, J.M.: Enabling explainable fusion in deep learning with fuzzy integral neural networks. IEEE Trans. Fuzzy Syst. **28**(7), 1291–1300 (2020)
18. Otte, C.: Safe and interpretable machine learning: a methodological review. In: Moewes, C., Nunberger, A. (eds.) Computational Intelligence in Intelligent Data Analysis. Studies in Computational Intelligence, vol. 445, pp. 111–122. Springer, Heidelberg (2013). https://doi.org/10.1007/978-3-642-32378-2_8

19. Ross, C., Swetlitz, I.: IBM's Watson supercomputer recommended 'unsafe and incorrect' cancer treatments, internal documents show. STAT+, 25 July 2018. https://www.statnews.com/2018/07/25/ibm-watson-recommended-unsafe-incorrect-treatments/

20. Samek, W., Wiegand, T., Müller, K.-R.: Explainable artificial intelligence: understanding, visualizing and interpreting deep learning models. ITU Journal: ICT Discoveries - Special Issue 1 - The Impact of Artificial Intelligence (AI). Commun. Netw. Serv. 1, 1–10 (2017)

21. Schweizer, B., Sklar, A.: Associative functions and statistical triangle inequalities. Publ. Math. Debrecen 8, 169–186 (1961)

22. Shapley, L.S.: Theory of capacities. In: Contributions to the Theory Games (AM-28), II, pp. 307–318 (1953)

Deep Attributed Graph Embeddings

Elisabetta Fersini[(⊠)] , Simone Mottadelli, Michele Carbonera,
and Enza Messina

University of Milano-Bicocca, Viale Sarca 336, 20126 Milan, Italy
{elisabetta.fersini,enza.messina}@unimib.it,
{s.mottadelli2,m.carbonera}@campus.unimib.it

Abstract. Graph Representation Learning aims to learn a rich and low-dimensional node embedding while preserving the graph properties. In this paper, we propose a novel Deep Attributed Graph Embedding (DAGE) that learns node representations based on both the topological structure and node attributes. DAGE a is able to capture, in a linear time and with a limited number of trainable parameters, the highly non-linear properties of attributed graphs. The proposed approach outperforms the current state-of-the-art approaches on node classification and node clustering tasks at a lower computational costs.

Keywords: Attributed Graph Embedding · Semantic proximity · Structural proximity

1 Introduction

Graphs are increasingly present in our daily life, where we have to deal with different types of large networks ranging from social communities to scientific collaborations. Most of the existing machine learning tasks on complex and sparse graphs, such as node classification, node clustering and link prediction, can benefit from the learning of suitable graph representations through *Graph Embedding* [1], which reduces the node representation space while maintaining the graph properties. The majority of the graph representation learning approaches derive node embedding by preserving few structural properties [2–6], while disregarding that nodes are frequently characterized by attribute information. During the last years, a number of approaches have tried to create a richer representation for attributed graphs, exploiting both the relational structure and the attributes associated to the nodes [7–10]. Although the above mentioned approaches represent a fundamental contribution to the graph embedding state of the art, they can capture the highly non-linear properties of attributed graphs at the expenses of the number of trainable parameters and/or increasing time complexity. The proposed approach, Deep Attributed Graph Embedding (DAGE), learns a representation in fully unsupervised settings, that is able to scale to large and complex structures, for both directed and undirected homogeneous graphs. The main contribution of the paper is three-fold:

V. Torra and Y. Narukawa (Eds.): MDAI 2022, LNAI 13408, pp. 181–192, 2022.
https://doi.org/10.1007/978-3-031-13448-7_15

– a model that is able to capture the highly non-linear properties of attributed graphs, showing outperforming results with respect to the most recent and promising approaches;
– the number of trainable parameters is less or equal than other effective approaches available in the state of the art, while ensuring better performance on node classification and node clustering tasks;
– the time complexity for the proposed model is linear with respect to the number of nodes, compared with the quadratic time necessary for the most recent and promising approaches in the state of the art, making DAGE suitable for large scale networks.

The rest of the paper is organized as follows. In Sect. 2, an overview of the state of the art is presented. In Sect. 3, the proposed Deep Attributed Graph Embedding (DAGE) is detailed. In Sect. 4, datasets, performance measures, experimental settings and experimental results are reported. Finally, in Sect. 5 conclusions and future work are presented.

2   Related Works

In the last twenty years, a lot of research work has been done in the field of graph embedding, mainly focused on designing increasingly effective and efficient algorithms for embedding graphs. The substantial differences between these algorithms reside in how they define the properties of the graph to be preserved and how they maintain these properties in the embedding space. Broadly, graph embedding algorithms can be divided into three categories: *matrix factorization based methods, random walk based methods* and *deep learning based methods*.

Among all the techniques for performing graph embedding, the methods based on *matrix factorization* were the first to be introduced in the literature around the 2000s. These methods are based on the idea of representing the graph properties in the form of a matrix and of factorizing this matrix to obtain the node embeddings. Examples of matrices used to represent the properties of the graphs include the node adjacency matrix [11–13], the Laplacian matrix [5], the node transition probability matrix [14] and the Katz similarity matrix [15]. Even though this method provides an effective way of preserving also the node attribute information, it is very expensive in terms of time complexity.

In the last decade, new methods based on *random walks* began to be proposed. The main contribution that these methods bring to research is the idea of solving the graph embedding problem in such a way that if two nodes tend to co-occur in paths of fixed length in the graph, then these nodes should be mapped close together in the embedding space. Roughly, random walk-based methods first sample a set of fixed length paths from the original graph and then apply some machine learning techniques to generate the node embeddings by preserving the information carried by these paths. In 2014, Perozzi et al. [2] proposed DeepWalk, a random walk-based method that exploits the neural language model Skip-gram [16] for generating the node embeddings. Like all random walk-based methods, DeepWalk first samples a set of paths from the graph. This is achieved by uniformly sampling a node among the neighbors of the last visited node until the predefined length of the specific path is reached. Every sampled path is interpreted as a sentence, in which the words correspond to the nodes occurring along the path. The embedding is finally generated by using the traditional Skip-gram models. More recently, Grover et al. [6] introduced Node2Vec, an approach that similarly to DeepWalk, is able to generate meaningful node embeddings by first sampling a set of paths from the original network and then employing the neural language model Skip-gram on the sampled paths. Unlike DeepWalk, Node2Vec is more flexible with respect to the path sampling strategy. Two hyper-parameters regulate the visit of the nodes, which can follow a strategy that is more oriented in depth or in breadth.

Finally, *deep learning* based methods represent the most promising state-of-the-art methods in numerous downstream tasks. Starting from the raw features in input, the deep models extract increasingly high-level features as they progressively proceed deeper into the network. Structural Deep Network Embedding (SDNE) by Wang et al. [4] is a deep learning- based method that uses deep autoencoders to preserve jointly both the first-order proximity and the second-order proximity of the original graph. Deep Neural Networks for Graph Representations (DNGR) [17] is a model that combines the ideas of random walk-based methods and deep autoencoders in order to solve the graph embedding problem, while preserving the higher-order proximity of the original graph.

Some very recent approaches belonging to the deep learning are mainly focused on dealing with not only the structural properties of the graph, but also to consider the attributes of the nodes when creating their embeddings. Examples of attributed graph embeddings approaches are *CAGE* [8], *DANE* [10] and GAT2VEC [18]. While CAGE is a deep model that preserves both the topological structure and the node attribute information of the input graph by means of a constrained optimization problem, DANE generates the node embeddings by jointly optimizing the semantic proximity, the second-order proximity and the first-order proximity of both semantics and network structure using autoencoders. GAT2VEC [18] is a hybrid method which is based on random walks for learning a node vector representation from a bipartite graph structure of nodes and attributes. This model is able to leverage multiple sources of information through early fusion that is subsequently processed through a single neural layer. A recent related work [19] is focused on creating an embedding representation on attributed hypergraphs, where an edge can link any number of vertices both from a structural and attribute point of view.

Although the above mentioned approaches represent a fundamental contribution to the graph embedding state of the art, they can capture the highly nonlinear properties of attributed graphs at the expenses of the number of trainable parameters and/or increasing time complexity. In order to address this issue, we propose DAGE, which learns a representation in a fully unsupervised settings also scaling to large and complex structures for both directed and undirected homogeneous graphs.

3 Deep Attributed Graph Embedding (DAGE)

3.1 Basic Definitions and Preliminaries

The main goal of the proposed model is to map nodes of an attributed graph into a low-dimensional embedding space, by preserving not only the relational structure but also the attribute information. More formally, an **attributed graph** is defined as $G = (V, E, W, A)$, where $V = \{v_1, \ldots, v_n\}$ is the set of nodes, $E = \{(v_i, v_j) \mid v_i, v_j \in V\}$ denotes the set of *edges*, $W \in \mathbb{R}^{|V| \times |V|}$ is the adjacency matrix such that W_{ij} represents the non-negative weight associated with the edge $e_{ij} = (v_i, v_j) \in E$ and and A is the node attribute matrix such that $A_i = (A_{ik})_{k=1}^n$ is the attribute vector associated with node v_i.

In the proposed model, detailed in the next section, two main proximity measures are introduced to be subsequently preserved during the embedding estimation, namely second-order and semantic proximity. The *second-order proximity* considers how similar the neighborhood structures of two given nodes are. More formally, let $W_i = (W_{ik})_{k=1}^n$ be the vector representing the i-th row of the adjacency matrix W. Then, the second-order proximity between two nodes v_i and v_j can be measures as the similarity between W_i and W_j. To compute the second-order proximity, a cosine similarity could be exploited.

Additionally to the second-order proximity, which will preserve the relational structure of each node, the semantic proximity needs to be preserved so that if two nodes have similar attributes, their embedding representation should be similar. In particular, the *semantic proximity*, or attribute proximity, between two nodes v_i and v_j can be measured as the similarity between their attribute vectors A_i and A_j.

3.2 The Proposed Model

The aim of the proposed model is to learn, in unsupervised settings, the embeddings of nodes belonging to an attributed graphs, by leveraging both the relational structure and the attributes associated with each node. In particular, given an attributed graph, the proposed model aims at learning a function $C_G : V \to \mathbb{R}^m$, where $m \ll |V|$, to preserve both the second-order and the semantic proximity. To address this challenge, a novel Deep Attributed Graph Embedding (DAGE) is proposed, whose architecture is reported in Fig. 1. In the proposed architecture, the two branches denote autoencoders that can capture the highly non-linear relational structure and the non linearity of the node attributes. More precisely, the autoencoder related to the relational structure contains three layers: the input layer, the hidden layer and the output layer. The training of the autoencoder, in their general form, consists in finding the parameter set Θ_R that minimizes the following reconstruction loss:

$$\mathcal{L}(\theta_R) = \frac{1}{n} \sum_{i=1}^n \|\hat{W}_i - W_i \odot B\|_2^2 \tag{1}$$

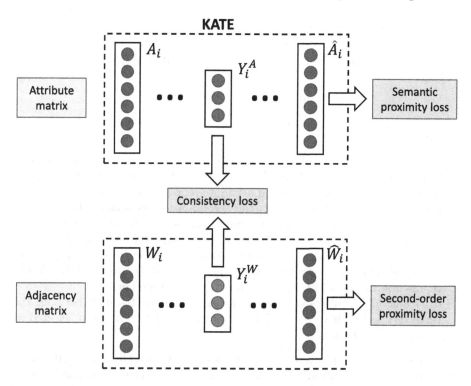

Fig. 1. DAGE architecture. It consists of two autoencoders that are trained to reconstruct the node attributes and the adjacency matrix of the input graph, respectively.

where W_i is a row of the adjacency matrix and B regulates the sparsity of the learned representation. The encoder and the decoder functions can be expressed as a multi-layer neural network, whose hidden layers are $Y_i^W = \sigma(HW_i + b)$ and $\hat{W}_i = \sigma(\hat{H}Y_i^W + \hat{b})$ respectively, where H and $\hat{H}$ are the encoder and decoder weight matrices, b and $\hat{b}$ are the bias vectors. According to the encoder-decoder general architecture, Y_i^W is the hidden representation of the node relational structure derived from the encoder, while $\hat{W}_i$ is the corresponding reconstruction from the decoder. Concerning the autoencoder related to the attribute information, the K-competitive Auto-encoder for TExt (KATE) [20] has been adopted. This approach has been specifically selected in order to have a fair comparison with other approaches of attributed graph embeddings that represent the most promising state-of-the-art solutions [8]. The parameter set of the KATE autoencoder is denoted as θ_A.

Given the set $\Theta = \{\theta_A, \theta_R\}$ of parameters related to the neural networks for the attribute information and the relational structure, the proposed model minimizes the following loss function as a function of Θ for obtaining a consistent representation of each node:

$$\mathcal{L}(\Theta) = \alpha \sum_{i=1}^{n} ||(\hat{A}_i - A_i) \odot B_i^A||_2^2 + \beta \sum_{i=1}^{n} ||(\hat{W}_i - W_i) \odot B_i^W||_2^2$$
$$+ \gamma \sum_{i=1}^{n} ||Y_i^W - Y_i^A||_2^2 \tag{2}$$

where:

- $||(\hat{A}_i - A_i) \odot B_i^A||_2^2$ denotes the semantic proximity term related to the node attributes, where the Hadamard product, with the hyper-parameter B_i^A, regulates the sparsity of the learned attribute representation;
- $||(\hat{W}_i - W_i) \odot B_i^W||_2^2$ represents the second-order proximity related to the relational structure, where the Hadamard product, with the hyper-parameter B_i^W, regulates the sparsity of the learned relational representation;
- $||Y_i^W - Y_i^A||_2^2$ denotes a consistency term that allows different aspects of the same node to be maintained. In particular, it is used to bring latent representations of structure and semantics closer together;
- α, β and γ are hyper-parameters that regulate the trade-off between the three terms. In our case study, the hyper-parameters have been selected as uniformly distributed.

The semantic proximity, in our investigation, is obtained by KATE [20], which is an autoencoder specifically designed for textual data, whose main contribution is related to the introduction of a hidden layer in which neurons compete with each other so that each neuron becomes specialized in recognizing specific data patterns. In this way, KATE addresses both the sparsity and the Zipf's law distribution issues and it is able to extract more meaningful representations from texts. As regards the second-order proximity, the core model to preserve the topological structure (second-order proximity) of the input graph is a deep autoencoder that is trained to reconstruct the rows of the adjacency matrix of the graph. In this case, the deep autoencoder present in [4] has been adopted.

Considering that both KATE, for the attribute proximity, and the deep autoencoder, for the second-order proximity, generate a latent representation for each node i of the graph, which can be denoted by Y_i^A and Y_i^W respectively, these dense and low-dimensional vector representations must be consistent so that different aspects of the same node should be maintained. In order to enforce this property, a trivial method would be to concatenate Y_i^A and Y_i^W as the final embedding result. However, this method does not guarantee consistency between the two modalities. Another common approach is to enforce the two branches to share the same encoding layer via parameter sharing, i.e. $Y_i^A = Y_i^W$. Nevertheless, this approach is too strict and the hidden layer neurons would have too many input and output connections, since the networks are fully connected.

To address this problem, DAGE tries to bring the embedding spaces Y^A and Y^W closer together by adding a consistency term in the objective function that penalizes dissimilar latent vector representations of the same node. In other words, given a node i, the model generates the embeddings Y_i^A and Y_i^W in such a way that they are as close as possible. In this way, the structural embedding Y_i^W will also contain information related to the attributes of the i-th node, and the same happens for Y_i^A. At the end, Y^A and Y^W will be very similar and, therefore, the final embedding for the i-th node will be given by either Y_i^A or Y_i^W. In our investigation, the final embedding is taken from Y^W. An advantage of taking only one of the two representations is also that this halves the number of latent features describing each node, further reducing the dimensionality of the node representations. The optimization process related to the proposed model can be performed by using *stochastic gradient descent*, or other possible variations, relying on the computation of the partial derivatives of the parameters.

4   Experimental Analysis

In order to evaluate the performance of the proposed approach[1], four benchmark datasest have been used: M10, WIKI, CITESEER and CORA. The datasets have been divided into training and testing sets by randomly selecting a percentage of labeled nodes. Table 1 reports the main statistics of the graphs.

Table 1. Dataset statistics.

Dataset	Nodes	Edges	Attributes	Labels	Average clustering coefficient	Attribute matrix density
CITESEER	3312	4660	3703	6	0.2430	0.0086
CORA	2708	5278	1433	7	0.2932	0.0127
M10	2035	3356	2000	7	0.2352	0.0032
WIKI	2405	12761	4973	17	0.4165	0.1301

The experimental evaluation has been conducted on two different tasks. The first task relates to **node classification**, where the goal is to predict for each node the corresponding label. Once the embedding representation is obtained, a linear Support Vector Machine[2] is firstly induced making use of the training data and then the learned model is exploited to predict the labels on the test data. The performance has been measured in terms of *micro-averaged F1-measure* [1].

The second task concerns **node clustering**. After having learned the node embeddings, the *K-means* [21] algorithm is executed with the hyper-parameter k equal to the number of classes in the considered dataset. The performance has been measured in terms of *Rand Index* [22].

$$Rand\ Index = \frac{a + d}{a + b + c + d} \qquad (3)$$

---

[1] The source code of DAGE is available at https://github.com/MIND-Lab/DAGE.

[2] We employed the default parameters provided by the *Scikit-learn* Python library, training all the investigated models using the same SVM configuration `scikit-learn.org/stable/modules/generated/sklearn.svm.LinearSVC.html`.

where:

- a is the number of node pairs (v_i, v_j) such that v_i and v_j are associated with the same label and have been clustered in the same group;
- b is the number of node pairs (v_i, v_j) such that v_i and v_j are associated with different labels, but have been clustered in the same group;
- c is the number of node pairs (v_i, v_j) such that v_i and v_j are associated with the same label, but have been clustered in different groups;
- d is the number of node pairs (v_i, v_j) such that v_i and v_j are associated with different labels and have been clustered in different groups.

The proposed approach has been compared with two recent and most promising state-of-the-art approaches, i.e., Constrained deep Attributed Graph Embedding (CAGE) [8] and Deep Attributed Network Embedding (DANE) [10]. These two benchmark approaches have been selected for two main reasons: (1) they belong to the most recent state of the art and (2) they have been shown their superior capabilities with respect to other pure graph such as SDNE [4], LAP [5], DeepWalk [2] and Node2Vec [6], and attributed graph embeddings TriDNR [7] and Gat2Vec [9]. The considered models have been trained using small batches of size 128 and with enough epochs for the corresponding loss functions to converge, using the Back-propagation algorithm [23], in conjunction with Adam [24] that is an algorithm for first-order gradient-based optimization of stochastic objective functions that is based on adaptive estimates of lower-order moments.

4.1   Node Classification

We report in Tables 2 and 3, the results for the node classification task where the performance have been measured in terms of micro-F1 score. Each experiment has been performed 10 times and the corresponding results have been reported by showing their average results.

The results show that the proposed approach is able to significantly outperform both CAGE and DANE when performing a node classification task. Considering the 36 training scenario (i.e., 9 different percentage of training data for each of the four datasets), DAGE always outperforms CAGE and it obtains remarkable results in almost the comparison with DANE. The only benchmark where DANE performs better than DAGE is the WIKI dataset. In fact, when a limited amount of training data is used (from 0.1% to 0.4%), DANE achieves better results than DAGE. Interestingly, the WIKI benchmark has denser attribute matrices compared to the other datasets, suggesting that DANE is more effective when the data is denser, as opposed to DAGE that seems to be more effective in sparse conditions. This can be explained by observing that the loss function of DAGE in Eq. 2 addresses the sparsity issue at the level of both network structure and node attributes by introducing specific penalty terms, helping the model to achieve a good classification performance especially in such conditions.

4.2   Node Clustering

Table 4 reports the performance comparison of the considered models, on the node clustering task, in terms of Rand Index. *DAGE* significantly outperformed

Table 2. Micro-averaged F1-measure on Cora and Citeseer datasets.

% training data	CORA			CITESEER		
	DAGE	DANE	CAGE	DAGE	DANE	CAGE
0.1	**0.7193**	0.6546	0.5745	**0.6742**	0.6335	0.5169
0.2	**0.7569**	0.6894	0.6194	**0.6989**	0.6766	0.5369
0.3	**0.7758**	0.7099	0.6407	**0.7109**	0.6925	0.5458
0.4	**0.7905**	0.7099	0.647	**0.7177**	0.694	0.5489
0.5	**0.7914**	0.7295	0.6581	**0.7246**	0.6938	0.5581
0.6	**0.7983**	0.7295	0.6672	**0.7245**	0.7055	0.5600
0.7	**0.7995**	0.732	0.6681	**0.7197**	0.7008	0.5579
0.8	**0.8085**	0.7408	0.6756	**0.7243**	0.7029	0.5531
0.9	**0.8081**	0.727	0.6741	**0.7241**	0.697	0.5638

Table 3. Micro-averaged F1-measure on M10 and Wiki datasets.

% training data	M10			WIKI		
	DAGE	DANE	CAGE	DAGE	DANE	CAGE
0.1	**0.8790**	0.7557	0.7444	0.6599	**0.7052**	0.6364
0.2	**0.9047**	0.7663	0.7722	0.6901	**0.7282**	0.6629
0.3	**0.9103**	0.7739	0.7783	0.7183	**0.7458**	0.6832
0.4	**0.9160**	0.7766	0.7830	0.7386	**0.7468**	0.6855
0.5	**0.9222**	0.7894	0.7953	**0.7613**	0.7601	0.6957
0.6	**0.9302**	0.7926	0.7961	**0.7636**	0.7613	0.6993
0.7	**0.9211**	0.7921	0.8020	**0.7903**	0.7723	0.6985
0.8	**0.9209**	0.771	0.8017	**0.7896**	0.7713	0.7019
0.9	**0.9275**	0.7863	0.8147	**0.795**	0.7544	0.7021

Table 4. Node clustering performance in terms of Rand Index.

Dataset	DAGE	DANE	CAGE
M10	**0.8143**	0.7298	0.7472
CITESEER	0.8034	**0.8166**	0.7487
CORA	**0.8350**	0.7930	0.7761
WIKI	**0.9029**	0.8969	0.8928

in all the computational experiments and *DANE* on the majority of the available datasets. Only in the case of CITESEER dataset, DANE ouperforms DAGE. Analysing the characteristics of the network, it emerges that CITESEER is composed of 438 connected components (against 78 for CORA, 1 for M10 and 45 for WIKI). In particular, it is possible to notice that the largest component has more than 63% of the overall number of nodes and, consequently, the other connected components consist of a very small number of nodes. This suggests us that DAGE could suffer from the presence of multiple connected components.

4.3 Trainable Parameters

A further interesting remark about DAGE relates to the number of parameters needed for creating the embeddings, especially compared with the other approaches. DAGE has less number of parameters than DANE, but equal to CAGE as reported in Table 5. However, at the same computational cost for determining the parameters of the models, DAGE remarkably outperforms CAGE, achieving a significant improvement both for node classification and node clustering tasks. Compared to DANE, DAGE achieved an excellent performance using less than 40% of the parameters of DANE and it is more efficient in terms of both space and time complexity. In other words, DAGE is more straightforward to train as it uses a smaller number of neural network parameters, still achieving a significant performance.

Table 5. Trainable parameters related to the considered dataset.

Dataset	DAGE	CAGE	DANE
M10	8.14×10^5	8.14×10^5	1.67×10^6
CITESEER	1.36×10^6	1.36×10^6	5.13×10^6
CORA	9.14×10^5	9.14×10^5	1.71×10^6
WIKI	1.29×10^6	1.29×10^6	6.03×10^6

Furthermore, an interesting insight can be derived by observing the loss functions of the DAGE and DANE. In particular, the proposed DAGE model preserves only the second-order proximity and the semantic proximity, whereas DANE tries to maintain also the first-order proximity at the levels of both the network structure and the node attributes. This difference makes DAGE more efficient than DANE, because the time complexity at every epoch of DAGE is linear with respect to the number of nodes n, while DANE has a computational complexity cost equal to $O(n^2)$, as at every epoch the model needs to consider also the pairs of nodes. This makes the proposed approach particularly suitable for scaling on large scale graphs.

5 Conclusions and Future Work

In this paper we proposed DAGE, a model aimed at creating an embedding representation of nodes in attributed graphs. The experimental evaluation on two benchmark datasets has shown significant improvements with respect to two recent and promising state-of-the-art models, showing its good robustness with respect to the size of the training data and remarkable performance even in the case of limited ground-truth data, also with a reduced number of parameters to be trained.

As future work, the role of hyper-parameters and higher order proximity measures would be investigated. Furthermore, although the model has achieved promising results, it is still a transductive approach, i.e. it is not applicable to dynamic networks, as the addition or deletion of even just one node in the graph no longer permits to generate the node embeddings. This because the architecture of DAGE strictly depends on the number of nodes in the graph. This means that the model must be re-trained every time a change occurs in the graph topology. Therefore, it would be of paramount importance to study a mechanism for making the model no longer transductive.

Finally, in order to study the behavior of the model on networks with different structural properties (e.g., assortativity and clustering coefficient), it would also be helpful to consider other benchmark datasets, such as biological networks and communication networks, also considering other machine learning tasks, as for example link prediction, node clustering and network visualization.

Acknowledgments. This work has been supported by the project "ULTRA OPTYMAL - Urban Logistics and susTainable tRAnsportation: OPtimization under uncertainTY and MAchine Learning" funded by the MIUR Progetti di Ricerca di Rilevante Interesse Nazionale (PRIN) Bando 2020 - grant 20207C8T9M.

References

1. Goyal, P., Ferrara, E.: Graph embedding techniques, applications, and performance: a survey. Knowl. Based Syst. **151**, 78–94 (2018)
2. Perozz, B., Al-Rfou, R., Skiena, S.: DeepWalk: online learning of social representations. In: Proceedings of the 20th ACM SIGKDD International Conference on Knowledge Discovery and Data Mining, pp. 701–710 (2014)
3. Tang, J., Meng, Q., Wang, M., Zhang, M., Yan, J., Mei, Q.: LINE Large-scale information network embedding. Proceedings of the 24th International Conference on World Wide Web, WWW 2015 (2015)
4. Wang, D., Cui, P., Zhu, W.: Structural deep network embedding. In: Proceedings of the 22nd ACM SIGKDD International Conference on Knowledge Discovery and Data Mining, pp. 1225–1234 (2016)
5. Belkin, M., Niyogi, P.: Laplacian Eigenmaps and spectral techniques for embedding and clustering. In: Proceedings of the 14th International Conference on Neural Information Processing Systems: Natural and Synthetic, pp. 585–591 (2001)
6. Grover, A., Leskovec, J.: Node2vec: scalable feature learning for networks. In: Proceedings of the 22nd ACM SIGKDD International Conference on Knowledge Discovery and Data Mining, pp. 855–864 (2016)
7. Pan, S., Wu, J., Zhu, X., Zhang, C., Wang, Y.: Tri-party deep network representation. In: Proceedings of the Twenty-Fifth International Joint Conference on Artificial Intelligence, IJCAI 2016, pp. 1901. AAAI Press (2016)
8. Nozza, D., Fersini, E., Messina, E.: Cage: constrained deep attributed graph embedding. Inf. Sci. **518**, 56–70 (2020)

9. Sheikh, N., Kefato, Z., Montresor, A.: GAT2VEC: representation learning for attributed graphs. Computing **101**, 03 (2019)
10. Gao, H., Huang, H.: Deep attributed network embedding. In: Proceedings of the 27th International Joint Conference on Artificial Intelligence, pp. 3364–3370 (2018)
11. Roweis, S.T., Saul, L.K.: Nonlinear dimensionality reduction by locally linear embedding. Science **290**(5500), 2323–2326 (2000)
12. Nourbakhsh, F., Rota Bulo, S., Pelillo, M.: A matrix factorization approach to graph compression. In: Proceedings of the 22nd IEEE International Conference on Pattern Recognition, pp. 76–81 (2014)
13. Ahmed, A., Shervashidze, N., Narayanamurthy, S., Josifovski, V., Smola, A.J.: Distributed large-scale natural graph factorization. In: Proceedings of the 22nd International Conference on World Wide Web, pp. 37–48 (2013)
14. Cao, S., Lu, W., Xu, Q.: GraRep: learning graph representations with global structural information. In: Proceedings of the 24th ACM International Conference on Information and Knowledge Management, pp. 891–900 (2015)
15. Ou, M., Cui, P., Pei, J., Zhang, Z., Zhu, W.: Asymmetric transitivity preserving graph embedding. In: Proceedings of the 22nd ACM SIGKDD International Conference on Knowledge Discovery and Data Mining, pp. 1105–1114 (2016)
16. Mikolov, T., Chen, K., Corrado, G., Dean, J.: Efficient estimation of word representations in vector space. arXiv preprint arXiv:1301.3781 (2013)
17. Cao, S., Lu, W., Xu, Q.: Deep neural networks for learning graph representations. In: Proceedings of the AAAI Conference on Artificial Intelligence, vol. 30 (2016)
18. Sheikh, N., Kefato, Z.T., Montresor, A.: GAT2VEC: representation learning for attributed graphs. Computing **101**(3), 187–209 (2019)
19. Longcan, W., Wang, D., Song, K., Feng, S., Zhang, Y., Ge, Yu.: Dual-view hypergraph neural networks for attributed graph learning. Knowl.-Based Syst. **227**, 107185 (2021)
20. Chen, Y., Zak, M.J.: KATE: K-competitive autoencoder for text. In: Proceedings of the 23rd ACM SIGKDD International Conference on Knowledge Discovery and Data Mining, pp. 85–94 (2017)
21. MacQueen, J., et al.: Some methods for classification and analysis of multivariate observations. In: Proceedings of the fifth Berkeley Symposium on Mathematical Statistics and Probability, vol. 1, pp. 281–297. Oakland, CA, USA (1967)
22. Rand, W.M.: Objective criteria for the evaluation of clustering methods. J. Am. Stat. Assoc. **66**(336), 846–850 (1971)
23. Kelley, H.J.: Gradient theory of optimal flight paths. Ars J. **30**(10), 947–954 (1960)
24. Kingma, D.P., Ba, J.: ADAM: a method for stochastic optimization. In: In: Proceedings of the 3rd International Conference on Learning Representations (2015)

Estimation of Prediction Error
with Regression Trees

Eva Armengol[(✉)]

Artificial Intelligence Research Institute, (IIIA, CSIC), Campus UAB,
Camí de Can Planes, s/n, 08193 Bellaterra, Barcelona, Spain
eva@iiia.csic.es

Abstract. Prediction is a common task useful in data analysis. The
goal is to predict the value of a variable in terms of the values of
other variables. The most used technique for solving prediction task is
regression analysis that approximates the data at hand by means of a
poly- nomial function. Because data can be represented as a cloud of
points, the approximation by means of a polynomial function has error.
Most of authors try to search for techniques allowing a more accurate
prediction than the one produced by the regression model. In this paper
we propose a completely different approach. Our goal is, given a predictive model, use regression trees to establish the error of the measure
proposed by the predictive model.

Keywords: Multivariate regression models · Regression trees

1 Introduction

In machine learning there are two kinds of predictions that can be made: 1) the
prediction of the class to which an object belongs, and 2) to predict the value
of a variable. Problems of the first type are known as *classification problems*;
those of the second type are known as *prediction problems*. In fact, classification
problems can be seen as a special case of prediction problems since the difference
between both kinds of problems is the type of the variable of interest. Classification problems can only predict values of categorical variables, called *classes* (for
instance, the animal X is a *mammal*), whereas prediction problems predict the
value of continuous variables (for instance, the temperature for tomorrow will
be 30 °C). The present paper is about prediction problems since our goal is to
predict the value of a continuous variable. Commonly, the target variable, also
called *dependent variable* is calculated by constructing a regression model that
relates it with other variables, called *independent variables*. Thus, given a dataset
with examples described by a set of independent variables $\{v_1, \ldots, v_n\}$ and V_D,
the dependent variable known for all the examples of the dataset, a regression
model $\mathcal{M}$ is constructed using all the examples. In that way, the model $\mathcal{M}$ can
predict the value of V_D for unseen objects.

© The Author(s), under exclusive license to Springer Nature Switzerland AG 2022
V. Torra and Y. Narukawa (Eds.): MDAI 2022, LNAI 13408, pp. 193–202, 2022.
https://doi.org/10.1007/978-3-031-13448-7_16

There are many regression models that could be used to predict a variable depending on the variables we choose. Commonly, a criteria to select relevant variables is by means of feature selection methods [8] taking into account the correlations of the independent variables between them and also with the dependent variable. In machine learning it is common to minimize some loss function, that usually is the sum of squared errors [7].

There are two different approaches to minimize the error, both based on *ensemble methods* [9,16]. Breiman [2] introduced the *Bagging predictors*, a method that generates several versions of a predictor and then aggregates all these versions. The idea is to generate datasets of the same size than the original one but with only a selection of examples that are duplicated. Then, for each one of these datasets a decision tree with some constraints of depth and attributes is grown. Notice that this procedure is carried out in parallel since each dataset is independent of the others. Finally there is an aggregation step to provide only one outcome. This method detects the elements in the dataset that cause the highest perturbations in the result and use them as a feedback to reduce the variance and hence, the prediction error. This technique improves the performance of predictive models [3] but it is computationally expensive.

Boosting is a family of algorithms that are able to convert weak learners to strong learners [5,6,12,13]. Differently than bagging, boosting works sequentially. The first step is to construct a model from the original dataset a model. Then each example is associated with a weight, where misclassified examples have a highest weight than the correct classified examples. The modified dataset is used as input of another classifier and so on until a satisfactory accuracy is reached. Boosting focuses on examples that are difficult to predict.

Feher [14] proposes a mixture of regression trees and regression models. His approach consists on growing a regression tree where each node is a regression model instead a set of examples as usual. The regression model is evaluated and, the node continues the expansion according that evaluation.

In the present paper we propose a completely different approach. From a predictive model satisfying the set of requirements appropriate for the domain at hand, we propose to analyze it by means of regression trees in order to detect areas of the model where its outcome is acceptable in terms of the error, and other areas where the outcome will not be acceptable. Thus, we propose to use the regression model to obtain a value for the dependent variable and then to give the probability that such outcome will be acceptable or not. To illustrate the procedure, we will consider that the predictive model is a Multivariate Regression (MR) model. However this does not mean any kind of constraint since our approach works taking into account only the results of the predictive model.

The paper is organized as follows. Section 2 briefly describe regression trees. Section 3 describes the methodology we propose. Section 4 describes the experimentation with the proposed methodology. Finally conclusions and future work.

```
ID3 (examples, attributes)
    create a node
    if all examples belong to the same class return class as the label for the node
    otherwise
            A ← best attribute
            for each possible value vᵢ of A
                    add a new tree branch below node
                    examples_vi ← subset of examples such that A = vᵢ
                    ID3(examples_vi, attributes - {A})
    return node
```

Fig. 1. ID3 algorithm for growing a decision tree.

2   Regression Trees

One of the most common techniques used in supervised machine learning is *Decision Trees* introduced by Quinlan [10] who proposed the well-known ID3 algorithm (see Fig. 1). Roughly speaking, the goal in growing a decision tree is to make a partition of the set of examples E to obtain several disjoint subsets S_i where all the examples of S_i belong to the same class C_i. This technique is specially useful for classification tasks, where the domain examples E are described by a set of attributes (i.e., variables) $A = \{a_1, \ldots, a_n\}$ and labelled according to its membership to a set of classes C. The value of these attributes may be *categorical* (i.e., a label) or *continuous* (i.e., a real number). Depending on the type of these values, decision trees are named as *Classification trees*, when the values are categorical; or *Regression trees*: when the values are continuous. The classes are labels and, as a such, represented by categorical values (or, sometimes by a finite set of integer values 0,1, ..., k). The goal in growing a tree is to create a domain model predictive enough to classify future unseen domain objects.

A key issue of the construction of decision trees is the selection of the most relevant attribute to split a node. In regression trees it is common to use the Gini's index [1]. The Gini's index measures the impurity degree of a set where 0 means the set is pure (all the elements belong to the same class); 1 is the maximum impurity (random distribution of the elements among the classes); and 0.5 means an equal distribution of elements over some classes. When growing a decision tree, the best attributes are those with lower Gini's index.

The formula to calculate the Gini's index is the following:

$$G = 1 - \sum_{i=1}^{n} (P_i)^2$$

where P_i is the probability of an object to be classified to a particular class.

3 Methodology

We assume that a predictive model P has been constructed by means of any technique considered appropriated for solving the problem at hand. Our approach is to construct a regression tree modelling the performance of P based on the prediction error. In other words, the idea is to define labels indicating whether or not the difference between the real value and the value proposed by P is acceptable. In that way, when P proposes a value, the tree indicates the accuracy of such value. Let us explain in detail our approach.

Let E be the set of examples from which the prediction model has been constructed, and let A_k be the variable to be predicted, we propose the following steps:

1. Determine a set of labels $\{L_1, \ldots, L_n\}$ associated to the difference we are willing to accept between the real value and the predicted one (this will be explained later in more detail).
2. Let DS' be a new dataset initially empty.
3. For each object $O_i \in E$,
   (a) Use the model P to predict a value v_{p_i} for A_k of O_i.
   (b) Compute $D_i = |vreal_i - v_{p_i}|$, i.e., the absolute difference between the real value of A_k and the one predicted by the model P.
   (c) Create a new object O'_i having exactly the same values in all the attributes (except A_k), and with a new attribute, namely the *class*, that has as value the label associated to the difference D_i.
   (d) Store O'_i in DS'.
4. Grow a regression tree using the objects in DS'.

To use regression trees is necessary that the class attribute has categorical values. In our case these values are labels $\{L_1, \ldots, L_n\}$ that we can define according to the knowledge we have about the domain. Thus, let us suppose that we want to predict a temperature and let us suppose that we are willing to accept an error of $3°$ although an error of $6°$ could be also acceptable. In that case, we could define three labels $\{good, acceptable, unacceptable\}$ in the following way:

- *Good* if $|real - aprox| \leq 3°$
- *Acceptable* if $3 \leq |real - aprox| \leq 6°$
- *Unacceptable* if $|real - aprox| > 6°$

Depending on the domain, the number of class labels could be different, therefore it is important to analyze the domain at hand and determine ranges of acceptable and unacceptable errors. Once the set of labels has been determined, we can proceed with the training step. For each object obj_i of the dataset, the model P is used to obtain a value for A_k. The second step is to compute the difference $|real - aprox|$ and associate a class label to obj_i. At the end, we have a set of objects with attributes having continuous values and with a categorical class label, so a regression tree can be grown.

The regression tree gives a model of the error produced by the predictive model P. Given that in the most of cases the leaves of the tree are not discriminant, i.e., objects in a leaf can belong to different classes, we can give a probability for each class label. In the next section we illustrate the procedure with an example.

3.1 Example

To illustrate the procedure we use the dataset *Bias Correction* from the UCI repository [4]. This dataset has 7750 objects described by 25 continuous attributes. The goal is to predict the minimum and the maximum temperatures for the next day. We will consider here only the problem to predict the minimum temperature $(Tnext_{min})$. First of all we have to determine the error that we are willing to accept. Let us suppose we take the following thresholds:

– *Good* if $|real - aprox| \leq 0.9$
– *Acceptable* if $0.9|real - aprox| \leq 1.8$
– *Unacceptable* if $|real - aprox| > 1.8$

Now we use a predictive model to obtain an approximate value for $Tnext_{min}$. In particular we have used a Multivariate Regression model, however any predictive technique could be used. After the training step, we have obtained the regression tree show in Fig. 2. This tree has four leaves and only two attributes are used: Present_Tmin and LDAPS_Tmin_lapse. Let us suppose that the regression model proposes a value x for an object O. When O has Present_Tmin < 14.7 there is a probability of 0.97 that x be unacceptable. When Present_Tmin > 14.7 the probability of being unacceptable is very low (0.1, 0.1 and 0.13 respectively) meaning that the most of times the value x predicted by the model has a difference with the real value lower than 1.8. Particularly, the probability that $|real - aprox| \leq 0.9$ is, respectively 0.61, 0.75 and 0.52. Notice that when Present_Tmin > 26.35 the probability of having a difference lower than 0.9 has decreased with respect to the other paths of the tree. A different point of view is to consider than when Present_Tmin > 26.35, the probability of $\leq |real - aprox| \leq 1.8$ is 0.87 (i.e., the sum of the probabilities 0.52 and 0.35 of being *good* and *aceptable* respectively). In that way the user can decide whether or not the value proposed by the predictive model is useful for his purposes and the percentage of error that could accept according to the application at hand.

The threshold we take for the acceptability of the error is important to assess the accuracy of the value proposed by the predictive model. Let us suppose that we want to distinguish only between acceptable and unacceptable differences. Figure 3 shows how changes the tree taking different thresholds of acceptability. Left hand side tree in Fig. 3 takes the difference $|real - aprox| \leq 0.9$ as acceptable and unacceptable otherwise. Focusing on the probabilities we see that for all those examples with Present_Tmin < 14.9 the result of the predictive model is not acceptable. Concerning the examples such that 14.9 < Present_Tmin < 26.25 there is a probability of 0.62 that the value proposed by the predictive model be

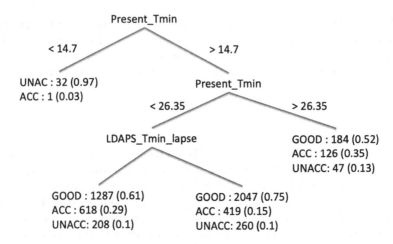

Fig. 2. Regression tree for the dataset Bias Correction taking three class labels. Numbers in parentheses are the probabilities for each path.

acceptable. For those such that Present_Tmin > 26.25 it is no clear whether or not the value could be accepted. This means that the tree gives not a valuable information about the performance of the predictive model in that situation.

The right hand side of Fig. 3 shows the tree grown taking $|real - aprox| \leq 1.5$ as acceptable and as unacceptable otherwise. Notice that this tree gives information more useful than the one in the left hand side. Thus, when Present_Tmin < 14.7 the result is unacceptable with probability 0.97 and when Present_Tmin > 14.9 the probability of being acceptable ranges from 0.80 to 0.85 depending on the value of the attribute LDAPS_Tmin_lapse.

Summarizing, the user has to define thresholds of acceptability of the error of the predictive model, i.e., the difference $|real - aprox|$ and then grown the tree using the labels associated to the acceptability intervals. There is not any constraint about how many intervals of acceptability are adequate; however, from our experiments we have seen that, in general, two or three intervals are enough to get useful information about the predictive model performance.

4   Experiments

We conducted several experiments to show that with our approach it is possible to determine better the accuracy of the predictive model depending on the features of the input object. We have used the datasets shown in Table 1, all of them coming from the UCI Repository. Each dataset has been randomly divided in a training set (around the 70% of the objects) and a test set (the remaining 30%).

For all the datasets we have constructed a Multivariate Regression Model (MRM) based on the objects in the training set and taking into account the

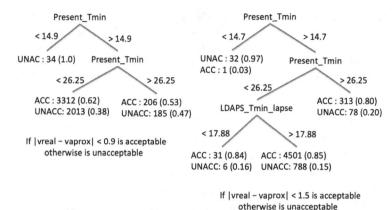

Fig. 3. Regression trees for the dataset Bias Correction taking two labels.

Table 1. Datasets from the UCI repository used in the experiments. the value m is the mean value of the difference $|real - aprox|$ where $aprox$ is the value proposed by the predictive model.

Dataset	Total	Training	Test	m	2 m
AirFoil	1503	1053	450	4	8
Bias Correction max	7750	5750	2000	1.5	3
Bias Correction min	7750	5750	2000	0.9	1.8
Fish	908	658	250	0.7	1.4
Residential building V9	372	272	100	130	260
Residential building V10	372	272	100	22.8	45.6
Red wine	1559	1149	450	0.50	1
White wine	4898	3448	1450	0.6	1.2

subset of variables that have been considered as relevant using LASSO Regression [11,15]. This step does not constrains the results since the construction of the model is independent from the tree assessing the validity of the predicted value.

We experimented with a discretization in two and three intervals. Because we have not a deep knowledge about these datasets in order to determine an accurate discretization, we have used MRM to asses the value for all the objects in the dataset and for each one of them we have computed the difference $|real - aprox|$. Let m be the mean value of these differences. For the discretization in three intervals we take the following labels:

- *Good*: when $|real - aprox| \leq m$
- *Acceptable*: when $m < |real - aprox| \leq 2m$
- *Unacceptable*: when $|real - aprox| > 2\,m$

Table 2. Comparison of errors of the predictive model (ϵ_{MRM}) alone and in combination with the regression tree (ϵ_{tree}) considering two discretization intervals. Columns $D \leq m$ shows the number of objects in the test set that are assessed as having an *acceptable* difference, i.e., $m < |real - aprox| \leq 2m$. Column $\%D \leq m$ shows the percentage of *acceptable* objects with respect to the total number of objects from the test set.

Dataset	ϵ_{MRM}	ϵ_{tree}	$D \leq m$	$\%D \leq m$
AirFoil	13.55	13.55	450	100
Bias Correction max	11.25	9.64	1960	98.00
Bias Correction min	14.35	12.65	1960	98.00
Fish	12.8	9.90	212	84.8
Residential building V9	26.00	7.89	90	90.00
Residential building V10	6.00	6.00	100	100
Red wine	11.33	11.21	437	97.11
White wine	10.34	10.19	1443	99.52

and the discretization in two intervals is: if $|real - aprox| \leq 2m$ then the value is *acceptable* otherwise it is *unacceptable*. Table 1 also shows the acceptability thresholds we have taken in the experiments.

Using the labels given by the discretization, regression trees have been grown. The tree was then used to assess the accuracy of the value proposed by the MRM for the objects in the test set. Tables 2 and 3 show the results when we consider a discretization with two and three intervals respectively. The column ϵ_{MRM} is the error of the predictive model MRM computed as the percentage of objects in the test set for which $|real - aprox| > 2m$. The column ϵ_{tree} corresponds to the percentage of error of the tree, computed as the percentage of objects that have an approximated value considered as *good* (i.e., such that $|real - aprox| \leq m$) or as *acceptable* (i.e., such that $m \leq |real - aprox| \leq 2m$) but that actually the difference is unacceptable (i.e., such that $|real - aprox| > 2m$). The column $D \leq m$ represents the number of objects of the test set classified as *good* or *acceptable*, and the column $\%D \leq m$ is the percentage that they represent. Let us explain in more detail the meaning of these columns.

Given an object Obj for whose we want to estimate the value of a variable A_i, the predictive model MRM proposes a value that has a probability of ϵ_{MRM} of being unacceptable. In a discretization in three intervals, when the tree assesses a difference as *good*, the probability of error is ϵ_{tree}. In a discretization with two intervals the error ϵ_{tree} is the percentage of objects assessed as *aceptable* but that are actually *unacceptable*. Notice that using two discretization intervals (Table 2) for the datasets AirFoil, Residential building V10, Red Wine and White Wine, both errors ϵ_{MRM} and ϵ_{tree} are similar. However, using three intervals (Table 3) the majority of datasets have ϵ_{tree} lower than ϵ_{MRM} with the only exception of AirFoil.

Table 3. Comparison of errors of the predictive model (ϵ_{MRM}) alone and in combination with the regression tree (ϵ_{tree}) considering three discretization intervals. Columns $D \leq m$ shows the number of objects in the test set that are assessed as having an *good* difference, i.e., $m < |real - aprox| \leq 2\,m$. Column $\%D \leq m$ shows the percentage of *good* objects with respect to the total number of objects from the test set.

Dataset	ϵ_{MRM}	ϵ_{tree}	$D \leq m$	$\%D \leq m$
AirFoil	13.55	9.37	363	80.67
Bias correction max	11.25	11.25	2000	100
Bias correction min	14.35	11.58	1545	77.25
Fish	12.8	7.14	168	67.2
Residential building V9	26.00	18.42	76	76.00
Residential building V10	6.00	5.10	98	98.00
Red wine	11.33	9.77	174	38.67
White wine	10.34	9.84	559	38.55

An important aspect to take into account is for how many objects occurs than $\epsilon_{tree} < \epsilon_{MRM}$ and which percentage they represent. For instance, the datasets Red Wine and White Wine in Table 3 have a clear improvement concerning the error. According to the column $D \leq m$, 174 out of 450 objects for the Red Wine test set and 559 out of 1450 objects for the White Wine test set are assessed as having a *good* value. As column $\%D \leq m$ shows, this represent only a percentage around 38% of both test sets. This means that for those datasets the use of regression trees is not useful. Conversely, for all the other datasets the tree improves the error of the MRM model using both two and three discretization intervals.

5 Conclusions

In the current paper we propose to improve the outcome of a predictive model using regression trees. Differently than other approaches that propose combinations of techniques to get more accurate models, we propose to analyze the predictive model using regression trees. The main idea is, given an approximate value proposed by the predictive model, determine the probability that such value is similar enough to the actual value by mean of acceptability intervals. We assume that the user has a good knowledge about the problem and that he is capable to determine the maximum difference between the actual and the predicted value that could be acceptable.

As future work we plan to use the approach described in the current paper to real problems. Also, our intuition is that sometimes there are several predictive models that could be combined to predict a value. We want to analyze how our technique could be useful in such situations.

Acknowledgments. This research is partially funded by the project Isinc PID2019-111544GB-C21 from the Spanish Ministry of Science and Innovation. Author also thank to Àngel García-Cerdaña his helpful comments.

References

1. Breiman, L., Friedman, J., Stone, C.J., lshen, R.A.: Classification and Regression Trees. Chapman and Hall/CRC Press, New York (1984)
2. Breiman, L.: Bagging predictors. Mach. Learn. **24**(2), 123–140 (1996)
3. Breiman, L.: Using iterated bagging to Debias regressions. Mach. Learn. **45**, 61–277 (2001)
4. Dua, D., Graff, C.: UCI machine learning repository (2017)
5. Freund, Y., Schapire, R.E.: A short introduction to boosting. In: Proceedings of the Sixteenth International Joint Conference on Artificial Intelligence, pp. 1401–1406. Morgan Kaufmann (1999)
6. Friedman, J.H.: Stochastic gradient boosting. Nonlinear Methods and Data Mining. Compu. Stat. Data Anal. **38**(4), 367–378 (2002)
7. Goodfellow, J., Bengio, Y., Courville, A.: Deep Learning. MIT Press, Cambridge (2016). http://www.deeplearningbook.org
8. Kuhn, M., Johnson, K.: Applied Predictive Modeling. Springer, New York (2013). https://doi.org/10.1007/978-1-4614-6849-3
9. Opitz, D., Maclin, R.: Popular ensemble methods: an empirical study. J. Artif. Intell. Res. **11**, 12 (1999)
10. Quinlan, J.R.: Induction of decision trees. Mach. Learn. **1**(1), 81–106 (1986)
11. Santosa, F., Symes, W.W.: Linear inversion of band-limited reflection seismograms. SIAM J. Sci. Stat. Comput. **7**(4), 1307–1330 (1986)
12. Schapire, R.E.: The boosting approach to machine learning: an overview. In: MSRI Workshop on Nonlinear Estimation and Classification, Berkeley, CA, USA (2001)
13. Schapire, R.E.: Explaining AdaBoost. In: Schölkopf, B., Luo, Z., Vovk, V. (eds.) Empirical Inference, pp. 37–52. Springer, Heidelberg (2013). https://doi.org/10.1007/978-3-642-41136-6_5
14. Fehér, T.: Using regression trees in predictive modelling. EMI Prod. Syst. Inf. Eng. **4**, 15–124 (2006)
15. Tibshirani, R.: Regression shrinkage and selection via the lasso. J. R. Stat. Soc. Ser. B (Methodol.) **58**(1), 267–288 (1996)
16. Zhou, Z.-H.: Ensemble Methods: Foundations and Algorithms,1st edn, Chapman & Hall/CRC, New York (2012)

Author Index

Printed in the United States
by Baker & Taylor Publisher Services